THE NATURE & GENESIS OF RELIGIOUS EXPERIENCE

The Nature and Genesis of Religious Experience

DEEPA DAS

GIAN PUBLISHING HOUSE
New Delhi-110002

GIAN PUBLISHING HOUSE
5, Ansari Road
Delhi-110002.

ISBN : 81-212-0421-6

Icssr Consultant : Chandmal Sharma

This publication is financially supported by the ICSSR. The responsibility for the facts stated, opinions expressed or conclusions reached, is entirely that of the author and that the ICSSR accepts no responsibility for them.

PRINTED IN INDIA

Published by Mrs. Gayatri Garg for Gian Publishing House,
New Delhi 110002
Printed at New Goswami Printers, Ghonda, Delhi-53.

For my parents, teachers and every other person who made this possible

Contents

Preface

Although human intellectual pursuits have revealed many unknown and unbelievable facts humankind has yet to arrive at an appropriate all-comprehensive definition of religion. It is still not clear whether religion necessarily involves God, the concepts of soul and after life, moral codes, etc.

Alongside any intimacy shared with religion, many human achievements have often propagated an attitude of disaffection towards, and estrangement from, religion and religious life. The method, approach and practice of religion is apparently at variance with the scientific temper. And the difficulty in reconciling them is founded on the perpetual conflict between scientific naturalism and religious super-naturalism. The progressive attitude of mind is frankly empirical, while the religious temper is persistently traditional and often dogmatic, bound by myths, rituals and superstitions. Empiricism which is at war with our religious traditionalism is bound up with science, and upon science the progress of civilisation is greatly dependent. Science is simply the specialised effort of scientists who concentrate upon achieving knowledge of things around us, in order to ensure their proper use and manipulation.

Approached in various ways, religion can be treated in the most diverse manners. Mystics, moralists, agnostics, humanists, etc., represent some of the different approaches to religion. This, however, should not lead to the conclusion that they are individually absolute as it is possible for the same person to adhere to views expressed by more than one approach. The diversity of opinions and reactions to religion are best explained by the fact that religion is variously approached by humankind in accordance with environmental conditions, mental make up and individual inclinations.

From each perspective, the place, validity and meaning of religion, and its relevance to life, varies. Mystics, for instance, abandon any attempt at comprehending the problem and rather indulge in pure intuitional contemplation, assuming the forms of vision and ecstacy. Mystics prefer to see religion in the context of human communion with the supernatural. The moralists try to point out the close relation between God and duty, preaching the sermon of the categorical imperative. Unlike these, the scientist is in search of the ultimate cause of creation and in one's endeavour to explain facts and phenomena of existence, reduces everything to a cause-effect series. The atheist's standpoint dismantles the structure constructed by the mystics, and calls their visions and ecstasies nothing but aberrations of the human mind. The agnostics' pet argument is that the 'finite cannot know the infinite', thereby doing away with the problem, or, shirking the responsibility of solving it.

Pratt has identified four typical aspects of religion in his *The Religious Consciousness* : *A Psychological Study*. He makes out the four aspects to be : (*i*) the traditional, which imbibes its attitudes from the authority of the past—from parents, teachers, tradition, the Church, etc. ; (*ii*) the rational, which seeks to free itself altogether from authority and to base itself purely on reason and the facts of verifiable experience ; (*iii*) the mystical, which appeals to a particular kind of experience and a kind that is peculiarly subjective and hence not scientifically verifiable; (*iv*) the practical which lays emphasis upon the thing that must be done rather than upon the thing that must be believed or felt.

Religion then, has both the rational and the supra-rational or emotional elements. The former includes approaches that depend upon and frequently fall back on the reasoning capacity and the senses in their pursuit of truth, while the latter subsumes those approaches primarily guided by emotive and intuitive factors in knowing truth.

Though there are forces that challenge the mystic's contentions, they do not, or cannot reduce the academic significance of religious experiences. The concern here is with the mystics' approach with particular emphasis on understanding and analysing their experiences in the light of their genesis.

This work is not interested in getting entangled with the question of validity and invalidity of religious experiences. Avoiding the controversy of truth and validity, it bases itself on the conviction that no evidence for the reality of religious experiences can be produced by any intellectual balance sheet of pros and cons, in a manner akin to that of the scientist. Such experiences have existential authenticity, because they have recordedly come to individuals irrespective of time, place, culture and conditions. Sharing the phenomenologists' view, the concern here is with religious experiences as phenomena, their meaning and conditions of origin. Let not existence and validity be the issue of contention – it is of grave importance to penetrate to the essence and know the source; I proceed with the assumption, until the contrary is proven, that persons having religious experience are sensible, rational people who are not always mentally ill and who are describing as best they can something they have really experienced. Based on these assumptions an objective and indepth study of the nature, genesis and motivating factors of religious experiences has been made besides examining their prevalence, their correlates and their consequences in contemporary society. The problem of expression as a significant aspect of these experiences also feature in the discussion.

Religious experience as a subject being vest makes it a fomidable task to give a comprehensive account and analysis of what has been academically achieved in this realm.

The focus herein is not on any particular religious creed or culture. I am, here concerned with religious experiences in general, as the objective is to evolve the factors to which the occurrence of religious experiences may be attributed such that their relationship is applicable to the whole of humankind and not just to any particular section of it. Though I have received sufficient light from the various approaches to religious experiences, *viz.*, psychological, philosophical, phehomenological, etc., yet in my treatment of the problems I have not restricted myself to any one approach in order to retain the objectivity of approach throughout the work.

Within the rubric of religious experiences comes its pronounced and bolder forms, meaning mysticism, revelation, prophetic insight, etc., apart from its milder forms like prayer, observation of rituals, etc. In the heirarchy of religious experiences, revelation and prophetic insight are placed at the apex because they are the sustaining ground of religion — as they are deemed to come from the Supreme Being or Beyond. The extravagant radical types of religious experiences consist of the study material in the present endeavour. The choice is in favour of the more intense types of religious experiences — those placed at the higher end of the heirarchical order — because they pose interesting problems unlike the milder types which are strictly subjective (as is clear in the case of prayer, worship, observation of rituals) insofar as they tend to be acts limited to the fulfilment of personal desires and ends, not extending beyond the self.

Comprising of seven chapters the study commences with an exposition of the nature of religious experiences. Some of their distinctive characteristics are necessary constituents which I have termed 'primary' and the other set of characteristics — 'secondary' — are their occasional accompaniments and are appropriately referred to as the concomitants of religious experiences. Scrutiny of the means of attaining religious experiences shows how it is possible for these experiences to occur spontaneously and also be 'created'. The study of the means is a further pointer to the probability of some psychological and extra-psychological agents that lie at the root of religious experiences. The psychological bases are broadly divisible into the psychic structure, determined by the environmental conditions, the subconscious and unconscious realms as also one's inclinations, subjective make up and personality traits. In the context of extra-mental agents that may facilitate the occurrence of religious experiences directly or as catalytic agents, the religious potentials of psychedelic drugs and Hindustani Classical Music have been explored. The book closes with a discussion of the communicability of religious experiences. It transpires that their expressions are either spontaneous or deliberate and only the latter form of expression has knowledge bearing capacity while the former is more an indicator of one having the experience.

A wide range of books and articles have appeared on the subject, a sizeable fraction of which comes in the form of biographical sketches, psychological investigations, anthropological studies, historical reviews, devotional work, and philosophical inquiries concerning the congnitive status and objectivity of such spiritual experiences. Few publications have, so far, dealt with the question of the genesis of religious experiences and the likely motivating factors instigating the genesis.

This wide array of sources mentioned above, provide a substantial part of the material referred to for this study. However, the study of religious experiences has been revolutionised as it no longer is cent percent dependent on this kind of material — this has been supplemented, especially in the West, by the questionnaire method and findings of laboratory experiments. Psychoanalysis and the medical sciences have also revealed much about the working of the human brain and physiology which is very relevant to the particular perspective from which religious experiences are being examined in this book. The emotional experiences resulting from the inhalation of nitrous oxide was recorded before James's 'Varieties' was written, and since then, the altered states of consciousness produced by drugs and meditational practices have increasingly asserted their role and relevance in any study of religious experiences. Aldous Huxley, W.H. Pahnke, Masters and Houston, etc., have made studies of the religious or seemingly religious experiences ensuing from the ingestion of psychedelic drugs, all of which have uncovered the unknown and the unexpected about them.

This book is the modified version of my doctoral dissertation submitted to the Banaras Hindu University. I would like to record my gratitude to the university for allowing me to publish it and also to the Indian Council of Social Science Research for supporting me with a grant to publish it.

The greatest support that I have received in preparing this volume is from my parents, who were always by me. It is difficult to adequately acknowledge my gratitude for their loving and patient encouragement, which has been the constant source of inspiration for me.

For the idea of this work and the initiative to write it, for the friendly encouragement and competent advice during the work, I am immensely indebted to my supervisor, Dr. R.S. Misra, retired Professor and Head of the Department, Department of Philpsophy, Banaras Hindu University, without whose valuable attention and guidance this work would never be a reality.

I am specially thankful to Dr. K.C. Gangrade, retired Professer and Head of the Department of Instrumental Music, Faculty of Performing Arts, Banaras Hindu University, for having very generously given me time to read and comment on the sixth chapter.

I take this opportuuity to express my appreciation and gratitude to the staff of the Sayaji Rao Gaekwad Library, Banaras Hindu University, the departmental library of the Department of Philosophy, Banaras Hindu University, and the National Library, Calcutta, for their very kind co-operation and help. Mr. Gautam Chatterjee of the Sayaji Rao Gaekwad Library was particularly helpful and I am most grateful to him for his ever-ready willingness to help.

The material made available by Sir Alister Hardy, Mr. Edward Robinson, of the Religious Experience Research Unit, Manchester College, has been of great value, and I feel highly obliged to them for their kindness.

I owe a very special 'thank you' to my friends Sindhu, Sumita and Sunira for all the help they have rendered in various ways, during all the phases of preparation of this volume. Without their assistance it would not have been possible for me to prepare this work single-handed.

Deepa Das

I take this opportunity to express my appreciation and gratitude to the staff of the Sayaji Rao Gaekwad Library, Banaras Hindu University, the departmental library of the Department of Philosophy, Banaras Hindu University and the National Library, Calcutta, for their very kind co-operation and help. Mr. [illegible] Chatterjee of the Sayaji Rao Gaekwad Library was particularly helpful and I am most grateful to him for his ever ready willingness to help.

The material made available by Sir Alister Hardy, [illegible] Edward Robinson of the Religious Experience Research Unit, Manchester College, has been of great value and I feel highly obliged to them for their kindness.

I owe a very special thank you to my friends [illegible] Sharma and Sunita for all the help they have rendered [illegible] during all the phases of preparation of this work. Without their assistance it would not have been possible for me to prepare this work single-handed.

Deepa Das

1

The Nature of Religious Experience

The nature of religious experiences may be explained in terms of their origin as well as in terms of their essential features. Essential features would imply the distinguishing features of these experiences by which they could be identified as religious experiences. Origin, on the other hand, deals with the question of how these experiences come to humankind; what triggers them as it were. Prior to examining either of these aspects, the relationship between religious experience and religion needs to be delved into briefly. In doing so, the significance of one in relation to the other is expected to emerge.

Religious Experience and Religion

Humanity is still puzzled by religious experiences. It persists to be a subject of concern for both theologians and philosophers, in so far as its credibility remains in doubt, because, on final analysis religious experiences merge into the subjective realm.

Regarding the subject of the possibility of interaction between natural and supernatural agents, the question—'Can religions be said to be based on religious experiences ?'—naturally arises. There are those who say that religion is not concerned with truth or falsehood; "religious experience *is* religion, and the whole of it."[1] A similar trend of thought is evident in Radhakrishnan's *An Idealist View of Life*[2]. Professor Daya Krishna in upholding this view, says, "The core of all religions is religious experience got through withdrawal, aspirations, and invocation of grace."[3] This shows how religions do fall back on religious experience as the unique source that support and hold their foundation in stability.

If this be so, religious experience becomes the root of religions--without it, the basic tenets of religion would be wavering in uncertainty. In agreement with this, Frits Staal states: "If mystical experiences are removed from the realm of religion, this would of course affect the notion and interpretation of religion itself. For it is not open to doubt that such experiences, when interpreted as divine inspirations, become the sources of many religious ideas and phenomena, if not of entire religions."[4] Religious experience, apparently, constitutes an important, if not essential, element in the religious consciousness of both religious geniuses and the ordinary believer.

However, the tension between the mystic's private religious insight and orthodox tradition, needs to be explained. According to traditional or conservative religious authority, religion is founded on revelation, which comes from Beyond; contrasted to the significance of this source, religious experiences pale out. In fact, the theological approach does not give importance to subjective religious experiences. The *Mimaṃsa* school in Hinduism provides a good example, according to which the Vedas are the life and soul of religion.

Evidently, religious experiences cannot be brushed aside as mental abberations or mere hallucinations; they contain more meaning than is usually attributed to them. Perhaps their claims to a peculiar and direct insight into truth should not be hastily rejected without first trying to understand them.

Living in a world of objects, one primarily turns to experience or sense perception in order to know the world.

Experience is useful in demonstrating any matters of fact and existence, where logic is of little use. The hall-mark of empiricism is its emphasis upon facts. It insists upon starting from facts and ending in facts. The rationalist way, on the contrary, is limited to a certain extent, as it is capable of proving only those truths that are analytic and ultimately tautological. Rationality is nothing but a form, an ideal constitution which experience may embody. Without experience, therefore, there would be nothing to reason about. Experience is primary and one can know the world through sense perception and conceptual reasoning. Religion is nothing but a part of experience, a mass of sentiments and ideas. The sentiments are unshifting and the ideas are a changing and struggling force. This struggling and changing force seems to lead human beings towards some eternal principle.[5] Santayana, from this, seems to entertain the possibility that religious experiences may be instrumental in revealing to humankind, God.

This brings us to the God-problem. One of the avenues of approach to the problem may be from the standpoint of one's own religious experience. "More private but still dramatic manifestation of God in vision and dream, by inner voice, numinous feeling, mystical or ecstatic experience have also convinced many of the reality of God."[6] John Hicks also said that, "God, if he exists, is not an idea but a reality outside us; therefore if he is to be known to men, he must manifest himself in some way within their experience."[7] Upholders of this view claim that a knowledge of God by direct awareness or acquaintance is possible through religious experiences. For those unconvinced by the traditional proofs for the existence of God, religious experience may provide the authentic evidence for establishing God's existence. Thus religious experience has come to be the sole means of penetrating to the essence of God, bridging the shores of finite and infinite.

Thus far the focus has been on theistic mysticism, but a word must be added about its non-theistic counterpart. For example, Buddhism is a godless religion with a profound mystical tradition. The mystic end which they call *nirvāṇa* is the state of self-realisation and attainment of *bodhi* is marked by one's complete detachment from, and indifference to, anything mundane. According to the non-theistic traditions, the subject-object distinction is obliterated and all is resolved into a oneness in religious experiences. Religious experience involves an intense and vivid appreciation of the unseen world, and an absorption of the self into it. In both instances religious experiences mark a quest for union with the beyond. And, for such direct and immediate contact with the unseen, due preparation is necessary. This naturally implies the mystic way and the whole apparatus of practical religion which is closely bound up with the production of religious experiences.

This approach is in tune with the claim that human beings are gifted with esoteric powers which leads us directly to the portals of truth. It is believed that certain kinds of knowledge, particularly the knowledge of God, come not through the laboured efforts of reflective thinking, but through direct insight and intuition. Sometimes the powers of reason may be transcended to open up a direct approach to God, or bring about an immediate union with reality, so that truth is felt, apprehended or grasped, as if in a flash.

The original impetus in the formation of most of the great religions has come from inspired individuals, the founders, and these in turn appear to reflect a general tradition in which the recurring inspirational excitation of a person seems to have no mean part to play. The personal attitudes, hopes, fears, and beliefs of religious prophets colour the basic structure of the religion. From this perspective religious experience is the root of religions. But institutionalised religion is likely to be barren unless its tenets are verified in the experience of the believer. In this way religious experiences are those very personal experiences which strengthen the foundation of believers.

Believers may be either—the blind believer or the questioning or introspective believer. Unlike the former, it is important, for the latter, to feel or realise whatever has been laid down by prophets and seers. For the believer religious experience "allows for a first hand understanding of religion as an actual force in human life, in contrast with religion taken either as church membership or as belief in authoritative doctrines."[8]

Stressing this, W.H. Clark says, "Yet it is doubtful whether religion would have survived the centuries without those immediate experiences of the presence of God that are to be marked not only among the great, but also in the ordinary believer during his moments of inspiration and uplift."[9] Therefore, the origin of religions may be traced in the religious experiences, and for their growth and survival they are dependent on the satisfactory affirmation of the tenets by the individual religious experiences of the believer—i.e., the subject may be approached from the standpoint of one's own individual religious experiences.[10] Personal religious experiences, as the claim stands, are all the "evidence" available in support of one's religious beliefs.

These claims associated with religious experience (*i*) that it is the basis of religion, (*ii*) that the survival and promulgation of religions depend greatly on the personal experiences of believers, and (*iii*) that it is adequate proof for authenticating the existence of God, or is the valid source for the knowledge about God, make it liable to scrutiny.

Religious Experience : Characteristics

This leads to the question, 'What are the characteristics that make up the essentials of a religious experience ?' A subsequent query is whether religious experiences are different from, or distinct from other experiences. And if they are, what are their distinctive features ?

Many writers have enumerated the quintessentials of religious experiences, and there seem to be little difference among them about their basic features. All of them attach some qualifying characteristics by which religious experiences stand out as distinct from other experiences, and, it is only in the case of the fringe characteristics that differences tend to arise. The important and interesting feature is that in spite of such a wide variety of experiences within the frame of varying traditions, environment, and mental make up, there is general agreement as to the fundamental characteristics of religious experiences; their recognisable similarities in the different ranges make them form a distinctively determinable realm having certain characteristics. Regarding this, Stace opines that "there will be a central nucleus of typical cases which are typical because they all share an important set of common characteristics. But there will be borderline cases. These are usually, or often, called "mystical experiences" because although none of them possess all the common characteristics of the nucleus, some of them possess some of these characteristics, others, others."[11] Stace has attempted to diagramatically express what he means.

True class relation of a set of common characteristics

Fig. I*

Accentuating the importance of borderline cases he says, "If we should find that the universal core in the central nucleus consists of the common characteristics *a*, *b*, *c*, *d* and if a critic were to bring up one of the borderline cases and say, "This is what people call a mystical experience, but it does not share all these characteristics *a*, *b*, *c*, *d* we should have no answer. But if we have taken the preliminary precaution of recognizing borderline cases we, shall have an answer to that critic."[12] However, the occurrence of the basic features justifies our calling the attached experience a religious one.

The study of religious experiences falls naturally into two parts, of which the first and more fundamental is the study of these experiences; the second being a study of their interpretations offered by mystics and others.

In order to facilitate a complete understanding of the nature of religious experiences, the characteristics have been divided into primary and subsidiary. Here primary characteristics constitute the quintessence of the experiences

* Fig. I : W.T. Stace, *Mysticism and Philosophy*, London, 1961, p. 46.

under examination, while the subsidiary ones are those that often accompany such experiences, but not always. The primary characteristics are more the distinguishing marks of these experiences, showing clearly their difference from other kinds of experiences. The secondary features, however, enable others to know of the occurence of the experience, its impact on the subject and also the intensity with which the experience had come. The secondary characteristics, being the manifestations of the experience, are the means by which various aspects of the experience may be gauged. This crucial point is closely associated with the problem of expression and cognitivity and will feature for discussion in a subsequent chapter.

A scan through the biographies of mystics and mystical writings reveal the consequences of religious experiences; viz., the birth of certain feelings which result in beliefs and convictions. In addition to these, the experiences also have some impact on both the psychological faculties and physical capabilities, i.e., the very being of the experiencer. These resultants will be discussed in the latter half of this chapter.

Primary Characteristics : Beliefs, Assertions, Feelings and the Quintessence of Religious Experiences

It seems fair to commence a study of the nature of religious experiences with the four Jamesian characteristics as basic, because they not merely provide the starting point for the ensuing discussions but also because there are many others who share the same view. The four characteristics identified by James are : (*i*) Ineffability, (*ii*) Noetic quality, (*iii*) Transiency, and (*iv*) Passivity.[13] Based on his observations Happold added the following to the Jamesian four : (*i*) a consciousness of the Oneness of everything, (*ii*) the sense of timelessness and (*iii*) the conviction that the familiar phenomenal ego is not the real I.[14]

As far as ineffability is concerned, the general consensus is that religious experiences are inherently difficult to express and explain. Regarding this James is known to have remarked :

"The subject of it immediately says that it defies expression, that no adequate report of its contents can be given in words. It follows from this that its quality must be directly experienced; it cannot be imparted or transferred to others."[15] It has almost universally been asserted that religious experiences do not succumb to analysis and description, because no language is suitable enough for the purpose. The ineffability of religious experiences is adumberated in the works of W.H. Clark, J B. Pratt, R.C. Zaehner and F.C. Happold, among others.[16]

Wittgenstein in his *Tractatus* has shown that reports of religious experiences without trivialising or destroying the very things which are sought to be explained, defended or clarified, is not possible. Wittgenstein, however, did not intend to dismiss religious experiences as nonsense. All he maintained was that mystics ultimately resort to silence as words distort the original experience, because, language pictures or mirrors the world. And the experiences under consideration seem to belong to a world beyond the one manifest to us by our senses. Naturally, any discussion relating to experiences from a world beyond falls well outside the scope of human language.[17] The usual practice is to describe the effect of the experience or comment on it, thereby importing an element of interpretation. Explanations and descriptions are unconscious interpretations in terms of the tradition in which the individual is trained, and, the frame of reference adopted is also determined by heredity and culture. The fact that any explanation of religious experiences is determined by one's personal preconceptions, plainly reveals the incompetency of such explanations.

Stretched to a further extent, the practical difficulties faced in the course of explaining a religious experience, compels the mystic to take recourse to silence. "The deeper and more intimate a spiritual experience, the more readily does it dispense with signs and symbols. Deep intuition is utterly silent."[18] Buddha exemplifies this best—when asked to speak on the nature of '*nirvāṇa*', he answered with the mystical silence.

According to Tennant one class of experiences are ineffable and "defy expression or articulation, reduction, translation into terms of imagery or thought, even for the experient himself. In them the mystic knows 'he knows not what'; yet memory of them persists. As they are ineffable, not to say incommunicable, these experiences must ever remain occult as to their nature. They cannot, therefore, be amenable to description as deliverances of truth ... "[19]

The noetic quality of religious experiences "are states of insight into depths of truth unplumbed by the discursive intellect. They are illuminations, revelations, full of significance and importance, all inarticulate though they remain; and as a rule they carry with them a curious sense of authority for aftertime."[20] In these experiences there is an immediate presentation of truth fortified by the accompanying sense of certainty. Truth comes to the individual as self-established (*svatāssiddha*), self-evidencing (*svasamvedyā*), and self – luminous (*svayam-prakāsa*), requiring no external means of verification. The feeling of immediacy and absolute certainty is universal and intersubjective in the sense that they attach to certain experiences, whoever has the experience. Even though such experiences are not expressible "in the language of the intellect ... one who has undergone mystical experience is convinced with absolute certainty that he does know."[21] The same thing is implied by Radhakrishnan when he says "It is pure comprehension, entire significance, complete validity."[22] He renders further support by calling mysticism 'integrated thought' – it brings things together, i.e., integrates them, instead of, as in analytical thought, breaking them into parts.

A peculiar sense of certainty accompanies religious experiences – certainty of the self-revealing and knowledge bearing nature of the experiences. This specific quality of religious experiences has probably led William Pepperell Montague to consider mysticism a well founded means of knowledge that is beyond doubt and explanation. There is the fullest affirmation on the part of the individual of one's involvement in receiving non-sensory impressions, which yield truth unmediated by understanding, ideation, or reason. " ... mystics claim with great unanimity the possession of what James calls a 'noetic quality' of mind, an individual illumination which gives them a powerful assurance of the reality of their religious experience."[23] These experiences, for mystics, are face to face presentations of truth, and this is how knowledge may be acquired through religious experiences. What James has called 'noetic quality' some others have preferred to call 'illumination'. Yet other names for it are 'intuition' and 'immediate knowledge'.

It is interesting to note that the scale being generally tilted in favour of the noetic quality in the strictest sense, does meet with disfavour from the likes of Tennant and George Santayana. For the former "Knowledge of ineffable truth, is a contradiction in terms."[24] George Santayana does not doubt that religious experiences are, but does question the claim of their being inherently noetic.

'Transiency' and 'Passivity' are treated as lesser important as compared to 'ineffability' and 'noetic quality' by James. Transiency refers to the momentariness of the experience, and of this James says that they "cannot be sustained for long."[25] Normally religious experiences last for an hour or half an hour, to a maximum of two or three hours, after which they fade out. They are imperfectly reproduced in memory, but on recurrence they can be recognised. Happold, though he holds the same view, adds that "The following of a particular way of life can, however, increase their frequency. At that stage of the Mystic Way known as the illuminative Life, they can be very frequent and, it would seem, controllable."[26]

Mystics in describing their experiences have used language to imply the transiency of their experiences. "The vision lasted a few seconds and was gone; but the memory of it and the sense of the reality of what it taught has remained during the quarter of a century which has since elapsed. I knew tha. what the vision shewed was truet"[27] "The transiency and momentariness ... is insisted on habitually by St. Gregory in such expressions as these : The contemplation is enjoyed by stealth and scantily, by stealth and in passing, delicately, suddely, not fixed but by snatch ... "[28]

By way of summing up this characteristic its necessary concomitants may be listed as—(*i*) the experience lasts but for a short duration, (*ii*) after the experience things shift back to the original state, (*iii*) faint impressions of the experience remain in the memory, (*iv*) ability to recall and recognize similar experiences when they occur, and (*v*) there is a feeling of grief that the experience should be over in a short while. Despite this, it does leave some lasting impact on one's life.

'Passivity' according to "James refers to the fact that the subject . . . feels himself in the grip of a power other than himself. He feels that his thoughts and his feelings, even his bodily motions, are somehow not the product of his own efforts but that of another . . ."[29] James himself admits that "the oncoming of mystical states may be facilitated by preliminary voluntary operation . . ." Yet in spite of this, "when the characteristic sort of consciousness once has set in, the mystic feels as if his own will were in abeyance, and indeed sometimes as if he were grasped and held by a superior power."[30] All this goes to show that the insight is gained through a kind of identification of the knower with the known; the known being, some superior transcendental being. Whatever happens to the experiencer at this stage is not accountable by the person because one is overpowered by some being outside one-self. After the experience is over the experiencer may have faint memories of what happened albeit one was wholly involved in the experience.

Happold means very much the same thing in stating : "when they occur, mystical states invariably carry with them a feeling of something given."[31] It is quite natural to have this standpoint, because what the individual knows comes to one spontaneously and not simply by virtue of one's own efforts. This givenness may explain certain definite phenomena, peculiar to religious experiences, like prophetic speech, automatic writing or the mediumistic trance.

Coe is of the opinion that, passivity is a corollary to the means adopted by mystics to attain a state of detachment so that they remain uneffected by external stimuli. It must be noted that Coe is one of them who believes in the possibility of creating an atmosphere favourable for the occurrence of religious experiences. Individuals attain to this state by concentration and withdrawal of attention from the activities and sense stimuli of daily life. Passivity is spelt out in the bodily responses, and unresponsiveness to ordinary incitements—an overall indifference on the part of the aspirant to objects and doings in the sense world. So, narrowing of attention and concern are aids to passivity.

Some more characteristics have been appended to the basic four disscussed so far. According to Happold another mark of religious experiences is "the presence of a *consciousness of the Oneness of everything*. All creaturely existence is experienced as a unity, as All in One and One in all."[32] Once the consciousness of the Oneness of things creeps in, things begin to lose their individuality resulting in the unique experience of unity. "It is a condition of conciousness in which feelings are fused, ideas melt into one and other, boundaries broken and ordinary, distinctions transcended."[33]

In many of our experiences, we apparently touch another dimension of existence than the sensible and mere 'understandable' world. These sorts of experiences lead to a greater unity—such as cannot be grasped in the course of ordinary experience. They affirm a greater unity than is acknowledged or felt. Happold elucidates the point by citing the example of the *Tao*, *yin*, and *yang*. *Tao* is the Primal Meaning and Undivided Unity behind everything from which spring the opposite principles of phenomenal reality—*Yang* (light) and *Yin* (darkness). All opposites which are visible in phenomenal experiences merge into unity. In sense perception there is no escape from such dualities and differences, but "In mystical experience the dilema of duality is resolved. For to the mystic is given that unifying vision of the One in the All and the All in the One."[34]

The Advaita Vedantins have the approach that one principle in which every other thing unites is the Brahman. They are guided by notions which lead to their denial of the reality of the world of senses. What is known of the temporal world is unreal as one is overcome by *avidya* or ignorance. When an individual is rid of ignorance one's vision is in focus revealing to one the inevitable unity. Samkara warns against the temptation to regard as real what is unreal. He accepts the empirical reality of the world, which is negated only when perfect insight or intuition of the oneness of all is attained. In the context of mysticism's belief in unity, and its refusal to admit opposition or division anywhere, Russell questions : "Is all plurality and division illusory ?"[35] The consciousness of oneness comes when "the bonds of the personal nature of life seem to have fallen away from us and we experience an undivided unity."[36]

Closest to this apprehension of Unity, is the feeling of a presence, which is emphasised by mystics of all times and places. There is, as it were, in the human cousciousness a sense of reality, a feeling of objective presence, a perception of what we may call 'something there' in a way far deeper and significantly than possible by any of the senses. Religious experiences produce the sense of the presence of a being or reality through other means than the ordinary perceptive processes or the reason. It is the *sense* or *feeling* of this presence. not the belief in it, neither the result of the senses, nor a conclusion reached by discursive thought; it is, instead, an immediate and intuitive experience. When the experience comes, the mystic is convinced of an impressive Presence, more concretely real than what one's eyes see, one's ears hear, or one's hands touch. This is a mystery which breaks in upon the human scene.[37]

To this sense of presence is attached religious and theistic significance by the mystics. The theistic interpretation of this presence is often qualified by words like 'absolute', 'real', 'supernatural', 'divine' etc. We may believe in the Beyond. or in God, on less direct grounds reached by mere circuitous paths; and then reasonably interpret religious experience in terms of the theistic concept and world-view. The theists arrive at God from the bases formed by the 'apprehension of unity', and the 'feeling of a presence'. Thus it is affirmation of the reality of what may be called the supernatural, terming it 'God', that determines the religious quality of religious experience. According to Patrick, "the God idea resolves itself into the idealisation of certain fundamental and characteristic values which have ranked high in human experience, particularly power, righteousness, love, justice, and personality. These are the things which appeal to us as of supreme worth, and God is the embodiment or personification of these ideals."[38] These lines evince how the idealisation of certain values results in the God idea; treating God as the repository of all values in their purest and perfect state.

The climax of religious experiences is apparently union with God, the ultimate reality, so intimate that self-conciousness vanishes, and the feeling tone is said to be utterly satisfying. The direct acquaintance with God is accompanied by a feeling of immediacy and certainty. The religious experiences lead upto the direct essence of God, and to the facts of the spiritual world, lying beyond the phenomenal world, embodied as religious truths.

The object confronted in religious experiences is understood to be the absolute limit to which, at least here on earth, human awareness can be extended, as it is the ultimate reality, knowable by insight, the unmediated perception of a higher coherence within the materials of one's more or less usual knowledge. Elmer O'Brien thus points out that

(*i*) the object confronted in mystic experience is thought, by the mystic to be somehow ultimate.

(*ii*) the manner of confrontation is immediate, direct.

(*iii*) The confrontation is always different from the familiar exercise of either sense perception or of reasoning.[39]

A study carried out under the auspices of the Religious Experience Research Unit, Manchester College, Oxford, provides the phenomenology of certain kinds of visionary and ecstatic experience, based on a thousand contemporary first-hand accounts, Sir Alister Hardy defined his requirements by using quotations when he made public appeal for accounts of a certain type of religious experience. Timothy Beardsworth who conducted the study affirms his approach to be phenomenological, "i.e. concerned with each individual's exact description of his experience (assuming that he is telling the truth), regardless of whether what seemed to him to happen "really" happened or not" The author further points out that no inferences have been drawn, instead the study "provides a great deal of quotation, comparison and contrast."[40]

In his chapter 'A Feeling Of Unity With One's Surroundings', based on the accounts received, he draws out the changes in appearance of surrounding, change of mood, change in relation to surroundings, and attitude that followed. He also discusses the cognitive state, the way in which the onset of the experience was marked, the ineffability of the experiences, the language used in general, the duration of the experience, and the nature of the object with which unity is felt.[41]

The fifth chapter in the same volume deals with 'The Sense of Presence'.[42] In the accounts of experiences received "there is emotional dependence. There is always this affective personal relationship implied .... The presence is felt to exist only in relation to oneself, as the cause of an emotional effect on one."[43] Further, "The two things—feeling of "presence" and emotional "response" to it are tied indissolubly. To experience it is to react to it."[44] The presence may be experienced as pleasing, disturbing, not comforting, etc., all of which may be externally apparent from the subject's emotional reaction of warmth, shame, fear, respectively. In this way, the presence which is felt to exist only in relation to oneself, as the cause of an emotional effect on one, explains how it is possible to feel something without perceiving anything. Beardsworth's study sheds light on the location of the presence, the prevailing moods and circumstances, the effects of the experience, and the nature of the presence felt.

A further characteristic appended by Happold is the sense of timelessness. Time itself, as shown by Happold, is an indefinite factor. Normally our experiences fall into a time series to include always a past, a present, and a future Time seems to melt into a state of timelessness in religious experiences. "Whatever time may be, and it is a mystery, the experience of the mystics are not understandable unless one is prepared to accept that there may be an entirely different dimension from that of clock time or indeed of any other sort of time. For the mystic feels himself to be in a dimension where time is not, where 'all is always now'."[45] According to Russell "A ... mark of almost all mystical metaphysics is the denial of the reality of time. This is an outcome of the denial of division; if all is one, the distinction of past and future must be illusory."[46] Further, "Bound up with the sense of oneness and the sense of timelessness there is another characteristic of mystical experience, the conviction that the familiar phenomenal *ego* is not the real I."[47]

The view propounded by Happold finds strength in the Indian concept of *Jivātman* and *Paramātman*. The *Paramātman* is Brahman or absolute, while the individual self is the *Jivātman*. The popular saying of the Upanisbads, '*Tat tvam asi*', 'That thou art', suggests an unqualified oneness between the self that underlies any person and Brahman. This oneness is realised when *avidyā* is removed and the phenomenal ego is cancelled, to be viewed as one with *Ātman*. The crux of Indian philosophy is that God created human beings in his own image, and it is for them to realise this underlying oneness. The temper of Indian philosophy is therefore a perpetual aspiring towards something higher and more real. The spirit of aspiration is conspicuous in relating the *Jivātman* and *Paramātman*' *mokṣa*, the finite and the infinite, etc. And all these form the base of Indian mysticism. Thus, the highest ideal expressed in the Indian texts is the realisation of the ultimate oneness of *Jivātman* and *Paramātman*. This claim finds its place in Christian writings also, though not quite in the same form. In Christian mysticism it appears under several names, the *spark*, the *centre*, or *apex of the soul*, and *the ground of the spirit* Eckhart seems to be saying that at the 'apex of the mind' there is a divine spark which is so closely akin to God, that it is 'one' with, not merely 'united to' Him.

An account given by Mlle Vé, would bring home to us the noted characteristics of religious experience. "She states that she was neither conscious of her body nor of her own identity; above all, the impression of time was lost, she seemed to be plunged in timelessness, in eternity. Combined with this she felt the essential reality of a presence which she was disposed to call that of the Life of God."[48]

According to Evelyn Underhill there are four other characteristics of equal significance. At times it becomes apparent that her approach, in part, contradicts William James, and those who share his views. Her first contention that "True mysticism is active and practical, not passive and theoretical,"[49] clearly shows the difference of approach between James and herself. Underhill's further contention is that mystics must learn by 'doing'. 'Doing' here does not imply merely the active purification of one's daily life, but, for best results, a rigorous course in meditation. There have been occasions when she says that mystical achievement is partly an 'act of surrender', which bears the under current of passivity.

According to Miss Underhill, the aims of mysticism are "wholly transcendental and spiritual. It is in no way concerned with adding to, exploring, re-arranging, or improving anything in the visible universe."[50] The spiritual and transcendental nature of the aims of mysticism does not reduce its importance. As long as humankind claims to have such experiences they retain their significance. But, if, as Underhill maintains, the mystic experiences are God-centred and separate from the worldly affairs, the gap between the world of senses and the world beyond is not reduced.

There has been an expressed interest in relating the 'phenomenal' and the 'noumenal' by knowledge acquired in the course of religious experiences, e.g., the noetic quality leads to knowledge of reality which supposedly elevates one's level of knowledge and helps further one's knowledge of truth; passivity implies submission or merging of the phenomenal ego with the One Self, which affects the individual's life style and attitude towards problems of cosmic significance. By this we realise the close link there is between what we perceive through our senses and what comes to us as immediate insight.

The changeless one for the mystic is "not merely the Reality of all that is, but also a living and personal object of Love; never an object of exploration."[51] The language of the mystic is suggestive of the experience of the ultimate in one's encounter with God. In this sort of an experience the mystic's yearning is fulfilled, and feeling of total submission comes. This feeling brings forth love — the love which Underhill speaks of as the ultimate expression of the self's most vital tendencies.

The last of Underhill's characteristics goes thus, "Living union with this One . . . is a definite state or form of enhanced life. It is obtained neither from an intellectual realization of its delights, nor from the most acute emotional longings. Though these must be present, they are not enough. It is arrived at by a definite and arduous psychological process—the so-called Mystic Way—entailing the complete remaking of character and the liberation of a new, or rather latent, form of consciousness which imposes on the self the condition which is sometimes inaccurately called "ecstasy", but is better named the Unitive State."[52] This rather lengthy passage appears to epitomise the most important aspect in her description of mysticism.

James and Underhill seem to be at variance in expressing their characteristics of religious experience. The Jamesian approach has been investigatory, untouched by any religious bias, whereas Underhill is a strong supporter of the credibility of religious experience—in the words of Clark "a partisan of the mystics."[53] The former's interest was directed to testing the authenticity of such praeternatural experiences. Johnson is of the opinion that "James was seeking to discover what is unique in the religious experience of individual persons, however varied and abnormal they might be. For in this way he hoped to find what is most personal and authentic in religious experience no matter how extreme it appears by conventional standard."[54]

What appears to be differences on the issue of passivity between James and Underhill is explained by C.A. Coe as the same thing viewed from two perspectives. The concentration of attention necessarily requires a narrowing of attention. Here is involved an element of control which can be achieved by effort and practice, and this holding of the mind at just the right point is, in a sense, intense activity. Hence it comes to pass that both passivity and activity are attributed by mystical writers to the same mental state.[55]

Clark has briefly summarised the foregoing discussion by integrating the various points raised in describing the characteristics of religious experience. "Mysticism is a definite but sporadic state of the religious consciousness partly active and partly passive, involving an experience so usually personal as to defy description in any but the most figurative and cryptic language. It involves the apprehension of a transcendental presence which radically influences the individual's point of view and way of life. The consequent passionate devotion to this presence tends so lead to an extremely unworldly value system. These values foster extravagant behaviour which nevertheless stimulates integration of the psyche centred on this devotion."[56]

Secondary Characteristics : Behavioural Responses to, and Psycho - Physical Effects of Religious Experiences

Some other characteristics have been mentioned as concomitants of religious experiences in the writings of mystics and religious scholars. Most of them, however, accompany religious experiences occasionally and neither necessarily nor always. The history of religious experiences and mysticism includes accounts of psycho-physical phenomena that unmistakably hold a prominent place in the lives of mystics. These phenomena have been noticed, though not accorded the status of characteristics of religious experience. This attitude is probably because the psycho - physical reactions are more pronounced in some cases and totally absent in others.

The psycho - physical reactions of religious experience deserve attention because they definitely contribute in moulding the thoughts and life style of the experiencers. Moreover, the variance of degree in persons should be considered as a variance in the manifestation and not in what is actually felt. This point is well illustrated by the example of people with the capacity to face shocks with sufficient coolness and others who react strongly to the slightest shock, which is dependent on the individual's temperament, and capacity to face a situation. Besides this, people differ in their expressive capabilities. So, considering these differences as prevalent in human beings, it is possible to enumerate and analyse the significance of the psycho - physical concomitants of religious experience, as (*i*) Mental Effects, and (*ii*) Physical Effects.

It is predominantly observed that mystics have noteworthy reactions to their experiences, whether momentary and unconscious, or life—changing or conscious. The experience of God or some higher being — call it the sense of a presence — is held to be evocative of emotional attitudes that tend to be qualitatively unique. In an experience of confrontation with the object of aspiration, the individual reaches the apex of self - fulfilment, thereby attaining the height of satisfaction. It is only natural that the feeling of self - fulfilment and extreme satisfaction should issue forth emotional and physical responses. The state of enthusiasm and excitement of highly - wrought religious emotion, is liable to manifest itself by way of physical and mental changes. The individual's response is the reaction of the whole self in its relation with reality—that reality of which only one is absolutely certain.

Any variance that is noticed in the expression of responses to religious experiences is attributible to the determining conditions like, human inclinations and temperament, cultural and social background, the subjective emotional framework, and the nature of experiences and events in an individual's life. Pathological extremes are by no means characteristic of all the mystics; and, when they do occur, they are seldom regarded even by those who experience them as of the first importance. To understand mysticism all right one must take into consideration the whole life of the mystic, including both the recurring states of ecstasy and the periods intervening between them or subsequent to them.[57] Psychologists have sought to associate the psycho - physical reactions with the psychological factors prevailing in human beings and their lives. Thus the only importance that these phenomena have received is from the psychologists who attempt to utilise them for investigation of the psychological factors conditioning an individual's disposition to such reactions.

In Christian writings we often come across the term 'divided self' or 'sick soul' — implying certain strains and conflicts going on within the self. These strains are profound and recurrent, taking forms like a distaste for usual worldly pleasures but inability to find adequate substitutes for them; restlessness caused by inadequate exercise of sensual and social instincts, or lack of occupation adequate to executive capabilities giving a feeling of life's emptiness ; a sense of personal unworthiness because one has failed to reach a victorious conclusion against sinful desires; changeability of mood with self - criticism for inconsistency, and similar instances. Such people are more susceptible to conspicuous psycho - physical reactions to their religious experiences. For them their religious experience indicates the path to unification of self, a commanding certainty displacing doubts, and a sense of purposiveness substituted for discordant impulses. This whole situation leads to the conclusion that though psycho - physical reactions are not uniform in kind and degree, religious experiences tend to produce serenity, poise, composure and an organised will. The individual sails into a sheltered harbour of stability from the tempestuous seas of internal conflicts. Thus, the hold religious experience has upon humankind is in its practical efficiency in soothing troubled emotions and stabilising the will.

A wide range of reactions, both physical and mental, are noticed to occur during and after a religious experience. The commonest among these are ecstasy, trance and rapture. In each of these states the person shows typical behavioural tendencies.

The three states, ecstasy, trance and rapture, are difficult to treat separately, and have been taken together to explicate the specific nature of the psycho - physical concomitants of religious experiences. The dictionary meaning of 'ecstasy' goes thus : "an overpowering emotion or exaltation; a state of sudden, intense feeling."[58] It is, as it were, a feeling of great joy and spiritual upliftment. "Ecstasy is a word which covers a multitude of things, from alcoholic intoxication and possession by demons to the raptures of Plotinus. Ecstasy of the quiet contemplative type is different from the wild excitement induced by physical means and indulged in for its intoxicating effects. All experience of God when it becomes intense is ecstatic, though every ecstatic emotion is not an experience of God."[59]

According to Selbie "The chief characteristics of the ecstatic state are intense emotional excitement, loss of normal self - control, insensibility to external impressions, and increased powers of vision and audition. It expresses itself sometimes in complete calm and in feeling of rapturous communion with the divine, sometimes in violent manifestations of emotion."[60]

But, what goes on with regard to one's bodily and mental state, which colour one's emotions, is of no interest to the individual. Neither is one in this condition conscious of one's emotional expressions, nor is one able to carry out the smallest activities of body or mind, as a feeling of bondage prevails. Leuba contends that in the extreme form of ecstasy all ideas vanish, there remaining no source of further suggestion, and the mystic either returns to ordinary conciousness or lapses into normal sleep. "In a fully religious ecstasy the subject is 'withdrawn from the bodily senses and is carried away unto God and afterwards is restored to his mortal members."[61]

In a state of rapture one is so carried away in thought and feeling that one is unaware of other things. With religious experience the person is so fascinated and spell bound, that one is in the grip of the experience, losing touch with surrounding objects, persons and activities. This state is accompanied by the spontaneous expression of extreme happiness, joyousness, enthusiasm and eagerness. Likewise in trance the beginning lies in narrowing of the consciousness, followed by loss of control over the voluntary muscles. The trance state is akin to that of the hypnotic state, in so far as their expressions are concerned. A trance state is a half - conscious state, seemingly between sleeping and waking, in which ability to function voluntarily may be suspended. Another way of looking at it is taking it to be a temporary state in which a medium, with suspension of personal consciousness, is controlled from without. It is during this state that the mystics indulge in maximum involuntary body movements. There is, as it were, alienation of the whole person from every other thing in the world. All attention is diverted and centred around the object of experience, with no concern for anything else.

In all three states there are apparently two dominating features—(*i*) the person's total involvement in the experience, and resulting incapability to control expressions, and (*ii*) the feeling of joy, peace and elation that comes effortlessly to the person. Both these tendencies result from the unique experience of one's union with the reality.

We frequently meet with instances of these states in the writings of Christian mystics. They are agreed that these states are beyond anything comprehensible to ordinary consciousness Peculiarly enough, all mystics, though they mention it, do not go through these phases. St. Augustine was one whose elevated states did not produce any pronounced psycho - physical effects. Yet, the phenomena, with their alienation of the senses, were familiar to him. Some like St. Teresa, are so constituted that they frequently go into ecstasies and trances.

A noticeable feature of the exalted states is that they are often marked by a feeling of depression, and it is a mistake to suppose that these states are experiences of every nice and soothing feeling. The mystics do go through a dry period as far as ecstasies, raptures and trances are concerned. The sufferings of individuals during these periods are of many sorts. St. John has distinguished them into three kinds : loss of delight in any creature; the feeling of one's distance from God and the memory of the joy of ecstasy which is no longer to be had ;

and, inability to 'mediate' or to excite oneself to poious emotion by the use of the imagination. St. Teresa's chief source of pain seems to have been a recurrent doubt as to whether her mystic experiences were not the product of illusion or the work of the 'Wicked One'. The phenomena of depression is due to an impoverishment of the emotional life through its over stimulation during the periods of ecstasy and trance. The former joy is remembered and longed for, but does not come, and this ushers in fits of disappointment and depression.

From the accounts given above it is indicative of the fact that all these states ensuing from religious experiences are marked by specific characters. Definite nervous, and psycho-physical changes occur, from which we can detect the effect of religious experiences on the human constitution. Though most of the effects or responses are subjective, they are at times evident from the modifications and changes in behaviour, activity, and sometimes from physical appearances. The list of effects of, and responses to, religious experiences has been formulated under the heads 'mental' and 'physical'. The commonly known 'mental' effects are as follows :

1. Forgetfulness
2. Insensitivity to external stimuli, to the extent of increase in the capacity to bear electric shocks
3. Detachment and indifference to worldly objects and affairs, thus giving no importance to intellectual doubts
4. Introversion
5. No experience of time transition
6. No awareness of self
7. State of spiritual delight and ineffable peace
8. An inrush of vitalising energies, enhanced appreciations, enjoyment, bliss, etc.

9. Feeling of certainty—that the objects and affective states bespeak an enfolding presence

10. Periods of terrible depression, darkness, apparent abandonment by God — a typical phenomena as latent in the writings of Christian mystics

11. Certain traits develop, which all come within the general class 'saintliness' :

    (a) A feeling of being in a wider life than that of this world's selfish interests

    (b) A sense of the friendly continuity of the ideal power with our own life, and willing self-surrender to its control

    (c) Immense elation and freedom, as the outlines of the confining selfhood melt down

    (d) A shifting of the emotional centre towards loving and harmonious affections

These traits that build up 'saintliness' have their corresponding practical consequences.[62]

Nervous instability and even some nervous and mental imbalances are sometimes exhibited by mystics. They tend to be apathetic about personal health, comforts, family affairs, and in general, to their environment.

Some of the conspicuous physical expressions usually to be found among mystics are as listed below :

1. Loss of control over voluntary activities and bodily movements and speech.

2. Vivacious and often rhythmic movements of the body.

3. Frequent and violent alterations of emotion have corresponding physical behaviour.

4. In the state of depression, restlessness, inability to concentrate in any particular activity, etc., prevail.

5. The individual's each activity seems to be controlled from without.

6. In a state of mental peace and serenity, there is relaxation of muscles.

7. Physical tolerance to bear external shocks and pains increases.

8. Involuntary muscular reactions of many sorts give an impression that one's body is being partly or wholly controlled by a will other than one's own.

Thus from the time of union or attainment of the mystic goal, termed 'spiritual marriage', the individual engages in a life of activity guided by a power which cannot be recognised as one's own. Delacroix goes to the extent of theorising that their "action is guided not by the conscious will but by the subconscious forces of the psycho - physical organism."[63]

Besides reactions and manifestations, mystics are said to acquire powers of both body and mind. In this connection, Radhakamal Mukherjee is known to have claimed that records of premonition, precognition, clairvoyance and telepathy, from the mystics of all creeds and times, are available. "The hypothesis is that when the ego side of the pure mind becomes, through the process of abstract concentration, free from the disturbance of the sensory and organic processes, the omniscient pure mind operates and apprehends phases or states of reality which are not bound to the spatio - temporal system of relations."[64] When there is an illuminating experience of knowledge, a tendency of self - abandonment grows spontaneously.

The tendencies in mystics so far enumerated have been sufficient cause to be evaluated as escapism. This may be justified when understood as a psychological evaluation of the attitude of individual mystics. For the very same tendencies, religious experiences have been paralleled with hysteria and mental degeneration. The similarities of expression of hysterics, mental patients, religious experients and drug addicts have led to many confusions and controversies.

It is indeed true that such emotions and raptures are erratic and unpredictable There is no assurance that every experient will undergo the same emotional upheaval to produce identical psycho - physical manifestations. At the same time, the experience is often detected and distinguished from others by virtue of the external manifestations which are unconscious manifestations. Regardless of whether external manifestations are detectable or not, detachment and comprehensiveness of attitudes and feelings as well as efficiency of attention gradually supercede emotionalism and bring the mystic to a unitive stage. Clearly then, integration of sentiments and attitudes provides the foundation of an intuitive perception of unity. This in turn is responsible for emanating calm, peace, pure joy and bliss in the individual who experiences the unity of being. "In the mystic experience one becomes freed of all his old established meanings; he is lifted out of the ruts of all his ordinary thinking; he is shaken loose from all his mental habits ; his mental system is melted down into a fluid state; he becomes filled with a theory of free, uncontrolled impulses so numerous and diverse that they hold one another in abeyance, producing a quivering mass of sensitivity to the total undiscriminated situation."[65]

A question that arises at this point is whether these characteristics are evinced in all kinds and degrees of religious experiences. For instance, do they characterise prayer, worship, observance of religious norms or rituals ? Talking of these characteristics the more intense kinds of religious experiences, which are best exemplified by mystic episodes, are referred to. By religious experience is implied its more intense forms; those at the upper end of the heirarchical order, like mystic experience, prophetic insight and revelation.

So, overtly this type of experience may be equalled with ecstatic experiences. This does not imply that all ecstatic experiences are instances of religious experience because their sources or origins are so diverse that they make their content equally diverse. Their external manifestation may appear to be the same but inwardly or qualitatively they may be very different from each other. However, when religious experiences are of the ecstatic type, they are bound to be marked by the mentioned characteristics—if not all at the same time, majority of them at least.

The psycho - physical concomitants, then, are significant as characteristics of religious experience, though they may not belong to the category of essential characteristics. That is precisely why they have been treated as secondary or subsidiary characteristics. By highlighting the nature of the psycho - physical characteristics a few important issues have been brought to light. (a) Whether it is possible to have religious experiences by practising prescribed methods, as given in Yoga. (b) What sort of personalities usually have religious experiences? (c) The secondary characteristics cause certain reactions in the subject having religious experience—what are the changes they bring about in personality, and what is the social significance of these experiences? (d) The role of the conscious and unconscious mind states in the occurrence of religious experiences. (e) The question of external agents like drugs and music as affective factors that induce or stimulate religious experiences. (f) The problem of expressibility of religious experiences. Each of these issues will feature for discussion in the following chapters.

REFERENCES

1. F.R. Tennant, *Philosophical Theology*, Vol. I, Cambridge. 1928. p. 330.

2. S. Radhakrishnan, *An Idealist View of Life*, Bombay, 1971, p. 70 "All the religions owe their inspiration to the personal insights of their prophet founders."

3. Daya Krishna, 'Religious Experience, Lauguage, and Truth', in Sidney Hook (ed.), *Religious Experience and Truth—A Symposium*, London, 1962. p. 233.

4. Frits Staal, *Exploring Mysticism*, Penguin Books, Middlesex, 1975. p. 184.

5. George Santayana, *Reason in Religion*, New York, 1962. p. 12.

6. John Hicks, *Philosophy of Religion*, New Jersey, 1973. p. 30.

7. *Ibid*. p. 49.

8. *Encyclopaedia Britannica*, Macropaedia, 15th Edition, 1974, Volume 15, p. 647.

9. W.H. Clark, *The Psychology of Religion*, New York, 1958. p. 415.

10. In the words of Radhakamal Mukherjee: "Accordingly the individual element is an indispensable part of every religion; mysticism, which is essentially the reaction of the individual, vitalizes what has been a social product and tradition; without it, religion fails to be a constructive factor..." Radhakamal Mukherjee, *The Theory and Art of Mysticism*, Delhi, 1960. pp. 11-12.

11. W. T. Stace, *Mysticism and Philosophy*, London, 1961. p. 46.

12. *Ibid*. p. 47.

13. William James, *The Varieties of Religious Experience: A Study In Human Nature*, New York, 1961. pp. 299-300.

14. F.C. Happold, *Mysticism A Study and an Anthology*, Middlesex, 1977. pp. 46-48.

15. William James, *Varieties of Religious Experience: A Study In Human Nature, op. cit.* pp. 299-300.

16. It is Clark's opinion that "the mystic has difficulty in communicating his experience ... The mystic says that he has had a perfectly definite experience but that he cannot explain it by any words he has available." W.H. Clark, *The Psychology of Religion, op. cit.* pp. 267-268 Pratt in keeping with this has remarked: "In fact the ineffability of the experience is one of its most prominent characteristics." J.B. Pratt, *The Religious Consciousness: A Psychological Study*, New York, 1921. p. 346.
    Affirming this R.C. Zaehner says, "Mystics of all schools insist that their experiences are not reducible to words ..." R.C. Zaehner, *Mysticism Sacred and Profane*, New York, 1971. p. 36.

Happold says, "it defies expression in terms which are fully intelligible to one who has not known some analogous experience." F. C. Happold, *Mysticism A Study and an Anthology, op. cit.* p. 45.

17. Ludwig Wittgenstein, *Tractatus Logico-Philosophicus,* Translated by D.F. Pears & B.F. McGuinness, London, 1978. 6.522, p. 73 and 7, p. 74.

18. S Radhakrishnan, *An Idealist View of Life, op. cit.* p. 79. Pratt in quoting Caroline Stephen renders support to this aspect of silence : "The deeper we go the fewer will be our words, and the less will any need of them be left. As we enter the innermost chamber of our hearts, words, and it may be even thoughts, are left behind ..." Caroline Stephen, *Light Arising,* p. 91. Quoted in J.B. Pratt, *The Religious Consciousness : A Psychological Study, op cit.* pp 346-347. Mlle V́e, a Swiss lady whom Flourney studied, is recorded to have refrained from describing her experience because "She feels herself so completely unable to describe her experience that she does not attempt it. She can only characterise it as a new emotion . ." R.H. Thouless, *An Introduction to the Psychology of Religion,* Cambridge, 1956 (2nd Edition, reprint, 1956). p. 252.

19. F.R. Tennant, *Philosophical Theology,* Vol. I, *op. cit.* p, 314.

20. William James, *The Varieties of Religious Experience : A Study In Human Nature, op. cit.* p. 300.

21. F.C, Happold, *Mysticism A Study and an Anthology, op. cit.* p, 45,

22. S. Radhakrishnan, *An Idealist View of Life, op. cit.* p. 73.

23. W.B. Selbie, *The Psychology of Religion,* Oxford, 1926. p, 253.

24, F.R. Tennant, *Philosophical Theology,* Vol. I, *op. cit* p. 315.

25. William James, *Varieties of Religious Experience : A Study In Human Nature, op. cit.* p. 300.

26. F.C. Happold, *Mysticism A Study and an Anthology, op. cit.* pp. 45-46.

27. Quoted from William James, *Varieties of Religious Experience : A Study In Human Nature, op. cit.* p 314. 'Butler's use of expressions like 'in the flash of a trembling glance', 'barely touched it with the whole beat of the heart', 'briefly, and hastily, and as it were in passing', 'can it be endured for long', speak of the transiency of religious experiences. Dom Cuthbert Butler, *Western Mysticism,* New York, 1966. p. 47.

28. Dom Cuthbert Butler, *Western Mysticism, op. cit.* p. 81. Corroborating this characteristic of religious experiences Radhakrishnan remarks. "The moments of vision are transitory and intermittent." S. Radhakrishnan, *An Idealist View of Life, op. cit.* p. 74.

29. W.H. Clark, *The Psychology of Religion, op. cit.* p. 270.

30. William James, *Varieties of Religious Experience : A Study in Human Nature, op. cit.* p 300.

31 F. C. Happold, *Mysiicism A Study and an Anthology, op. cit.* p. 46.

32. *Ibid.*

33. S. Radhakrishnan, *An Idealist View of Life, op. cit.* p. 72.

34. F. C. Happold, *Mysticism a Study and an Anthology, op. cit.* p. 47.

35. Bertrand Russell, *Mysticism and Logic and Other Essays*, London, 1953. p. 18.

36. R.C. Zaehner, *Mysticism Sacred and Profane, op. cit.* p.v.

37. C.J. Ducasse, *A Philosophical Scrutiny of Religion*, New York, 1953. p. 292.
Thouless recognise the sense of an intimate pervading presence to be one of the characteristics of religious experience. R.H. Thouless *An Introduction to the Psychology of Religion*, (2nd Edition, reprint, 1956,) Cambridge, 1956. p. 59.
According to Tennant, during, such experiences is aware of an "active presence, with which he is face to face and by which he is possessed so that his attention is no longer under his voluntary control, and that, as to the Reality of this presence, he has the maximum of certitude. F.R. Tennant, *Philosophical Theology*, Vol I, *op. cit.* p. 316.

38. G.T.W. Patrick, *Introduction to Philosophy*, London, 1968. p. 389.

39. Elmer S.J.O' Brien, *Varieties of Mystic Experience and Anthology and Interpretation*, Canada, 1964. pp. 4-6.

40. Timothy Beardsworth, *A Sense of Presence*, Studies in Religious Experience, The Religious Experience Research Unit, Manchester College, Oxford, 1977. p. viii.

41. *Ibid.* pp. 48-64.

42. *Ibid.* p. 116-128.

43. *Ibid.* p. 116.

44. *Ibid.* p. 117.

45. F.C. Happold, *Mysticism A Study and an Anthology, op. cit.* p. 48.

46. Bertrand Russell, *Mysticism and Logic and other Essays op. cit.* p. 17. "Past and present fade away in a sense of timeless being" during religious experiences says Radhakrishnan. S. Radkakrishnan, *An Idealist View of Life, op. cit.* p. 72.

 Expressions like, "All Time was Eternity" show the feeling of timelessness experienced by mystics.

 Thomas Traherne, *Centuries of Meditation III*; 1, 2, 3. Quoted from F.C. Happold, *Mysticism A Study and an Anthology, op. cit.* p. 369.

47. F.C. Happold, *Mysticism A Study and an Anthology, op. cit.* p. 48.

48. Robert H. Thouless, *An Introduction to the Psychology of Religion*, (2nd Edition, reprint 1956) Cambridge, 1956. p. 251.

49. Evelyn Underhill, *Mysticism*, London, 1911. p. 96. In keeping with Underhill, Dasgupta says of religious experience that "it is fundamentally an active, formative, elevating and ennobling principle of life." S.N. Dasgupta, *Hindu Mysticism*, Delhi, 1976. p.x.

50. *Ibid.*

51. *Ibid.*

52. *Ibid.*

53. W.H. Clark, *The Psychology of Religion, op. cit.* p. 273.

54. Paul E. Johnson, *Psychology of Religion*, New York, 1945. p. 27.

55. G.A. Coe, *The Psychology of Religion*, Chicago, 1916. p. 272.

56. W.H. Clark, *The Psychology of Religion, op. cit.*, p. 275.

57. J.B. Pratt, *The Religious Consciousness ; A Psychological Study, op. cit.* p. 430.

58. *The Random House Dictionary of the English Language*, Laurence Urdang, (ed.), New Delhi, 1975. p. 419.

59. S. Radhakrishnan, *Eastern Religions and Western Thought*, London, 1940. p. 77.

60. W.B. Selbie, *The Psychology of Religion, op. cit.* p. 263. "While ideation has been decreasing, emotion (at least in its relative proportion) has been increasing; and in fact throughout the ecstasy

the emotional element predominates and is of an intensity which seems far to exceed that of any emotion known to the mystic in any other condition." J.B. Pratt, *The Religious Consciousness: A Psychological Study*, *op. cit.* p. 416.

William James says, "Intellect and senses swoon away in these highest states of ecstasy." William James, *The Varieties of Religious Experience: A Study in Human Nature op. cit.* p. 323.

61. Dom Cuthbert Butler, *Western Mysticism*, *op. cit.* p. 51.

62. William James, *Varieties of Religious Experience*, *op. cit.* pp. 220-221

63. J B. Pratt, *The Religious Consciousness: A Psychological Study*, *op. cit.* pp. 439-440.

64. Radhakamal Mukherjee, *Theory and Art of Mysticism*, *op. cit.* p. 203

65. H.N. Wieman, *Religious Experience and Scientific Method*, London, 1971. p. 346.

2

Religious Experience : Origin and Means of Induction

Religious Experience as Spontaneous and Cultivated Experiences

Questions pertaining to the origin of religious experiences have been raised by many. Whether these experiences occur spontaneously or may even be made to occur is the issue uppermost in their minds.[1] At first glance it seems that religious experiences come of their own to individuals –spontaneonsly, effortlessly, as if by the grace and good will of some superior being. But, there are ample references and indicators in mystical writings that suggest the possibility of inducing such experiences by the true searcher, who follows a set of prescribed rules. Consequently then, "a distinction must be made between experiences which occur spontaneously (i.e., involuntarily) and those which are deliberately sought for by means of personal discipline. Some mystical insights appear to come to a man without his seeking for them, though an analysis of these involuntary experiences sometimes reveals the operation over many years of 'unconscious volition' ... But speaking generally, spontaneous religious experiences should be distinguished from those which come after long and often strenuous periods of physical and spiritual preparation."[2]

Grace and revelation occupy a significant position in the context of spontaneously occuring religious experiences. Christian thinkers are of the view that mysticism means supernatural intervention in the natural order—it is a gift of grace and revelation. Western monotheistic beliefs render that a mystical experience or state is the product of a special divine grace. Paul Tillich once told Agehananda Bharati that grace is something like a sudden successful mathematical solution.[3] Grace plays an important role not only as a state of things to be hoped or worked for, but also as explaining, quasi-casual factor, issuing from the charismatic figure who functions like God or any divine entity in the theistic forms of mysticism. "... the content of revelation is a body of truths expressed in statements or propositions Revelation is the imparting to man of the divinely authenticated truths. In the words of the *Catholic Encyclopedia* "Revelation may be defined as the communication of some truth by God to a rational creature through means which are beyond the ordinary course of nature."[4] It is perceived knowledge in which the subject is wholly passive. It is quite evident that much cannot be said about the spontaneous religious experiences save that they fall well outside the reach of human control.

Grace and revelation undoubtedly find a more prominent place in Western religion. Their pronounced status lends support in emphasising the active role of the other-than-human subject in religious experiences. To quote Meister Eckhart, a leading figure among Christian mystics, "The emptier your mind, the more susceptible are you to the working of His influence."[5] It is as it were by the grace of the 'Divine' that religious truths are 'revealed' to humankind. "... the whole of the Christian revelation is based on the assumption that it was, from all eternity, the munificent and gratuitous decision of the Lord to call man to an even higher destiny, not only to a natural but to a supernatural and Divine reward .... Man was, therefore, to be admitted into the sanctuary of the Divine self, to become a partner and an associate of God himself in His possession of Himself, to partake of the Divine and infinite beatitude, on the same footing and in exactly the same way as God Himself."[6]

The element of grace has been defined as "paramount and inalienable in all religious ...."[7] In grace there is co-operation between God and an individual. The grace of God can be attained only when the devotee acquires a receptive mood by purifying one's mind through the practice of prayer, concentration, and meditation and by making one's mind one-pointed in directing it to God. Only then can one feel the grace of God and His presence. Grace, according to Christianity, is of two separate kinds, viz., sanctifying grace and actual grace. The former is "the Divinely infused supernatural quality which permanently divinizes human nature to make it proportionate to its Divine end."[8] In other words, it may be said that sanctifying grace is an inherent perfection, understood to be subjected in the essence of man, which is not a moral participation in the Divine nature. From it the various complementary perfections which we know as 'gifts' and 'virtues' of the Holy Ghost branch out in the various faculties of the soul. Now we come to actual grace. Besides the supernatural superadded organism (habitual grace, virtues, and gifts) the human soul, in order to produce supernatural actions requires the help of actual grace. This form of grace is some internal, transient, supernatural impulse from God, which enables the human soul to perform supernatural action.

Contrasted to the experiences that come as "divine" gifts there are other contextually similar experiences that can be made to occur by subjective inputs and factors like desire, conditioning, effort, etc. S.N. Dasgupta has significantly remarked that "the highest reality or the ultimate realization and fulfilment (whatever may be their nature) cannot be attained by reason alone, but that there are other avenues to them, namely, the firm and steady control of will, the development of right emotions, or both combined, or by them both along with the highest functioning of reason."[9]

The much talked about stages of mysticism, in Christianity, presume the possibility of created religious experiences. Only, the stages break up the journey, to the end, into phases that are reached by due dedication and effort. The stages imply a gradual ascending to the end. If the experiences come of their own with no effort applied by the individual, how can the stages of religious experience be explained ? The spontaneity of the experience is characterised by completeness of experience, but, any graduated experience proves that the experience occurred by dint of personal effort. Even though it is not spelt out that the mentioned stages of mysticism imply a synthetic (artificial) creation of the experience, one can well understand it. In this way Christians too are of the opinion that experiences of the religious kind can be produced at will.

Eastern traditions find individuals playing a positive role in creating religious experiences. The mind must be rid of all worldly affairs by following a disciplined and controlled life accompanied by frequent practice of the prescribed exercises. "The main emphasis of Hindu religion is the potentiality of the divine in man. There is no unbridgeable gulf between God and man and between man and man. The vision supreme establishes universal kinship, the oneness of man in God. While the mystical side emphasizes the unity of man and God, the personal side points out how man is so different from God that he has to change himself before he can be admitted into the presence of the divine."[10] All this implies a certain metaphysical conception of God and the soul, and it implies further, a 'mystic way' of attaining union with the Absolute—the prime principle underlying every earthly creature and activity.

Religious ideas and experiences may be conditioned and even cultivated by personal desire and effort. There are varied religious moods and attitudes which the mystic deliberately seeks in order to find one's vision of God and to enrich one's spiritual consciousness. Different religious groups have employed methods of producing religious experiences, such as, fasting, flagellation, meditation, the mental and physical exercises of Yoga, and aslo submission to a spiritual teacher and guide.[11]

In some sense religion can be said to consist of concious ideas, hopes, enthusiasms; operating by grace and flourishing by prayer. When the religious inclination of an individual is conditioned or motivated by such ideas and aspirations and one is influenced by such trends of thought, the longing for union with God becomes an absolute necessity. In such an instance "the mystic starts with the idea of God which is a part of his social inheritance, and by meditation transforms God from an idea into a real presence."[12] The mystic's passion for the ultimate 'Thou' shrouds the physical world in darkness and unreality. Their zeal for the union suffices to sacrifice and disown material goods and existence as worthless, and rejection of the appeals of the senses as deceptive illusion. On the other hand, if the individual's religious grounding is devoid of this spirit, one does not feel the need for experiencing any higher being. In this way, the approach of religions makes all the difference, in so far as the necessity for religious experiences is made felt.

Varied opinions about religious experiences and mysticism have had diverse impacts on individuals with regard to the personal desire for experiencing some higher entity (God). Subjectively speaking, for some it is totally insignificant, for some, of some significance, and for others, of total significance. For the latter category, no religion makes full appeal unless it indicates some way by which one may experience what is believed to be an authentic commerce between human beings and the Ultimate. These persons are aware of an inner division, personal incompleteness, and the warring element of their nature, all of which give birth to a craving to return to some state of existence where they can be released from themselves and their limitations. It is how the varied opinions about these concepts have resulted in diverse impacts on individuals with regard to the desire for experiencing some higher entity, as an essential aspect of human existence.

The relegious background and religious aspirations of the individual are very important factors in achieving one's religious ends. The religious aspirations, in turn, vary according to the religious tradition and more according to personal interest and opinion of the individual. For instance, "The fact that Yoga, Taoism and many schools of Buddhism regard mystical experience as dependent on human effort, is related to their anthropocentrism, rationalism and relative independence of philosophical evaluation and religious—context e.g. of particular doctrines or rituals."[13] Thus, education, religious tradition, and mystical contemplation, as well as organic experiences, work upon the raw material of the individual's personal history and affective life, to result in an ineffable experience of reality.

Traces of suggested paths are evident in the writings of thinkers besides what is found in the literature of particular traditions. They have made suggestions, and on occasions prescribed the path, comprising of steps, leading to the experience sought. Miss Underhill's 'Mystic Way' is one such example.

It is the general opinion that the mind has to be purged of all mundane contents and freed of biases and partialities, before the commencement of any experience of God may be expected. Indian systems have gone a step beyond in attributing importance to physical exercises like posture, breathing, and to a certain extent physical deprivation and hardship—they all go a to long way in affecting the mind. They help steady the mind and empty it of its contents, which is the most congenial condition for religious experiences to occur. In this context Pratt remarks that, "It is probably the mystics of India who have most refined upon the art of influencing mental states by physical and psychological conditions."[14] "The idea that physical and mental exercises should be used in seeking the presence of God is possibly repugnant to many Christians. This is understandable when we realize that for many Christians their religion is essentially acceptance of its theological concepts plus a vague hope of the grace of God."[15]

Added to the above, the fact that the place of drugs, in this context, has been very significant – a fact evinced by historical records of religions - cannot be overlooked. R.C. Zaehner points out that "The real importance of Huxley's book* ... is that in it the author clearly makes the claim that what he experienced under the influence of mescalin is closely comparable to genuine mystical experience ... "[16] The gravity of the problem has reached optimum heights as drugs, music, physical exercises, etc., result in raptures and ecstasy akin to those that follow religious exeperiences. "It seems difficult to deny that there are numerous parallels and similarities between mystical and drug-induced states .... there are at least general similarities on the physiological, the behavioural and the experiential levels which it would be arbitrary to deny."[17] Thus, our problem is, 'Can we say that qualitatively religious experiences and experiences produced by triggers are similar ?' Their external manifestations that are observable apparently suggest their identity of nature. Can this be denied, and if so, on what basis ? "Whether the 'doors of perception' are opened by more traditional means or by LSD and other psychedelic drugs, the result is the same, and the result is, according to Leary, direct *religious* experience of the eternal being that pervades all that is ephimeral and transient."[18]

Though Huxley has been the first to argue for the relatedness of mysticism and drugs, this is a topic of deep concern for thinkers today. Being interested in studying the nature of religious experiences, we must be able to point out the distinctive features of religious experience so that the confusion between genuine and pseudo experiences may be obliterated.

* *Doors of Perception.*

Thus, in so far as we are able to examine and analyse religious experiences, second-hand, from the reports and writings of mystics, it is obvious that—(*i*) religious experiences come with suddnness and spontaneity, and, (*ii*) similar experiences are evoked by embracing different methods and techniques. Religious experiences, as understood so far, consist of two domains—a domain of phenomena that can be caused by human effort and also a domain of phenomena that occur spontaneously.

Means of Inducing Religious Experiences

The possibility of cultivating religious experiences points towards the further possibility that certain standard methods when adhered to would tend to produce such experiences. In fact, mystics, prophets and religious thinkers of both Eastern and Western traditions have more or less unanimously stressed the need for various forms of preparations as a preliminary stage towards attainment of religious insight. In spite of varying conditions and individual independence of inter-personal influences of each other, the suggested processes or methods of cultivating religious experiences are strikingly similar in content and spirit.

In the writings of individual thinkers there are two visible trends with regard to the possibility of cultivating religious experiences. There are some who, while acknowledging the importance of discipline and control on the way to religious experiences, have not specified any prescribed path but have exposed the general concepts and favourable conditions instrumental in creating religious experiences while there are others who defide the path. There are religious traditions that are more specific about the course that needs to be followed for attainment of religious experiences. The aim is to discipline the senses and passions of individuals, not always by complete suppression, but with regulated legitimate satisfaction by an objective integration of desires with a code of positive and negative duties. In other words, moods conducive to inducing religious experiences can be developed by acknowledging certain disciplinary and physical means. "Mysticism ... is also a skill. Skills can and must be learned ... The causal explanation of the mystical event is an analysis of training."[19]

It is expected that an examination of the alternative paths suggested by people of different walks, times, places and faiths will facilitate a derivation of the common denominators of the different methods for effectively inducing religious experiences. Further, such an exposition is of vital significance insofar as it enables us to evaluate the 'situation' on the way to arriving at any understanding of the psycholgical or extra-psychic factors underlying the artificial occurence of religious experiences.

Stages of ascent have been described by mystics. The characteristic feature of the 'mystic way' is progress, whether it is spelt out in stages or it is the gradual unfolding of the mystical powers. In her book *Mysticism*, Annie Besant has dealt with her 'Method of the Mystic'. The first part of it depends on conquering the senses, the emotions, the mind and the lower nature on the whole. To recognise the importance of these. one must realise that the spirit is one's Self, operative in the world of matter in order to subdue matter for one's own purposes, that one may be its master, not its slave. By conquest of the senses she does not mean destroying or killing of the senses but rather means that no sensation reaching one through the senses should have the power to swerve one from the path chosen by one's will.

Her further contention is that "The Mystic not only realises that Omnipotence living within himself which makes all difficulties easy and all burdens light, but he also has that perfect serenity and content which makes it impossible to crush him with sorrow ... he is content because he is seeing God in everything, and God is the Mystic's hope and joy ... "[20] It is important to vest faith in God, which becomes the source of all confidence and strength. The mystic develops tolerance and that sympathy which grows out of one's seeing God in everyone and everything around oneself. There is no desire to compel or control. Instead, respect for the divine spark in all emanates and accordingly, the mystic treats all as equals. Finally, the attitude of submission must be there, which is instrumental in bringing forth union with God. Thus, by emancipating oneself from one's personal limitations, one realises one's goal of bringing about a change in one's inward being or soul or spirit.

Evelyn Underhill refers to five steps in her 'Mystic Way.'* The first three and the fifth stages are similar to the ones taught by Christianity. But, she adds her own fourth step which she calls the 'Dark Night of a Soul', which is also pointed out by some Christian mystics. "Miss Underhill's five steps will serve to indicate by their names the general outlines of this progress. They are (1) Awakening, (2) Purification, (3) Illumination, (4) the Dark Night of the soul, and (5) the Unitive State or Spiritual Marriage—often referred to as marriage."[21] In the first step there comes the awareness of an universal principle with whom encounter is sought. This experience is usually abrupt and well-marked and accompanied by intense feelings of joy and exaltation. This is, however, tinged with dissatisfaction, caused by the realisation of one's finitude which, keeps one at an immense distance from the divine. This step is followed by Purgation, which is the negative path of renunciation. The general belief is that human life is distorted by the carnal desires and materialistic inclinations. Such distortion can be

* *Mysticism.*

eradicated by keeping away from the matters of the world, which helps purify the human perspective. The self in this step "attempts to eliminate by discipline and mortification all that stands in the way of its progress towards union with God ... it is a state of pain and effort."[22] Illumination is the contemplative state—once again in this state the self's joyful consciousness of the Absolute returns, though in an enhanced form.

After the awakening the desire for union arises, for fulfilling which, steps are taken to purify one-self by way of preparing oneself for receiving the experience With the occurrence of the experience the desire arises for recurrence of the experience, yet this is not always possible. The resulting dissatisfaction and discontentment at the loss of vision is the 'Dark Night of the Soul', also known as 'Mystic pain' or 'Mystic death'. When all efforts fail to restore the desired experience it is considered a period of 'Spiritual Dryness' for the aspirant. "The consciousness which had, in Illumination, sunned itself in the sense of the Divine Presence, now suffers under an equally intense sense of the Divine Absence : learning to dissociate the personal satisfaction of mystical vision from the reality of mystical life."[23] But this stage is only a temporary phase, ultimately leading up to the cherished union – the Unitive Stage. "In this state the Absolute Life is not merely perceived and enjoyed by the self as in Illumination : but is *one* with it. This is the end towards which all the previous oscillations of consciousness have tended. It is a state of equilibrium, of purely spiritual life; characterized by peaceful joy, by enhanced powers, by intense certitude."[24] Ramakrishna is said to have gone though this phase of despair—'Dark Night of the Soul' ; He passed twelve years in such agony waiting for the bliss of union with the supreme.[25]

St. Teresa, in her *The Interior Castle*, described "Seven Degrees of Contemplation" as the graduated steps to the attainment of union with God. The chief among these are pointed out by Leuba as (*i*) Meditation, (*ii*) The Orison of Quiet, (*iii*) The Sleep of the Powers, and (*iv*) Ecstasy, or Rapture, or Flight of the Soul. To begin with, a suitable subject of meditation must be chosen on which attention is fixed. This human effort is assisted by the grace of God in the meditative state. In the next stage the grace of God is intensified, and it is God who elevates the finite soul to union with Him. This and the following stage are both stages of imperfect union with God, which is the result of God's merciful grace. However, in the third stage, activity of the mental functions is much reduced and it is marked by a deeper absorption in God. In all these three states the identity of the experiencer is felt, but in ecstasy all awareness of individuality perishes – the soul here is completely absorbed in the enjoyment of union with God.

Thinkers like Pratt, Leuba, Radhakamal Mukherjee and R.C. Zaehner are agreed upon the fact that one does seek to unite with God or some higher principle, which desire actually inspires one to undertake the rigorous path to unity. J.B. Pratt has analyzed two kinds of methods - the positive and the negative. The value of the former method may be expressed by another common psychological term – auto-suggestion. Similarly, the negative methods and their psychological explanation may be summed up by the word 'inhibition'. The aim is to keep out from the mind the undesirable and to leave it free from all that is irrelevant and distracting. They are means by which the mystic's attention gets under control of the proper ideas and emotions, so that these may dominate one's whole mind and activity. Among the positive, the better known and practised ones, are the meditative and illuminative steps of the mystic progress. Achievement of meditation brings the mystic closest to fill realisation of the spiritual experience. External conditions like solitude, bodily posture, etc., increase and hasten the receptive state.

Pratt has suggested austerities for the emptying of the mind. These are the constituents of the negative mood. The mortification of the body like fasting and breath-control make up the negative method. By reducing the amount of food required the mind is left undisturbed to fix its attention upon God, whereby discursive thought process is checked. However, any of these austerities singly is not sufficient to produce religious experiences. "Asceticism, the mystic has used only as a tool for lopping off the rougher outer elements of diversity and sources of distraction; and the processes of meditation and contemplation are for the purpose of reducing the mind itself to unity. One idea after another is done away with, the rapidity of thought is stopped, and gradually the mystic approximates a condition of monoideism where one idea alone remains with its accompanying feeling tone, dominating the mind ... "[26]

According to Radhakamal Mukherjee, the highest expression of the normal human impulses is in the union of the finite soul with the infinite being. "The mystic sometimes seeks to reach higher levels of experience by a simplification of the mental life through starvation, isolation, use of narcotic drugs, and other physical means of ecstasy, through hypnotic processes and through intense delights and cutting pains."[27] Both mental and physical practices and disciplines are held to be effective in the production of the sought state. He does not believe that God can be found through the different arguments for His existence, but rather by emptying the mind and concentrating on God. All efforts on the part of the individual are directed to keep away from all irrelevant impression. By this method the individual is able to concentrate first on the idea of God, which one finally realises as a real presence.

"It must be admitted that there are certain religious cults that seek mystic experience in collective worship ... the Bamachari Tantrik cult in Bengal and Assam seeks to induce a state of ecstatic emotion through the collective incitement of the sex feeling... the emotion aroused is intense in character. As a consequence there is an inhibition of definitely directed motor responses a phenomenon which is usual in the case of all intensive emotions. Thus the purpose of isolation is served through the intensification of emotions."[28] "Orgiastic dances like those of the dervishes produce collective excitement, culminating in exhaustion and even loss of consciousness."[29] A more recent and contemporary version of a similar method is to be found in the teachings of Acharya Rajneesh. It is not only a similarity of teaching but Rajneesh also practices his method in group.

His method he calls psychotherapeutic. Humankind is undersome crisis and the Acharya has formulated his method for overcoming this crisis by studing and understanding human psychology. needs and drives. He claims his method to be more psychological than spiritual. It leads ultimately to the spiritual dimension, but it starts from psychology."[30] His method is based on catharsis. "We have layers and layers of suppressions, and unless they are released, thrown out, exhaled, nothing can be done as far as the inner journey is concerned. So my method works with catharsis...Unless the repressions in your mind are released, you cannot proceed further."[31] All other Indian methods are different in this respect. They have mainly taught the suppression of the desires and basic human requirements through the process of self deprivation, abstinence and self-mortification. But Rajneesh opines that such method cannot ensure a permanent revival—their effects are short lived and can give calm for the time being, but cannot transform. The reason for this Rajneesh attributes to the fact that these methods begin with all the suppressions and tensions within oneself, whereas he starts by releasing all tensions—by expressing everything that is inside.

To stir such a state of spontaneous expression, his first step consists of chaotic breathing. Chaotic breathing disturbs the suppressed being, which is followed by the stage of actual expression. "Whatever you want to express, express. But not to someone; just in a vacuum."[32] The third step is repeating the particular sound '*hoo*' for ten minutes. This sound hits the sex centre. When the sex energy is released from the sex centre, it becomes a biological phenomenon, but when it passes through the spine to be released from the head, it becomes spiritual transformation. This step is followed by the fourth step, when the person is completely relaxed. He is a witness, not doing any thing. It is the meditative stage.

Leuba is more concerned with ecstatic states which according to him are the highest attainable experiences for a mystic—what others have referred to as union with God. "The states are induced by means of drugs, by physical excitement, or by psychical means."[33] Though Leuba has granted that drugs have a prominent role in the production of religious experiences, they cannot be considered the exclusive grounds. The other means worth the name are "Deprivation of food and sleep, isolation, even active tortures ... Rhythmic bodily movements and shouting or singing," which "when long continued, yield results similar in several respects to that of alcohol ... and other drugs."[34] Yoga, drugs and the Christian means of inducing religious experiences have all been touched by Leuba.

Aldous Huxley's *The Doors of Perception* has drawn the attention of religious thinkers to the question of relatedness between drugs and religious experience. On the basis of personal experience he arrives at the conclusion that drugs are capable of producing praeternatural experiences which in essence are similar to those experiences described by the term 'mysticism'. Thus, Huxley's thesis that drugs have the potentialities of producing religious experiences has heralded in multitudinous views and experiments, with the idea of understanding the relationship from all perspectives.

Besides the views put forward by individuals, there are well-defined methods prescribed by different systems like Sufism, Yoga and Christianty. Their contributions in this field have been significant and need to be elaborated. Sufism is a system of Islamic mysticism offering "Steps toward union with God, as repentance, abstinence, renunciation, poverty, patience, trust."[35] The Sufis' method was restricted to ascetic discipline, which meant allegiance to the negative method of abstention from food and drink and other pleasures of life. Sufism is a "spiritual movement and a spirituality that grew out of the practice of a specific technique for attaining to mystical experience."[36]

The principal among the Sufi teachings, so far as mysticism is concerned, are as follows :

1. To win a sense of direct communion with the Absolute Being behind the phenomenal world, one should practice the quietistic virtues (poverty, austerity, humility, fortitude, and discipline), devote oneself to to the ways of inwardness (withdrawal, silence, solitariness, and self-examination), and keep in mind a constant awareness of God (with faith, awe, and desire).
2. It is useful to utter certain slogans (such as "Allah is here') as reminders of the mystic belief and aim, and as aids to concentration on the quest for unification.
3. If one follows these directions with sufficient perseverence, one will advance through the standard mystic stages of concentration, apprehension of the oneness of everything, sudden and unpredictable illumination, blissful ecstasy, sense of union with the Deity, and sense of one's own nothingness.[37]

Sufis then reach the end with the help of bodily discipline along with other exercises in rhythm, accompanied by swaying of the body. With the control of attention by repeating sacred phrases like '*La ilaha illa llah*' (there is no God but God), and '*Allah Allah*' so that a stage is finally reached when the whole being of the aspirant is fixed on the divine object without his knowledge. There are seven spiritual stages which a Sufi passes before realisation of the truth dawns upon him. First is *Talab*, (yearning) for union with God which quest demands complete renunciation of the world. Second comes '*Isqh*' (Love); the stage when one is not at peace, and one has to disown all desire for name and fame to facilitate full absorption in the object of pursuit. '*Marfat*' (Enlightenment) is the next stage when the devotee sees Him as the Supreme Effulgence in every particle of creation. Fourth is '*Istāghrak*' or '*Fana*' (Absorption) in which the height of despondency is reached—like unto the passage into the 'Dark Night of the Soul" of Underhill. Then comes '*Tauhid*' (Unity Consciousness) when God is experienced as the all permeating (Timeless) Unity amidst multiplicity (in time). This is followed by '*Hairat*' (Amazement). It is the stage when the seeker sees the glorious sight that leaves one dumbfounded. Herein comes presentation of stern reality, impressing the subject for life, paying the path to further spiritual advance. Lastly we have '*Fuqr Wa Fanā*' which is the stage of ego annihilation. It is here that the total effacement of body consciouness takes place, accompanied by rapture and ecstasy not merely momentary but firm and eternal. Man is reborn in Godhead. This is the mark of the Sufi goal and climax of realisation.

For those committed to the guidance of *shaikhs*, the spiritual teachers, it is impending upon them to abide by the rule, method and religious practice inculcated by the *shaikhs*. Accordingly, details of the path, (*Tariqa*) fixity and uniform character, are determined by the individuality of the teacher. Broadly speaking, the Path corresponds to the *via purgativa* of mediaval Christian mysticism. Hunger, solitude, and silenec are the chief weapons employed in the war against 'the flesh (*nafs*), on the path to union. In this way the ascetic and ethical discipline is divided into a progressive series of 'stations' (*maqamat*), which the learner must traverse, making oneself perfect in every one before advancing to the next.[38]

As in other systems, the path offered by Christianity is constituted of the same principles—the primary human urge for union with a higher being, followed by steps of preparation for the union. That Christianity is basically theistic, devotion oriented, wherein love assumes a dominant role, is reflected in the method of practical mysticism. From these facts about the systems emerge the method more as an unassailable corollary. It's mystic methodology, wherein the technique is practical, derives its content from a scheme of generic typology. The exalted being of God, that finitude impedes any awareness of the real, the illusory and superficial character of sense experiences along with the world around us, that union with the godhead is possible, are the themes that make up the practical aspect of religious experiences in Christianity.

The course outlined by Christianity is marked by three phases—purgative, illuminative and unitive. The way of purgation has as its two objectives complete detachment from, and renunciation of the sense word to result in the death of the egocentric life, and self-mortification. "By turning inward, away from the flux of phenomena, towards the centre of the soul, by putting aside all concepts and images, spiritual as well as bodily, in a state of stillness and passivity, it is possible to penetrate through these separating screens, and to see deeper into that which more completely *is* ..."[39] The essentials of the purgative stage are negation of human interests, or emptying of the mind, and prolonged fixation of attention upon a single object or word. The emptier the mind, the more susceptible does one become to the working of the felt presence. Therefore, withdrawal of attention from the activities and sense stimuli of ordinary life is followed by extra-ordinary concentration upon some object.

These, then, are the anticipatories that mobilize new revelations which illuminate and transform the finite soul, to culminate in union with God. In this way, the purgative stage is a prerequisite for the fortification of the human condition such that it may be entrusted with the challenge inevitable in the illuminative of meditative stage. This calls for the practice of the common expedient found in asceticism.

Having brought under control the human faculties, the aspirant's mind is set on the object of pursuit and looks upto it in a spirit of devotion, worship and adoration The illuminative stage involves prayer and contemplation. Here it ought to be pointed out that in Christianity love has a distinct role in the fulfilment of any relationship. Further, Christian love is identified with an experience of 'union' in which the distinction between lover and loved is supposed to be annihilated.

A deep justification for the practice of prayer is inherent in Christianity, like all religions. "Prayers, or "orisons", as they are called, as understood by the Christian mystics, primarily aim at communion, or union, with what they take to be a Divine Being. and are not requests for favours ...."[40] There is some variation in the way the degrees of prayer are described, but the usually acceptable division is as follows—recollection, quiet, and contemplation proper. Recollection commences with acts of meditation on some object or idea, in which imagination and thought play a predominant part. When imagination and thought begin to fade out, the subject enters into the prayer of quiet. It suffices to say that a deliberate effort of attention and concentration accompanied by an equal effort at bringing the mind to a state of complete stillness, results, at length, in the consciousness reaching a state marked by an immense increase in receptivity, a near complete suspension of the reflective powers, and, a strange indescribable silence. As the prayer of quiet becomes deeper, the stage of true contemplation is reached.

The state of contemplation involves a movement of consciousness towards a higher level as the result of the emergence and cultivation of powers lying latent in the individuals. A Christian mystic does not necessarily resort to any intoxicating or physical process, but "he does systematize fixation of attention technically called "contemplation".... It is not an effort to know anything new, but simply fixation of attention upon something already regarded as real and important. In Christian mysticism the common objects of contemplation are God and Christ ... "[41] Thereby Christian mysticism is marked by a minimal attention given to mere psychological mechanics, with more attention to idea contents. We may justly sum up by saying; "In the *state* of Contemplation there is found a self-forgetting attention, a humble receptiveness, a still and steady gazing, an intense concentration, so that emotion, will and thought are all fused and then lost in something which is none of them, but which embraces them all. Gradually, by a deeper and deeper process of self-merging, a communion is established between the seer and what is seen, between him who fells and that which he feels."[42] This union is the unitive stage.

A distinctive feature of most of the Indian traditions is their emphatic appeal to a variety of means for the attainment of union with the ultimate reality. Whether called *mukti*, *mokṣa* *nirvāṇa*, or *kaivalyā*, the same end is implied by each. Further, each is a developed path, which includes different exercises both of body and mind, harnessing of desires, control of will, concentration of mind with the help of *mantras*, acquiring spiritual guidance from a teacher, and so on. In addition there are the three paths of *Jñāna*, *Bhakti* and *Karma* as taught by the *Bhagavad Gīta*. Whether the path adopted is *karma*, *bhakti* or *jñāna*, the followers of all the three paths withdraw their attention from the sensual world and attempt at whole-heartedly fixing their concentration on the supreme object, surrendering all activities, physical and mental, to it. Therefore, all those desirous of attaining perfection must tread the path of discipline, austerity and renunciation.

The Upanishadic passage, *tat tvam asi*, 'That thou art', means that the individual self is one with Brahman, the supreme reality. It is up to the individual to realise one's oneness with the undifferentiated reality. Man is the manifestation of Brahman in a lower or imperfect form, though in essence the same. And, when one acquires such an awareness, the individual soul is freed from the bonds of misconception, and is said to have attained liberation or *mokṣa*. The state of the released soul is one of non-separation (*avibhāga*) from Brahman, which non-separation has been variously interpreted by different commentators. Only realisation of reality is capable of destroying *avidyā*, which enables one to move from the domain of *vyāvahārika satya* to attain *paramārthika satya*. In this way, when the egotistic self is delivered from bondage, it becomes illuminated and it is restored to its origin in pure Being, above all discriminations.

Suffice it to say, that it is characteristic of the Indian or Hindu tradition to offer systematic paths, starting at the grass roots and passing through gradual phases of self elevation till the end is reached. It remains to be seen what comprises the training and discipline of an aspirant. Without gradual self-development no marked progress can be effected in the individual's pursuit for liberation. In the words of Dr. S. Radhakrishnan, "The supreme good for man consists in the breaking down of the fetters that shut him out from the reality which he is. Freedom consists in the realisation of the Ātman in the individual soul."[43] This is in principle what should be the goal of humankind in compliance with its nature as related to the reality.

The Yoga system of Indian philosophy is synonymous with training in mystical insight—training that culminates in the union of an individual with the divine. "It is based on persevering exercise, and the diet, posture, breathing, intellectual concentration, and moral discipline vary slightly in the different systems which teach it. The Yogi, or disciple, who has by these means overcome the obscurations of his lower nature sufficiently, enters into, the condition termed *samādhi*, "and comes face to face with facts which no instinct or reason can ever know"".[44]

Yoga makes a distinction between the 'self' and the 'mind-substance' or 'thinking-substance' (*citta*), and the respective functions it ascribes to them. The self knows the objects of the world through the modifications of *citta* which correspond to the forms of the objects known. *Citta* always exists in the form of its states called *vṛttis*. The *Bhāṣya* describes the five classes of *citta* and comments upon their fitness for the Yoga leading to *kaivalya* as –

1. *kṣipta* (wandering): the *citta* characterised as wandering, because it is being always moved by *rajas*.

2. *mūdha* (forgetful) : the *citta* is overpowered by *tamas*, or passions, like that of anger, by which it loses its senses and always chooses the wrong course.

3. *vikṣipta* (occasionally steady) : The distracted or occasionally steady *citta*, is that mind which rationally avoids the painful actions and chooses the pleasurable ones. None of these can hope to attain the contemplative concentration.

4. *ekāgra* : The one-pointed is that kind of mind in which true knowledge of the nature of reality is present and

the afflictions due to nescience or false knowledge are thus attenuated and the mind better adapted to attain the *nirodha* or restrained state.

5. *nirudha* (restrained) : the restrained mind is that in which all mental states are arrested.

"It is the object of Yoga gradually to restrain the *citta* from its various states and thus cause it to turn back to its original cause, the kāraṇacitta, which is all-pervading. The modifications of the kāraṇacitta into such states as the kāryacitta is due to its being overcome by its inherent tamas and rajas ... "[45]

The modifications of *citta*, the cognitive mental states, may be classified under five heads, namely, *pramāṇa* or true cognition, *viparyaya* or false cognition, *vikalpa* or merely verbal cognition, *nidrā* or sleep, and *smṛti* or memory. All cognitive mental states and progresses (*cittavṛtti*) are included in these five kinds of modifications. "The task before the Yogin is, then, the suppression of the activity of the mind, the 'fluctuations of the mind-stuff are to be restricted.'"[46] Thus, Yoga means the cessation of mental functions or modifications (*cittavṛttinirodha*), identifying itself with mental modifications.

Patanjali's Yogasutras indicate eight steps, known as *Yogāṅgas*, that comprise the devices leading to the desired goal. Of these five are indirect and physical (*yama* or restrain, *niyama* or observance, *āsana* or posture, *prāṇāyāma* or breath-control, and *pratyahāra* or withdrawal of the senses) and three are direct or mental (*dhāraṇā* or attention, *dhyāna* or meditation, and *samādhi* or concentration). Cultivation of the habits of friendliness, compassion, complacency and indifference towards happiness, misery, virtue and vice are further aids for cleansing the mind as mentioned in the Yogasūtra I.[47]

The paths *karmayoga*, *bhaktiyoga*, and *jñānayoga* are given in the *Bhagavad Gīta* as the means of realising the truth—the first being the path of action, the second, that of devotion and the third the path of knowledge. *Karmayoga* ensures liberation through action without attachment, *bhaktiyoga* results in liberation through intense devotion to the personal God or the divine incarnation, and *jñānayoga* liberates through knowledge of the self and the Absolute Grouud of all being with which it is identical. Each is suited for persons of different temperaments, and in this way the *Gīta* leaves room for individual freedom of choice. In pursuing any path it is to be remembered that all duty must be carried out in a spirit of detachment, with no concern for its results.

Karmanyevā dhikāraste
mā phaleṣu kadācana
mā karmaphalaheturbhūr
mā te saṅgo stvakarmaṇi [48]

When desires are overcome, and the spirit is content in itself, the mind maintains stability in all states of sorrow, desire, pleasure, when good and evil do not evoke extremities in feelings, only then can a person be called fit to undertake the arduous task of self elevation (*Bhagavad Gīta*, II, 56-61). Details about restraints, observances, and then control of mind are taught in the sixth chapter of the *Bhagavad Gīta*, and the followers of these are regarded as best attuned to God. Sri Kṛsṇa then asks the aspirant to fix one's mind on Him, worship Him with devotion and reverence, and having thus disciplined oneself, keeping God as the end to be achieved, one merges with Him.

manmanā bhava madbhakto
madyājī māṁ namaskuru
mām evaiṣyasi yuktyaivam
ātmānam matparāyaṇah [49]

On similar foundational premises, the *Bhagavad Gīta* also expounds paths for God realisation.

Swami Vivekananda's *Raja Yoga* is more or less a synthesis of the three paths of the *Bhagavad Gīta*, based on the principles of bodily control and exercises, breath-control and meditation.

Discussions so far clearly show that :

- religious experiences can be created
- the mind, when brought to a certain level or state of being is provenly conducive to mark the onset of religious experiences
- it is possible to create such a favourable state of mind
- by following prescribed paths or adhering to some general principles such favourable mind states can be created by the effort of the aspirant coupled with some external agents that hasten or facilitate the process of attainment.

Being concerned with the question of origin and motivating factors, we are obviously required to consider those kinds of religious experiences which, for their occurrence, are not dependent on the subjective will alone. Subjective will or desire, as has been discussed at length in this chapter, is no doubt the first step towards realisation of any voluntary religious experience. But in the case of prayer, act of worship and the observance of rituals, the subjective desire and devotion are the sole motivating factors, because they seem to be at a lower level in comparison with their ecstatic counterparts. Moreover, these former types of experiences are often the result or manifestation of one's psychological need or satisfaction, which with the passage of time becomes a matter of habit. On the contrary, in the intense types it is basic that the desire moves hand in hand with the urge and effort to total self-submission or relegation of the self to the background, i.e., cultivating a state of egolessness in order to experience the true nature of the self and its oneness and union with the supreme self. When this has been achieved there seems to be some supernatural intervention prior to reaching the climax of the experience. Intervention by any supernatural order is evinced by the religious doctrines and warnings that have been revealed to prophets in their moments of insight. On the personal level also, these experiences elicit a good amount of certainty among those who have the experience.

Self-submission raises the question of the 'subject' to whom the self may be submitted. Putting it plainly, is there a referent, an object or person, in these experiences? This is indeed a very delicate issue. From our accounts and study of religious experiences it appears as if 'God' or some 'supreme being' is the referent of religious experiences, but as researchers we are in no position to affirm this because we are lacking the apparatus to substantiate the existence of any referent, and it is empirical folly to affirm the existence of something beyond the empirical. Therefore, the approach to the problem of referent in religious experience is based upon what is apparent or what is phenomenologically there in such experiences – as given by those who have the experiences.

The mystic methods reveal in them some underlying uniformity of rules and techniques employed for attaining mystical ecstasy. There may be differences in the number of steps to the end, but there is an unquestionable unanimity of principles on which the methods rest. Withdrawal of the self and contemplation are the fundamental steps that ultimately bring about religious experiences As the inwardness of the individual increases, thoughts and feelings are gradually separated from the social, material and sensuous context. Personal alienation from the affairs of the world minimises the impediments which stand between the individual and the end to be realised.

Progress in the inner life cannot be successfully achieved without detachment from, and indifference to, all things worldly and transient, and more than anything else, the individual ego or self. Fixation of attention is very important, though there is no rigidity about the object on which attention is to be fixed.

Independent of all conditions and creeds, the important thing is to free the mind, bring it to a stable and detached condition when it is no longer moved by any sense perception or object attractive to the senses. The objective of these practices is to inculcate concentration and total withdrawal of senses such that the mind becomes engrossed in its object in such a way as to produce a vivid awareness of its presence and an assurance of its reality that nothing can shake.

The aids to mystical discipline are solitude, postures, breathing exercises, guidance of spiritual teacher (*guru*), restrictions of food and sleep habits, rhythmic movement of body, repetition of desirable words (*mantras*), prayer, concentration, meditation and contemplation. These efforts are rewarded sooner when the aspirant is moved by the desire for religious experience. Preparing oneself for the religious experience involves in the first stage the necessity to inculcate the deep felt desire for the experience. This decides the mystic's goal and the mystic is able to visualise the ideal being aspired for. We can well see that there is a referent in a religious experience, which, prior to the experience, is the object contemplated or aimed at by the mystic. The object aspired for may be God or a realisation of oneness. The pre-conceived idea of God, which ultimately becomes the referent of the attained religious experience explains why a Hindu mystic experiences only the Hindu gods and a Christian mystic experiences Christ, and so on. But this is relevant only in the case of voluntary religious experiences and not the spontaneous ones. In fact, the exposition and ensuing discussion herein pertain to the realm of cultivated religious experiences.

The emphasis on ascetic practices should not be misunderstood. "The body, the natural impulses, the feelings, are neither to be crushed nor wantonly denied, but only to be mastered instead of allowed to rule thought and behaviour ... "[50] There are certain elements which in one form or another enhance spiritual realisation Moving through physical, intellectual, devotional and symbolic rituals of discipline, takes one toward the ultimate goal.

Further, there is some physiological common denominator in all the practical methods and this has been testified by their medical aspect The differences in the methods is only superficial and actually entails a difference of details only and not of principles. The significance and scientific working of the methods that have been practised down the ages has proved their meaningfulness, and they cannot be derided as superstitions or mere religious fancies.

On analysing the content of the different methodologies leading up to religious experiences it is possible to draw out the generally accepted factors that are instrumental in facilitating this. Once the common factors are determined an outline of a methodology devoid of any doctrinal colouring is obtained. As a consequence of the association between ecstatic intoxication and religious experiences, some of the ecstasy producing agents like drugs and music cannot be ignored. It is, therefore, incumbent upon us to study deeply the ecstasy producing capacity of drugs and music, to examine whether they can at all induce religious experiences.

REFERENCES

1. "Mystical theology, both in the East and West, has sometimes been divided over the issue whether the union with the divine is the result of one's unaided effort or suppernatural grace."

   Encyclopaedia Britannica, Macropaedia, Volume XII, 15th Edition, 1974. p. 789.

Swami Akhilanda asks a question "abont the place of God in spiritual realisat ion. Does the devotee have to do eveything himself to attain his answer to prayer for things and divine revelation or experiences, or is the grace of God active too ?"

Swami Akhilananda, *Mental Health and Hindu Psychology*, London, 1952. pp. 215-216.

2. G.S. Spinks, *Psychology and Religion ; An Introduction to Contemporary Views*, London, 1963. p. 152.

3. Agehananda Bharati, *The Light at the Center, Context and Pretext of Modern Mysticism*, New Delhi, 1977. p. 120.

4. John Hicks, *Philosophy of Religion*, New Jersey, 1973. p. 52 (*The Catholic Encylopedia*, New York, 1912, XIII, 1.)

5. J.B. Pratt. *The Religious Consciousness : A Psychological Study*. New York, 1921. p. 414 (Meister Fckhart's "Mystische Schrifteu", put into modern German by Landaur, Berlin, Schnabol : 1903, pp. 20-23.)

6. James Hastings (ed.), *Encyclopaedia of Religion and Ethics*, Volume VI, New York, 1937. p. 367.

As "The achievement is never wholly earned; as in the mystic there remains a saving measure of humility, so in the revelation these is a touch, if not mystery, at least divine generosity. And to it none can attain through knowledge....neither through any exercise watsoever. Only he with whom it pleases God to be united in his spirit, and whom it pleases to enlighten by Himself, can see God, and no one else." C.A. Bennet. *A Philosophical Study of Mysticism, An Essay*. New Haven, 1931. p 63.

7. Daya Krishna, 'Religious Experience, Language, and Truth', Sidney Hook (ed.) *Religious Experience and Truth-A Symposium*, London, 1962 P. 234.

8. James Hastings (ed.) *Encyclopaedia of Religion and Ethics*, Volume VI, *op. cit.* p 368.

9. S.N. Dasgupta, *Hindu Mysticism*, Delhi, 1976. pp. vii—viii

10. L.S S O'Malley, *Modern India and the West*, Oxford, 1968 p 342.

11. "...there are breathing exercises which tend to produce mystical states. In the same way there are many mental exercises, certain kinds of disciplined meditation and concentration, which are undertaken with the same end in view. Prayer, properly understood, is another name for these spiritual efforts to reach up to mystical experiences," W.T. Stace, *Mysticism and Philosophy*, London, 1961. pp. 24-25. Further, "solitude... is an absolute prerequisite for mystical development." Andrew M. Greelay, *Ecstasy A Way of Knowing*, New Jersey, 1974. p 59.

W.R. Inge points out that "Some have gazed intently or their own navels ; others have fixed their eyes on some bright object ; the Indians have made a special study of these experimental methods. The ecstasy, thus attained, is to be very pleasurable .... Hashish, alcohol, mescal may be employed." W R Inge, *Mysticism in Religion*, London, 1969. p. 35.

12. Radakamal Mukherjee, *The Theory* and *Art of Mysticism*, New Delhi, 1960. p. 168,

13. Frits Staal, *Exploring Mysticsim*, Penguin Books, Middlesex, 1975. p. 129.

14. J.B. Pratt, *The Religious Consciousness: A Psychological Study*, *op. cit.* p. 388.

15. Arthur Guirdham, *Christ and Freud : A Study af Religious Experience and Observance*, London, 1959. p. 89.

16. R. C. Zaehner, *Mysticism Sacred and Profane*, New York, 1971. p. 12.

17. Frits Staal, *Exploring Mysticism*, op. cit. p. 148.

18. R.C. Zaehner, *Drugs, Mysticism and Make-Believe*, London, 1972. p. 76.

19. Agehananda Bharati, *The Light at the Center, Context and Pretext of Modern Mysticism*, op. cit. p. 115.

20. Annie Besant, *Mcystiism*, London. 1914. pp. 26-27.

21. W.H. Clark, *The Psychology of Religion*, Now York, 1958. pp. 276-277.

22. Evelyn Underhill, *Mysticism*, London, 1911. p. 205.

23. *Ibid.* p. 206.

24. *Ibid*, pp. 206-207.

25. Kamakhya Prasad Singh Choudhary, *Modern Indian Mysticism*, Delhi, 1981, p. 89.

26. J.B. Pratt, *The Religions Consciousness: A Psyclological Study*, op. cit. pp. 414-415.

27. Radhakamal Mukherjee, *The Theory and Art of Mysticism*, *op. cit.* p. xii.

28. *Ibid* p. 113.

29. W.R. Inge., *Mysticism In Religion*, *op. cit.* p. 35.

30. Bhagawan Shree Rajneesh, *The Eternal Quest*, New Delhi, 1980. p. 38.
31. *Ibid.*
32. *Ibid*, p. 41.
33. J.H. Leuba, *The Psychology of Religious Mysticism*, New York, 1925. p. 8.
34. *Ibid*. p. 11.
35. Frank Gaynor (ed.), *Dictionary of Mysticism*, New York. pp. 175-176.
36. Elmer S.J. O'Brien, *Varieties of Mystic Experience, An Anthology and Interpretion*, Canada, 1964. p. 101.
37. Paul Edwards (ed.), *Encyclopaedia of Philosophy*, Vols. 7 & 8 London, 1972. p. 41.
38. James Hastings (ed), *Encyclopaedia of Religion and Ethics*, Volume XII, Edinburgh, 1958. p. 13.
39. F.C. Happold, *Mysticism a Study and an Anthology*, Middlesex, 1963. p. 60.
40. W.T. State, *Mysticism and Philosophy*, London, 1961. p. 24.
41. G.A. Coe. *The Psychology of Religion*, Chicago, 1961. pp. 270-271.
42. F.C. Happold, *Mysticism* a Study and an Anthology, *op. cit.* p. 70.
43. S. Radhakrishnan, *Indian Philosophy*, Vol. II, Bombay, 1977. p. 462.
44. William James, *The Varieties of Religious Experience, A Study in Human Nature*, New York, 1961, p. 314.

"The term Yoga, according to Patanjali's definition, means the final annihilation (*nirodha*) of all the mental states (*cittavṛtti*) involving the preparatory stages in which the mind has to be habituated to being steadied into particular types of graduated mental states." S.N. Dasgupta, *Yoga as Philosophy and Religion*, Delhi, 1973, p. vii.

According to Vijñānabhikshu's definition in the *Yogasarasamgraha*, "Yoga consists in the suppression of the functions of the thinking principle (mind) which leads to the absolute abidence of the Agent (*Purusha*) in his real nature. The partial suppression of the mental functions consequent upon the waking *state* (which include the conditions of Agitation and Ignorance) does not lead to the liberation of the form of *absolute* abidence in one's real nature." J.R. Ballantyne and Govind Sastri Deva, *Yoga Sutras of Patanjali*, Calcutta, 1963. Appendix.

45. S.N. Dasgupta, *Yoga as Philosophy and Religion, op. cit.* p. 94.

46. James H. Leuba, *The Psychology of Religious Mysticism, op. cit.* p. 39.

47. S.N. Dasgupta, *Yoga as Philosophy and Religion. op. cit.* p. 137. It is also true that "Through the practising of benevolence, tenderness, complacency, and disregard towards objects (i.e. persons who are respectively in possession) of happiness, grief, virtue, and vice, the mind become purified." J.R. Ballantyne & Govind Sastri Deva, *Yoga Sutras of Patanjali, op. cit.* p. 27.

48. *Bhagavad Gīta* II-47.

49. *Ibid.* IX-34.

50. C.J. Ducasse, *A Philosophical Scrutiny of Religion*, New York, 1953, pp 308-309.

3

Psychological Bases of Religious Experience I

Psychological Approach to Religious Experience: Some Problems

That there are certain antecedents of religious experiences is evinced by the fact that voluntary means and methods are taken recourse to in producing them. Any distinction drawn between spontaneous and deliberately induced religious experiences consequentially implies some responsibility shared by subjectivity in actualizing the experiences. However, it is not enough to attribute the occurrence and recurrence of the experiences to a set of causes within the human complex or external to it. There seem to be conditions lying latent and sometimes beyond an individual's control, which lend a hand in producing religious experiences. The psycho-physical alterations that follow a religious experience, sets the mind thinking whether these behaviouristic and mental reactions are products of specific evironmental conditions and causes lying within the consciousness.

One is a biological organism comprising of physiological drives, needs, potentials, and limitations. This represents the bodily aspect, while the other component is the mind. Both the mental and the bodily subsist in harmony through interaction. Derivable from the two components are the distinct attitudes that underlie our approach to the world of objects and experiences. The first is the practical attitude and the other the contemplative. And the formative roots of the scientific and artistic temperaments lie in these attitudes respectively.

Humankind being inextricably enmeshed in the universe is at all times in physical contact with the cosmos ; the cosmos impinges on it, absorbs it, permeates it and pervades it every second of its existence. Life lived is an interaction, manifested through variations and modifications in psycho-physical attitudes with both animate and inanimate objects that we encounter in the course of our existence. To this extent the contacts and reactions are confined to the realm of the profane. Their reactions to the universe sometimes find expression in forms that are obviously religious. In this way, the contacts and reactions of humankind surpass the profane to enter the sacred. The interaction and communication between humans and a higher principle constitute the basic feature of religious experiences.

From what has been said so far we arrive at certain questions, a few of which have been asked by Clark in his *Psychology of Religion*. (*i*) Can we trace religious experiences, however complex, back to some single tap root without which they could not exist ? (*ii*) If we find the sources are many, which of these sources serve as psychological impulsions and so can be thought of as real sources of religious experience, and which are simply modifying factors that influence the form and the manner of expression ? (*iii*) Similarly, which of these sources act as impelling drives and which are to be thought of as capacities whose presence is indeed necessary to a religious experience but which may or may not be exercised, depending on whether the drives stimulate their use ? [1] (*iv*) What type of personality makes the best percipient of religious experiences ? (*v*) What are the observable effects of religious experience on the individual as a whole ? (*vi*) Is a religious experience a complex that is ultimately explicable in terms of a cause and effect series ? And, finally, a question raised by W.P. Montague—Is there a basic intuition from which originate the beliefs and experiences on which mysticism is founded ? If there is, what is the nature of that intuition in psychological terms ? [2]

Religious experience is understood to grow out of many needs and interests basic in human nature. There is the affective or feeling root of religious experiences potentially in the moods, emotions and feeling states of an individual. Besides this, there are the dormant sentiments and inclinations that bring about such experiences. "In every mind ... there is an inherent bias of both selection and interpretation, dependent on disposition, heredity, environment and mental endowment."[3] This along with one's involvement in family and society builds up a harmonious system of social sentiments and relationships, which have positive contributions to make in the production of religious experiences. Temperament, tradition, suggestion, sensual urges in some cases, and the desire for security or escape in others, condition religious experiences. Religious experience is also stimulated by attitudes like aspiration, praise, adoration, and thanks giving, directed towards the 'Beyond'. It seems more a combination of attitudes or what is in the mind coupled with efforts to inculcate the favourable mind state that can effectively induce religious experiences.

Experience is seen as a human activity related to the purpose and interests of the one who experiences, and it is understood as an interpreted product of multiple transactions between human beings and the environment. Whatever one experiences derives its zest and co-ordination from the various loyalties in domestic and social life, the cultural and intellectual climate of the age, and one's personal emotional constitution and attitudes. On analysis, it is found that religious experience involves many aspects of the personality and also many environmental conditions and circumstances. In it, feeling, thought and will are all active and concerned. Religious experiences seem to be the outcome of individual motivation, in turn the resultant of one's particular neurophysiological state, and the environmental conditions encouraging or discouraging such tendencies. All this portrays the significance of considering the mystic as human and enquiring into the domain with which one's existence is closely associated.

Psychology in its concern with human experience and behaviour as its subject matter, aims at explicating their causes and consequences and inter-relation. Wundt specified the three-fold target of psychology as : (a) the analysis of the conscious processes into their basic elements; (b) to discover how these elements are connected ; (c) to determine their laws of connection. Psychology is the science which deals with human beings as emotional, volitional and rational organisms against the background of a social set up. Further, psychology has probed deep into experiences of all kinds. Based on observation of the external manifestations in behaviour and experience, psychologists set out to explain mental states and how they work in relatedness to the external manifestations. "In many ways, religious and psychological enterprises have parallel, if not overlapping, concerns. Both call attention to and offer conceptualizations about the relation of an individual to his total environment, about the process of coping with stress, and about ameliorating the human condition. It is not surprising, then, that each should be intrigued by the prospective insights of the other."[4] Therefore, the psychology of religion looks within human experience to understand what religious experiences are and what they mean to persons. A point of importance is made by Johnson when he says, "Not that psychologists have the answers to the questions theologians ask, but they are aware of the profounder depths in man and join in the search for truer understanding."[5]

" .. there are two more or less objective though indirect manifestations of mysticism for the psychologist to study. These are, first the spoken and written accounts of their experiences by the mystics themselves and second, the facts about their lives and observable behaviour."[6] Works on religious experiences have been divided on the basis of the source material used and method of approach—(a) those works based on the writings and biographies of religious individuals and observers, and (b) those works founded on experiments and researches In (a) the source matter is selected and interpreted by the writer, using psychological principles for their interpretation, while these selected facts are used as criteria for the development of psychological principles. Such an approach successfully fulfils the aim of laying the foundation for a scientific understanding of religion, but the method's limitations are exposed in its aim to use selected facts as criteria for the development of psychological principles. This is because, the fact of selection of material drawn from religious writings and biographies is determined by subjective choice and will, which is apparently an elaborate and systematized means of expressing personal views and most unsuited for deciding theoretical issues. For instance, in emphasising the age factor as a determinant of the subjective degree of religiosity, the writer is inclined to select extracts to support one's stand and refute opposed opinions. The same principle of selection and interpretation when applied to matter scientifically proved or experimentally established, makes the result authentic.

With the help of psychology it is expected that it would be possible to account for such human behaviour that may be commonly regarded religious. A psychological study would also include an attempt at seeing how far these experiences are explicable in terms of principles and hypotheses derived from the study of human behaviour as a whole. Thus, what is required of true research in the field to religion is to consider the findings of psychology and see how far they may sucessfully account for the religious in man. It is important to note that 'religious', involves factors like faith, belief, emotion, submission, humility, prayer, worship, conversion, etc. A complete study of religious experiences, therefore, demands at least, in part, the study of certain specific aspects of the mind which happen to be the storehouse of all emotive, intellectual and volitional capacities in human beings. That is, religious experience in order to be understood psychologically (or as a psychological phenomenon) should be viewed in the light of the general schemes of psychological theories.

But this may not be feasible in the case of some novel religious experiences, which remain unexplained by any psychological theories. If we attempt to fit religious experiences into the grooves of available psychological theories, we are faced with the danger of adopting a reductionist approach which does not do justice to deeper religious experiences. The reductive theories attempt to explain religious phenomena in terms of familiar psychological or social processes which often fail to provide the insight into all categories of religious experiences. In order to arrive at some comprehensive explanation of religious experiences, it is incumbent upon us to extend beyond the circumscription of the popular psychological theories.

It should not be the business of a psycholcgical investigation of religion to fit religious experiences into the pigeonholes of Freud or Jung, or into the categories of Gestalt or stimulus-response—as if they are the categories of understanding the psychological aspect of religion—but also to see what the data available from religious experiences themselves suggest. Our study of the psychology of religious experiences in this chapter will therefore be two fold.

1. We will attempt at shedding light on the psychological mechanisms that are operative in causing such experiences.
2. We will also take into account the responses that arise out of the experiences. Efforts will be directed towards studing the consequences and implications of religious experiences in so far as they have sociological and mental effects on the experiencer.

Some details about the methodology of the psychologist is necessary at this juncture. "He will have two methods of approach, the direct observation of the actual behaviour of individuals, which is easy to observe, record, and tabulate, but very difficult to interpret without guidance of a kind which this direct method does not itself provide, and, second, the information of the individuals concerned as to the motives, emotions, purposes, and ultimate meaning of their outward behaviour."[7] Psychologists face difficulty in obtaining precise evidence as to the inner nature of the experience being interpreted. The temptation to judge mysticism and religious experiences by externals is strengthened by the prevailing psychological difficulty already mentioned. Moreover, it is paradoxical that a psychologist's participation in religious experiences affords one profounder understanding of such phenomena, though at the same time one's involvement may imply a divergence from the supposedly objective standpoint of one's scientific brethern who are unaware of what practical mysticism means.

Any psychological study of religious experiences must be founded on the idea that the essential function of such a study is to observe the phenomena without concerning oneself with making judgments as to the truth of its propositions or trying to appraise its values. There is no doubt that one should adopt the aim of dispassionate study but it is doubtful whether this can be practically achieved. Moreover, it is also true that dispassionate study is not all that one has to do about religion—there are also important decisions to be made as to one's own commitment and one's opinions cast from experience. Preliminary dispassionate study may, however, contribute to make such decisions more reasonable. In addition, any dispassionate study has its own value in promoting the understanding of other view points. In the religious context, if it makes no direct contribution to religious enthusiasm, it does contribute to religious toleration. Any psychological study should do something towords correcting the balance by increasing tolerance and mutual understanding.

The temperament and experience of the psychologist are important factors "If he happens to be susceptible to mystical experience, he, like other mystics, is apt to have been convinced by the experience. Consequently, his estimate of the phenomenon is apt to be quite different from another's whose temperament and experience has kept him from any participation in the mystic life."[8] "Now contemporary psychology is committed to the method of illuminating experience from without rather than from within."[9] Therefore, the actuality is available to psychologists in translation as expressed behaviour and variations in bodily conditions, which gives us a psychology of religion investigating the psychological laws governing religious attitudes, though its object is not the truth about the divine, but the human reality in which belief in a divine revelation comes to be.

As "mystical experience is at least (whatever else it may be in addition to that) an experience which affects the mind ... the mystical experience may be said to bring about a mystical state, which as a state of mind or consiousness should be compared to the other states, e.g. the waking state, the state of sleep and dreaming, or the hypnotic state."[10] Psychology with its various devices is capable of conducting such a survey of religious experiences.

Psychic and Environmental Factors in Religious Experience

We are part of an universe which is in direct physical contact with us, even though we may be unaware of any such contact. "Rooted to the earth .... his life is sustained by biological and physiological cycles. His mood is affected by the weather and the barometric pressures. Gravity, the rotation of the earth on its axis—all of these may have a profound effect on his life."[11] Experiences, as such, may begin with the tentative initiative of the subject concerned; a fact necessitating a consideration of the subjective dimensions like personality and its determinants found in the social, cultural and general environmental structure, as related to religious experiences. Life histories of mystics and persons who have had religious experiences make it apparent that persons with particular personality traits are most susceptible to having experiences of the supernatural order, supposedly bridging the abyss between finite and the infinite. Ramakrishna is an example of this type of personality.

The question why one deliberately seek religious experiences elicits a twofold answer—firstly, it is because of something in the nature of oneself, and also because of something in the nature and potential of extra-mental factors. One's existence is based on the principle of homeostasis—meaning the tendency of the organism to maintain its stability. There are physiological and phychological homeostasis, the latter of which safeguards stability. It is maintained by the fulfilment of needs, drives mental and motives which, in turn, constitute the dynamics through which the human personality operates. Human dynamics or personality dynamics consist of the hypothetical functioning of the structure called personality, which is behaviour. A need is the state of tension or disequilibrium that results from some lack within the person. A felt need activates a person to perform such action that helps one get rid of tensions and achieve a state of equilibrium. From the need springs interest and whatever satisfies interest or need, has value. Taking the whole realm of behaviour, it is possible to trace reasons and explanations for the various modes of behaviour. The religious propensities and susceptibility of mystics who have religious encounters seem to be the resultant of their unfulfilled needs and desires. Such an imbalance of homeostasis is detectable in the mystic's attitude and overt behaviour.

Every act of an indivi dual is the externalisation of a fusion of various levels of human dynamics. Many and varied feelings, emotions, intentions and instincts combine to result in a single human activity. Actually, these fusions of mental energies form needs which become the driving and striving forces within us, seeking fulfilment Any behavioural pattern is, therefore, the overt expression of fulfilled or unfulfilled needs and drives. Further, the modes and patterns that the various levels of needs produce, account for the psychological structure of each personality.

A look into the lives of mystics reveal some conditions that result in their breakdown of psychological homeostasis which in turn generates their intense desire for religious experience. Examples of such cases are found in the lives of St. Bernard of Clairvaux, Catherine of Genoa, Mme Guyon, among others.

St. Bernard of Clairvaux belonged to a century packed with intellectual, cultural and social activities—it was a period of overall upliftment in European history. Of this twelfth century Renaissance the revival of spiritual and mystical life is an important and essential part. It was a period when all were deeply concerned with the problem of love, carnal as well as spiritual. "The century saw the emergence of that ideal of romantic love so vividly mirrored in its literature, and its mysticism is fundamentally the mysticism of love. The foundation stone of St. Bernard's mysticism is the love of God .... For St. Bernard God is love and the Mystic way is, for him ... a continous apprenticeship in love."[12]

Catherine of Genoa (1447-1510) between 13 and 16 was drawn to the conventual way of life, but before her desire could be realised her father expired, and she was married off for political ends. Failing to settle down to her new life she found it unbearable to pull on with apparently no escape of any kind from out of the dull oppression, the living death of her existence and of herself. Her extreme depression ended when came a dramatic crisis, which preceded by a long period of preparation during which glimpses of saintly life, of God as lover, of the ecstatic gift of oneself to Him, and through Him to humanity, had come and gone. The world had offered her nothing that could content her higher self. But to choose God meant a total renunciation of self. While making confessions, one day, she was hit suddenly by the immense love of God, accompanied by the penetrating sight of her miseries and sins contrasted to His Goodness. This almost broke her, when she was drawn away from the miseries and sins of the world, and kept crying " 'No more world, no more sins!' "[13]

Similarly, the life history of Mme Guyon (1648-1717) reveals some unfulfilled desires or at least some impediments to wish fulfilment, which left her discontented. After an unsuccessful marriage she began to feel the actual need of God. "The real world had refused her ; very well, she would return to the ideal would of her childhood, she would become the bride of Jesus."[14] As a child she was spritely, highly strung, passionate, extremely sensitive, and most of all, hungry for admiration. Influenced by the ideas and images of convent life she used to perform childhood devotions and this strain in her became pronounced when she was dissatisfied with her married life. A Franciscan monk advised her to seek God in her own heart and said she would find Him there. This bit of advice proved to be the turning point in her life.

"We know that before entering a holy life, our mystics were not content with existence as it was for them ; they felt needs that were not satisfied, and conceived ideals that could not be realized. Some of them were cruelly wounded in their self-esteem and, although married, were denied the spiritual as well as the physiological satisfaction of intimate companionship with a person admired, loved, and loving. In the mystical union they found a Presence that satiated the desires for self-esteem and self-affirmation, for affection and self-surrender, for intellectual harmony and moral perfection. They found or thought they had found the fulfilment of all their yearnings. And when they had returned to normal consciousness, they rejoiced in the momentous assurance of God's love and in the promise of his constant companionship."[15] It seems that "the existence of needs not fully satisfied elsewhere ... creates a felt need for religious satisfaction."[16] Thus, one of the main prompting factors has apparently been dissatisfaction with or inability to cope with life situations which paved the way for seeking religious satisfaction. From the accounts of the life histories of the above mentioned mystics, two factors emerge—(*i*). Breakdown of physiological and psychological homeostasis in persons is accountable for the appearance of religious traits and desire for union with or involvement with the 'more than human', and (*ii*) that there are certain factors (a) subjective and (b) environmental, which cause the failure to maintain stability.

Regarding the psychological background of mystics "Murisier declares that most mystics whose mental history is accessible to us have shown themselves in the early part of their lives to be victims of a radical and extensive instability. They have been subject to frequent and violent alterations of emotion : no middle path where feeling remains relatively uniform seems open to them. Further, they have lacked the power of making decisions. They are constantly torn between conflicting temptations : between society and solitude, abstinence and self-indulgence ... they are owned by, their impulses .... life with its crowding demands, impulses, feelings, sensations, is too much for them .... Proceeding by elimination and suppression the mystics succeed in putting the religious idea or emotion in supreme control, or rather in exclusive possession."[17]

Sometimes the experience of the natural world that includes the elements of malevolence, disorder, ugliness, pain and suffering, may determine the religiosity or religious leaning in an individual. The best example of this negative attitude towards the experience of nature is to be found in the case of Buddha, who was born as a prince and had all the benefits of his status laid before him. But Buddha gave up all this when he came face to face with the basic realities of life – disease, old age and death. His negative approach gave birth to the non-theistic Buddhist tradition. Buddha devoted his life to the quest for a means of escape from suffering and rebirth.

Though it is true that some people have taken to mysticism out of despair, fear, or because of social failure, others, like the Buddha, took to it despite their comfortable position in society. "In Hinduism, where the prevailing ideal results from a synthesis or compromise between the requirements of ascetism and of society, the mystical path of *saṃnyāsa* is generally advocated only for those who have gone through the entire gamut of social responsibilities."[18] The Indian system is such that persons who enter the mystic path are not social dropouts nor considered outside the social structure. Life has been divided into four stages, the last being the mystic one. The three stages prior to that enable one to go through every phase of life without exerting self restraint. So we see that recourse to the mystic way is optional and not always submission to the pessimistic strains and pressures.

The personality consititution of Ramakrishna was such (from his very childhood) that he evinced "marked leanings towards the mystical life, and showed signs of mystical temperament and great recaptivity for higher spiritual experiences. Temperamentally emotional a-d sensitive, he was very rich in his aesthetic sense. His *absorption* appears to be so complete that even a slight suggestion would send him into deep ecstasy and mystic rapture."[19] Ramakrishna is known to have had innumerable mystical encounters and most of this was based on his profound state of God-intoxication, his constant absorption in God-consciousness, his intimate communion with God and his 'divine madness' after God-realisation. He did not content himself by following one single path to God realisation—he experimented and succeeded with paths of different religions and sects.

On the subjective side religious experience "includes all man's psychical functions, feelings, will and thought ; on the objective side it has reference to a trans-subjective divine reality. It further involves a living relation of the subject to that reality in worship, fellowship, and service, the relation being controlled by a purpose viz., the conservation and enhancement of human values both social and individual, but culminating in utter devotion to the divine reality for its own sake as itself the ultimate value."[20] However, it must be remembered that religious experiences, though always obtained through individuals, always has a social setting. If this aspect is missed, we would tend to lapse into some form of individualism overlooking the continuity of human experience and the importance and closeness of social life.

The general basis of all religious experience rests on the fact that human beings have a dual nature, each representing distinct propensities—the shallower and the profounder—the former including the fleshy sensations, instincts, and desires, of egotism, doubt, and the lower personal interests. The profounder aspect is devoid of these tendencies. When the profounder aspect is pronounced, the person is more liable not only to have the desire for religious experiences but actually have such experiences. For a complete psychological purview personal unconscious factors, the life history of the individual, and many factors in the current social environment, as formative forces, must be discussed. Apparently, particular desires or thought prepare an individual for religious experiences—i.e., a subject's desire and mental activity, in general, count for the production of these remarkable phenomena.

Prior to any psychological study of religious experiences it must be noted that, "religious experience is conditioned by and derives much of its content from its social environment - i.e., the traditions, customs, beliefs, which constitute the social heritage of the time and place in which the individualfinds himself .... On the other hand, such traditions, customs, beliefs, are themselves vitally rooted in certain psychological motives, even though such motives operate to a large extent in the subconscious mind rather than in the full daylight of consciousness."[21] From a psychological point of view, factors active in the production of religious experiences are of two orders—(*i*) psychical and (*ii*) environmental. Both factors act either separately or conjointly to determine the nature and occurrence of religious experiences. Coe, as a psychologist of religion, stresses on "the influence of the particular religion or sect in which the mystic has his setting" and also "individual differences in original endowment or in induced psycho-physical condition"[22] as factors that must be taken into account while studying religious experiences.

We set off, then, with the assumption that there are three conditions which combine to produce religious experiences :

(*i*) stimulant (*ii*) set (*iii*) setting. By 'set' is understood the inherent characteristic of the subject, one's psychological make-up, one's personality on the whole. 'Setting' is the particular environmental condition, the socio-cultural climate in which the stimulant (whatever it may be) is operative. Both 'set' and 'setting' are determinants of behaviour, inclinations, attitudes, likes and dislikes.

"What correlations, if any, exist between mysticism or various varieties of mystical experience on the one hand, and religion, social class, education, age, occupation, ethnic background, region of the country, on the other hand ? Are there certain fundamental world views that are more likely to predispose some people to mystical episodes ? Are there experiences in childhood, adolescence, or young adulthood that facilitate or impede the development of mystical capabilities?"[23] A study of Catholic priests in the United States conducted by the National Opinion Research Centre showed that there exists a correlation between family tension during childhood and religious experiences in adult life. The defining features of the religious experiences described above were (*i*) an overwhelming feeling of being at one with God or Christ, (*ii*) a sense of being in the presence of God, (*iii*) a deep feeling of being personally loved by Christ here and now. This from Greelay is again a pointer towards the impact of personality and environmental situations, on both the content of religious experiences and their production. But this applies primarily to the desired and cultivated experiences and partly to the profound and powerful experiences that have forced themselves on individuals and prophets, resulting in complete conversion of their psychic set up. These latter experiences, cannot always be adequately explained either in terms of psychic or environmental factors, though they do constitute occasions for such mighty experiences.

The essence of the mystic attitude is the withdrawal of attention from the incidents and interests of common life, and the fixation of the attention on some one object. This is what is generally known as contemplation, a state from which everything in the nature of thought or reflection is excluded. What are the psychological traits that promote such tendencies—when the subject enjoys such self-denial ? In the words of C.D. Broad, "What are the ***genetic and causal conditions*** of the existence of religious experience ? Can we trace the origin and development of the disposition to have religious experiences (a) in the human race, and (b) in each individual ?"[24]

Mystics form a psychic type to be studied with respect, and this falls well within the jurisdiction of psychology of religion. Psychology enables us to discover within us certain feelings, impulses, cravings and beliefs, which actually supply us with the key to the meaning of religious experiences. It must be admitted that the study of the psychology of religion brings into prominence the subjective element - an element otherwise not within cognitive reach of outsiders. The features of religion and their connection with the acts of mind will elucidate how emotions of common life and the common ways of conduct and of thinking, extend into and influence religious experiences. Religious experiences suggest certain mental states which require a good deal of explaining, whose counterparts in day to day life are very familiar. There is no part of human psychical nature that can be labelled religious in the sense that it is that part *alone* which functions in his religious life and that it functions *only* in the religious life. Therefore, a step by step account of the elements that determine personality development is called for at this juncture.

Human beings are gifted with certain primary impulses which include fear, anger, curiosity, tenderness, gregariousness, acquisitiveness, constructiveness, hunger, disgust, self-assertiveness, self-abasement, sex, and perhaps a few others. Individuals differ as to the relative strength of different primary impulses and their modifications, owing to various forces in interaction, which result in habits (their most important form being sentiments), to make up the personality. Wright has listed a few points which we must bear in mind while dealing with the determinants of personality growth and fixation—(*i*) the self develops through intercourse with others, (*ii*) the self develops by the choices it makes and decisions it takes, and (*iii*) the self as a whole is determined in its constitution by its dominant sentiments. An adult's character consists of one's impulses and emotions as they have become organised into sentiments. In the course of interaction with other persons, in one's choices, in one's cultivation of sentiments and submission to them, the development of the self to a considerable extent goes on without one's full knowledge. Besides conscious growth, the development to a very large extent is due to subconscious processes and this is particularly true of religious experiences. "None of us develop our religious attitudes in isolation from our fellow men; from childhood to old age we are receiving from the behaviour of those around us and from what is said by them influences that affect on religious attitudes."[25]

While behaviour and personality traits in an adult are fixed upto a point by one's genetic make-up, considerable influence is rendered upon them by two separate environmental factors that at times operate in combination—(*i*) early childhood experiences, particularly the interaction between child and parents, and, (*ii*) influences of society at large. "There can be no doubt that the attitudes of parents are among the most important factors in the formation of religious attitudes. In several surveys of students in which subjects were asked what had been the most important influence on their religious beliefs, 'parents', 'home', or 'mother', were the most frequent answers given."[26]

Different circumstances in home life affect the child in different ways. There is a direct relation between the parents' behaviour and beliefs to the formulation of a child's personality or inclinations. It has been found that people who had a harmonious home life tend to have pro-religious attitudes. Argyle points out that "when parents hold differing religious beliefs, the children are less religious (e.g. Lenski, 1953). In this case the children tend to adopt the faith of the mother if anything (Bell, 1938), as would be predicted from the findings about the greater influence of the mother."[27] Mother's attitude and attention determine both emotional and intellectual development. A mother's absence or neglect causes disturbances in behaviour culminating in abnormal development. Such a deprived child experiences a feeling of insecurity or separation anxiety. For satisfying these lacking necessities, the child tends to develop religious leanings. Furthermore, "There is evidence that parents who are inconsistent in their behaviour toward children cause personality problems."[28]

Besides parents, opinions of others, like friends, associates and teachers, largely determine what a person values and places worth upon. Religious experiences focalize in an individual some existing socio-cultural standards and ideas apart from psychological determinants like home life. Depending on the particular educational system, the kind of educational institution, and the child's own psychological adjustments, experiences of academic success or failure can be either beneficial or destructive to one's developing personality. A secure child can accept failure as a learning experience, while one who has been rejected may not be able to deal with failure. In the course of personality development the socio-cultural background in which a child is reared has its own impact on the child. Working-class parents, for example, tend to use physical punishment to discipline their children while middle-class families rely more on reasoning, isolation, appeals to guilt, and other methods involving the threat of loss of love.

In a study Bronfenbrenner (1970) compared child-rearing practices in the U.S. with those in the them Soviet Union. In Russia, the state played a much larger role by providing advice and instruction to parents, as well as extensive systems of state-supported nurseries and schools in which the child spends a great deal of his time. In general, the family's role has been de-emphasised in an effort to foster "collective consciousness". Though Russian babies receive substantially more physical handling than their American counterparts, they are given little opportunity for freedom of movement or exercising individual initiative. Another striking finding was the prevalence, among Soviet parents, of the witholding of love as a disciplinary method. This technique is strongly encouraged by the state, with the objective of producing children with hi gh levels of internal control—children who are obedient, conscientious, industrious responsible—set to face life. As one might expect, however, the children do not exhibit much creative, innovative or impulsive tendencies.[29]

Apparently, these major forces impelling the development of personality do not operate on the individual in isolation. Certain incidents in a child's formative stage also have a great impact on one's personality traits. We do encounter persons with fear phobias, aversions, repulsion, or great liking for something, which is in apparent contradiction to one's overall personality. But they do form a part of one's being, and their existence can be traced to some traumatic experience way back in childhood days, leaving a vivid impression, to form part of one's personality.

The role of age and sex in the context of development of religious traits is no less important. " ... children are considerably religious, at first holding fairy tale beliefs, later accepting the standard ideas of their group (10-18). Intellectual doubts start at a mental age of 12, followed by emotional stress ; these conflicts are often resolved at about the age of 16 either by conversion or by a decision to abandon the religion of childhood."[30] No change of attitude towards religion is marked till thirty five, as this is the period in life when maximum involvement in worldly affairs occurs, which results in a tempory withdrawal from religious interests. After this period there is a steady increase of religious leanings until old age when belief in God and after life is most intense. Members of the fairer sex usually grow to be more religious as compared to their male counterparts. This is probably because of their temperamental make up, and partially because of their keen involvement in home life, which limits their ties with worldly affairs—a domain looked after by male folks. "Women are more religious than men on all criteria, particullarly for private prayer, also for membership, attendance and attitudes while differences in beilef are small."[31]

Allegiance to particular religions is a deciding factor of individual attitude towards religious experiences, and also the nature and content of these experiences. Consequently, the form of religious experience varies according to individual religious beliefs, faiths and practices and the diverse religious temperaments. "Some types of religion seem to be by their nature mystical, in the sence that they are directly and frankly oriented toward a mystical goal, so that the life of a faithful adherent of such a religion is expected to be a steady progress in mystical experience....In other types of religion, mysticism appears as something which, welcome as it may be, is regarded as exceptional."[32]

Spinks classifies religions as authoritarian and humanistic. The essential characteristic of the former is that it demands the surrender of the individual to some power transcending the human person. Voluntary Submission to a higher authority implies loss of sense of personal dissatisfaction and frustration, and by willing association with a Divine Power one achieves an exhilarating sense of fulfilment. The humanistic type emphasises the fact that the individual 'finds' one self by being in loving association with one's fellows. Religious experience for the humanistic type is an experience which receives its significance from one's relationship with others. As objective situations condition emotional responses, whatever God means to an individual will define one's religious emotions. The sense of or craving for a relationship with the divine ensues from the fact that religions variously emphasise the intellectual, moral and mystical elements. It is clear that individuals owing allegiance to different religions are bound to devolop diverse religious sentiments.

A factor deserving attention in connection with our area of study is the specific brain lobe which is predominantly active. Science admits eparate functions for the two lobes. "Although each hemisphere shares the potential for many functions, and both sides participate in most activities, in the normal person the two hemispheres tend to specialize. The left hemisphere (connected to the right side of the body) is predominantly involved with analytic, logical thinking, especially in verbal and mathematical functions....the right hemisphere (... connected to the left side of the body) seems specialized for holistic mentation. Its language ability is quite limited. This hemisphere is primarily responsibe for our orientation in space, artistic endeavour, crafts, body image, recognition of faces. It processes information more diffusedly than does the left hemisphere..."[33] They function as complementary organs but neither can replace the other. The two cerebral hemispheres communicate through the corpus callosum, which joins the two sides anato mically. To the devoloped left lobe are attributed the rationa - listic operations in human beings—linguistic, mathematical, intellectual—while the right lobe instigates the creative and instinctive attitudes—musical, imaginative, artistic. This is the ineffable side, which is mostly underdeveloped because most people are right handers. A developed right lobe in a left hander marks the individual to be sensitive and artistically bent, in contrast to a right hander. "There is also evidence that religious people tend to be right hemisphere dominant (Bakan, P. 'The eyes have it' *Psychology Today*, 4, pp. 64-7, 1971). This suggests that religious attitudes and ideas are primarily produced by the non-verbal right hemispheres, but are supplemented by the verbal activities of the left."[34] "The left hemisphere, which controls the right hand, seems to be able to operate well in an analytic manner, yet poorly in a relational mode. The performance of the left hand reversed that of the right can operate holistically, but does not have much capacity for verbal-analytic information processing. Ornstein mentions that the right-left specialization is based on right handers. This is because left handers are less consistent ; some have reversed sepecialization of the hemispheres, but some have mixed specialization—e.g., language in both sides. Some are specialized in the same way as right handers. Thus, this distinction of functions of the two brain lobes (as evident from the use of hand) may explain one's religious propensities."[35]

Based on the observations enumerated above, psychologists have formulated Personality Theories. The type theory approaches personality study by categorising people according to type. The basic elements of Jung's typology are two opposed characteristics—introversion and extroversion. The former is basically a shy person often withdrawn into oneself, especially during periods of emotional stress, and tends to be highly imaginative and intellectual. The extrovert tends to be out-going and sociable, preferring to deal with people rather than with ideas. One limitation of this theory is its tendency to categorise people into static types, while the other limitation is lack of concern about the immediate environmental factors that influence anyone. Implicitly it views personality as genetically determined, ignoring the fact that behaviour changes and develops over a lifetime under the influence of personal and social experiences. The Trait theory sought to categorise persons in terms of traits. But categorising people in this way means a list of traits so vast that duplication and a high degree of imprecision is the likely result.

Eysenck added another fundamental dimension of personality—stability—instability—to Jung's extroversion-introversion. Stability implies calmness, thoughtfulness and dependability. Instability characterises people who are moody, touchy, anxious, restless. In conjunction these four dimensions suggest the existence of four basic personality types - stable extrovert, unstable extrovert, stable introvert and unstable introvert. This approach has proved useful in identifying latent or manifest problems.

Among theorists of human behaviour, Freud has profoundly influenced the trend of modern ideas concerning the nature of human beings, as none before him seriously argued that events in childhood might have a bearing on adult behaviour and consciousness. The key to Freud's work is his concept of the unconscious. He believed that thoughts and feelings within awarerness represent a fraction of actual mental experience. A far larger portion of what goes on inside a person occurs without one's conscious knowledge. He introduced two types of unconscious drives or instincts, believed to be present in persons at birth. They are sexuality (eros) and aggressiveness (thanatos). Arousal or activations of these produce tension, leading to action for satisfying the unconscious drive. Freud deemed personality as having three aspects—the id, or pure unconscious instinct ; the ego, or reality principle ; and the superego, or conscience.

Neo-Freudians as reactionaries to the basic tenets of Freud have extended their own views. Jung proposed two kinds of unconscious, the personal unconscious and the collective unconscious ; the latter being inherited from ancestors. Adler stressed the importance of the social environment and introduced the concepts of compensation and inferiority complex. Horney was concerned with the effects of anxiety, especially childhood feelings of insecurity, on the personality. Phenomenological theories emphasise the uniqueness of each person and the subjective nature of one's experience.

It is seen how these wide range of factors complement and interact with each other in the development of a religious personality. Each personality theory is relatively reliable in terms of its own limited objectives. Recognising the role and significance of personality in the religious context, James devoted much attention, in his Gifford lectures, to the discussion of the religion of the healthy mind and the sick soul. "Human beings interpret their experiences not only in terms of belief but also in terms of their own personality, whether it be sick or healthy, introverted or extroverted. Both attitudes are equally real and each has its own type of religious experience ....Many a young man or woman...brought up in an evangelical tradition with its insistence upon the necessity of conversion, has been brought to the point of despair by failing to recognize that he is by temperament and disposition a healthy-minded soul trying to behave as if he were a sick soul."[36] The streak of optimism in the works of Walt Whitman inspired William James to make this distinction of religious types. He sees a need to "distinguish between...involuntary and...voluntary or systematic way of being healthy minded. In its involuntary variety, healthy-mindedness is a way of feeling happy about things immediately. In its systematical variety, it is an abstract way of conceiving things as good."[37] In the healthy-minded approach the ordinary contrast of good and evil vanishes into a higher denomination.

In contrast to the healthy-minded view of deliberately minimising evil, is the sick-soul that wilfully maximises evil. It is a morbid way of looking at any situation. "As the healthy-minded enthusiast succeeds in ignoring evils' very existence, so the subject of melancholy is forced in spite of himself to ignore that of all good whether for him it may no longer have the least reality."[38] In these two distinctive types of personalities we can well see their difference in approach to religious experiences. Their experiences and interpretation of experiences will be as per their psychological make up.

Sheldon, has distinguished between three types of temperament on the basis of stature and traits. According to him "any given individual is a mixture, in varying proportions, of three physical and three closely related psychological components."[39] The three physical components are endomorphy, mesomorphy and ectomorphy. The corresponding psychological components are visceratonia, somatotonia and cerebrotonic. (*i*) The Viscerotonic temperment is associated with a physique which exhibits breadth of body and weight. Such a physique is found to be characteristically amiable, tolerant, slow to anger, dislikes solitude, desires company and companionship when in trouble, enjoys good food and good family relationships, loves comfort and has an inclination to luxury. (*ii*) The Somatotonic temperament is found with a strong muscular body, an active and athletic physique. The characteristics associated with these physical traits are the courageous, combative, danger loving, indifference to pain, dislike for being in closed places, aptitude to be ruthless when pursuing some objective, strongly extroverted and when in personal trouble show a tendency to seek some active occupation as a means of dispelling 'gloom and despondency'. (*iii*) The Cerebrotonic temperament is generally found in those whose physique is of a highly nervous type both in build and in gesture. This type tends to avoid company, is emotionally restrained, dislikes open spaces, is introverted and when in trouble needs solitude.

Each of these three types has its own religious orientation. Viscerotonic types incline to sacramentalism, with solemn and elaborate worship in magnificient architectural settings. Owing to one's love of family relationships the cult of the Divine Mother and Child often figures prominently in one's religious devotions. Somatotonic types show strong inclination to make converts, a readiness to suffer martyrdom as well as to persecute others for a good cause. This type has a marked tendency to austerity, and a dogmatic insistence upon morality and good works rather than upon sacraments and rituals. The cerebrotonic type, being introvert, rarely experiences the convulsive sort of emotional experience that is so characteristic of somatotonic types. They make positive contribution in the contemplative life. "Psychologically, the history of mysticism is mainly the record of the cerebrotonic temperament, not that this temperament in itself produces mystical experiences but such experiences are most readily apprehended by those who have this particular temperament. This type often renounces, or seeks to avoid, ritualistic forms of worship as impediments to the soul's free encounter with the Divine....the cerebrotonic type regards the life of voluntary poverty as the most natural form of life, while he worships in churches almost devoid of ornament."[40]

Suggesting the importance of psychological factors in the attainment of religious experiences, Underhill states—"More than the apprehension of God...more than the passion for the Absolute, is needed to make a mystic. These must be combined with an appropriate psychological make-up, with a nature capable of extraordinary concentration, an exalted moral emotion, a nervous organization of the artistic type. All these are necessary to the successful development of the mystic life process."[41]

Efforts have been directed at exposing the way personality and temperaments influence religious experience and also how the personality traits develop under the influence of many forces. It is evident how religious experiences can be traced down to psysiological and psychological conditions of the individual. Thus far, personality has been viewed as the inciting factor of religious experiences and it remains to be seen how religious experiences affect the personality and overall life style of persons. Besides this, their social and religious impact will also be considered in the following section.

Religious Experience and Integration of Personality

"...just as our awareness of God sharpens our moral sensitivity, so conversely a sensitive conscience predisposes us to an awareness of God."[42] Similarly, religious experiences both condition and are conditioned by personality, when viewed from different perspectives. Therefore, it is necessary to examine what place religious experiences have in the development of human personality. We cannot afford to overlook the deeply entrenched religious ideas and experiences which play a significant role in the structuring and development of personality. What we are concerned with for the moment is the psychological interpretation of the direct intuition of the divine and unity, and their bearing on the life and development (religious in particular) of the individual.

Among the characteristic marks of religious experiences, as we have already seen, are the 'noetic quality' and 'a feeling of a presence', both of which are, perhaps, potentials that affect and alter personality and way of life. Noetic quality, as mentioned earlier, is the sense of certitude—that their contents are self-established, self-evidencing, and, self-luminous—that accompanies religious experiences.

A fractional consequence of religious experiences is alleged to be knowledge or well-founded belief about the nature of reality, e.g., that we are dependent on a being, that values are somehow conserved in spite of the chances and changes of the material world, and so on. By the term religious experience is described the feeling element in the religious consciousness - the feelings which lead to religious belief. To the unquestionable presentation of these experiences and the accompanying feeling of certainty, has been attached cognitive significance. But, there is yet another aspect which cannot be overlooked. This aspect is concerned with those correlates of religious experiences as found in human behaviour and experience, and these, one perfers to call the effects of these experiences. It is important to know how these experiences are endured by individual dispositions and how they contribute to the rest of life by becoming one with the traits of our nature and behaviour. The noetic quality affords far reaching consequences for the experient along with the conviction that the contents given in these experiences are authentic and indubitable.

Reference has also been made to the characteristic apprehension of Unity in religious experiences which imply the 'feeling of a presence', involving a perception of 'something there', in a way far deeper and significant than any other perception. This sense or a feeling of a presence and the gradual dependence on it are not the mere belief in it nor the outcome of reason, but are the immediate and intuitive experiences which under no circumstances can be questioned or doubted.

A more definite aspect of this 'feeling of a presence' depends on the individual, according to whom religious or theistic significance may be attached to it. It is this quality that gives rise to the interpretation of such consciousness as being the experience of God. Those for whom this 'feeling of a presence' means union with or communion with God are inclined to experience mental depressions when their experience of God ceases to occur. These periods of depression Underhill has called 'Dark Night of the Soul'—a period of trial marked by restlessness and distraction. More over, one who sets one's mind on the mystic way anticipates emancipation and freedom of the spirit from the bonds of the flesh, and until the process is complete and realized, there is bound to be struggle, turmoil, and pain. "...the typical mystic seems to move towards his goal through a series of strongly marked oscillations between "states of pleasure" and "states of pain"."[43]

The vividness with which the presence of God is felt, the intensity of joy which it affords and of sorrow which its absence brings vary largely with individual temperaments. Not only this, every consequence ensuing from religious experiences leaves an impact on the human mind. The person emerges from a smaller limited world of existence into a larger world of being. We, therefore, begin with the assumption that religious experiences leave a profound impression on personality, sometimes to the extent of completely reshaping life.

Pratt deems the milder form of religious experiences to be productive of joy and calm, unconnected with pain of any sort. But there is the heavier or sadder aspect of religious experiences, whose extreme type is either positive or negative. The latter, being the milder of the two, is due simply to the fact that the individual tends to overemphasise the importance of religious joy, expecting its return at a time when for some unknown reason it cannot come. Contrary to this, the positive sort of pain is the lack of joy of communion plus the intense feeling of being deserted by God and being separated from Him. This is usually connected with a sense of sin and unworthiness. God is felt far away, and the mystic concentrates all efforts to regain the lost sense of peace and joy. These acute bouts of pain, belonging mainly to the 'sick-soul' are to be found to some degree in intensely religious persons.

The tradition of mystical self-realisation is most attractive to persons who suffer from a sense of "divided self". Such persons undergo recurrent strains of the following kind—a struggle that one cannot defeat sinfulness, resulting in a deep sense of personal unworthiness and helplessness; distaste for the usual pleasures of life, with inability to find any substitute for them; restlessness and a feeling of life's emptiness; fluctuations of mood; persistent doubts with insistent but vain protest against uncertainty. All the mental strains just enumerated may find relief in mystical practices. "The divided self may become unified, a commanding certainty displacing doubt, a focus for the emotional life being established, a central purpose being substituted for discordant impulses, and executive steadiness being achieved. These results are not uniform in kind or degree, of course, yet on the whole the tendency of mysticism is toward serenity, poise, and an organised will."[44] It is a state of bliss, beatitude, joy or a sense of supreme value. The happiness of the healthy-minded religion, reaches the exalted state of ecstasy and rapture in mystic consciousness.

"Mysticism, impelled by such instinctive patterns as calm resignation, consecrated service, and the love of parents, of child, of friend, and man-woman love, or rather expressing herein the fundamental needs of the mystic's own nature, restore sanity and balance in emotional life. The goal of the types of ardent mysticism that cherish a personal God everywhere has been to establish such harmony and unity in inner life that both denial and enjoyment of things of sense become consecration, both pleasures and pains become offerings, and all deeds become sacrifices; the entire framework of life, with its bafflings and expressions, being fitted into God as the whole and the All."[45] The passage elicits a distinction between the effects imparted on the personality by spontaneous and created gious experiences. The spontaneous experiences occur with relino forewarning and takes the person unaware. Tinged with abruptness, the person is unable to acquire a grip over things and succumbs to the intense experiences. Under these circumstances religious conversion is likely to take place. And, it is well known that profound transformations of habit and dispositions are wrought in the soul by such intense religious experiences as conversion.

In all cases of conversion the individual undergoes sharp changes to emerge a changed person. Conversion consists in spiritual illumination and in a widening of the whole horizon of life. "we can define religious conversion as *that type of spiritual growth or development which involves an appreciable cha· ge of direction concering religious ideas and behaviour. Most clearly and typically it denotes an emotional episode of illuminating suddenness, which may be deep or superficial, though it may also come about by a more gradual process*."[46] Conversion may mean, (a) a voluntary change of attitude toward God, (b) the renunciation of one religion and beginning adherence to another or a change from one branch of religion to another, (c) individual salvation, which means repentance, faith, forgiveness, regeneration, etc., (d) becoming voluntarily religious as distinguished from mere conformity to the religious ways of family or creed, and (e) any abrupt transfer from one standpoint and mode of life to another. According to Coe, the term 'conversion' should be understood to refer to experience that seem to the subject of them to have the following marks : (*i*) The subject's very self seems to be profoundly changed, (*ii*) this change seems not to be wrought by the subject but that which comes upon the subject —control seems not to be self-control (*iii*) the sphere of the change is the attitudes that constitute one's character or mode of life, with the world acquiring a new meaning, (*iv*) the change includes a sense of attaining to a higher li^e or to emancipation or enlargement of the self. [47]

A characteristic prelude to conversion is a feeling of incompleteness which "is one of uncertainty, unrest, mistiness, a dazed feeling, distress, effort, struggle toward an indefinable something, longing for something out of reach, etc., which is followed by peace, happiness, a sense of harmony, a clearing away, a flash of light, freedom, entrance into the new life, and so on."[48] To be converted denotes the process, gradual or sudden, by which a self hitherto divided, and consciously wrong, inferior and unhappy, becomes unified and consciously right, superior and happy, in consequence of its firmer hold upon religious realities. What brings about and changes the way in which emotional excitement alters is dependent upon the constant change of our interests and a consequent change of place in our systems of ideas, from more the central to the more peripheral parts of consciousness and *vice versa.*

Oscillation of emotional interest means the emergence of the wavering and divided self, which calls for the intervention of religious experience for restoring stability. Thus, when discord between the deeper spiritual self and superfical worldly ego becomes intolerable, conversion is desired. Professor Coe "found that conversions took place in nine out of ten persons who combined these three qualifications :

1. expectation and desire for conversion,
2. temperaments of an emotional and sensitive as opposed to an unemotional and intellectual sort, and,
3. passive suggestibility (so as to be devoid of initiative when hypnotized) and with a tendency to automatisms.

With any one of these qualifications lacking, the probability that a person could experience conversion was reduced. Persons possessing the opposite of all three qualifications were temperamentally and constitutionally incapable of the particular form of awakening called conversion."[49]

There are two volitional types of conversion distinguished by Starbuck and William James—one involving effort and the other self-surrender. In the former, the necessity of making a resolute struggle in order to gain the larger life is felt, whereas the latter requires the individual to give up struggling—the self must passively submit, and permit the awakening sentiment to dominate consciousness entirely, and automatically to suppress all that is hostile to it. Both Starbuck and James insist that conversion is usually a process of struggling away from sin rather than that of striving toward righteousness. Pratt altogether denies this. However, on the whole, conversion experiences seem to guarantee a profounder development of character on the religious side. Therefore "it is a perfectly legitimate description of conversion to say that it is brought about by a change of ideas, or rather of emphasis. When certain ideas previously on the fringe of consciousness and dimly felt become central and vividly realized, what we call a conversion takes place".[50]

The question as to the relation and functions of the conscious and unconscious mind in conversion must next be considered. Both elements are present in all normal cases. Indeed, it is often said that there is no such thing as sudden conversion. When it appears to be sudden it shows itself as an unexpected decision to follow a certain line of conduct, or abandon certain practices which are habitual; what really happens is that this comes about as the result of a process of incubation in which certain psychic forces that suddenly manifest themselves have long been maturing and gathering strength.

Though conversion is the highest in order among resultants to show on personality, the milder forms appear as peacefulness, tranquility, joy, eradication of doubts, anxiety and humility, submission to a higher authority on the strength of faith—i.e., appearing in all forms of ethical and moral convictions and actions.

For the divided or sick soul, religious experiences become a desired objective, the attainment of which naturally results in a host of positive feelings. There is no doubt that the intense emotional upheaval provided by religious experiences leaves behind long lasting, sometimes permanent, impressions on the personality. The way of looking at things alters—hope, optimism, joy and peace become part of life. Unlike spontaneous experiences where the subject is taken by surprise, the subject who cultivates religious experience does so with certain ends in view, which necessarily implies a certain amount of 'expectation'. Something desired and expected is the result of subjective thinking—use of one's reasoning power—and whatever comes is received with gladness in a spirit of calmness. But the spontaneous kind of experiences give the subject neither time nor opportunity for reasoning—one is swept off one's feet, as it were, and made to react or respond intensely. We can see, then, how the spontaneous experiences leave a stronger image as compared to those resulting from created experiences. Moreover, in the mystical consciousness many degrees or types have to be admitted.

Apparently, then, religious experiences are therapeutic, in so far as they are capable of installing human balance. Their therapeutic capability is attributed to the fact that "religious feeling from earliest times has often manifested itself in admiration, awe, and even love of the supreme. This positive attitude has been stressed by Spinoza, who considers the religious feeling as a vitalizing force, which keeps the man of religion in an ever-happy state."[51] It seems that when "a religious insight is of critical personal importance ... the worshipper may try to spell out its meaning for his life – attitudes and his daily activities ; he may relate it to many other facets of his life .... "[52] Therefore, through religious experiences, one, by a sense of having obeyed and conformed, gets a sense of inner rightness and external security. Psychologically these experiencсs make life more peaceful within and more secure without because it resolves the confusions and uncertainties of the demands of society and strains of divinity latent in human being.

"The mystical experience involves a consciousness of God as a personal being so intense and vivid as to react powerfully on the personality of him who experiences it. It involves a degree of awareness and attention that constitutes in itself a deep religious experience and has a real educational value. It produces a sense of calm, strength, and courage that brings with it the conviction that the subject concerned has reached his true self-hood and increases his self-reliance and self-respect."[53]

According to Leuba religious experiences command passivity and subordination of the conscious intelligence, which is nothing but abdication of the highest human power, namely reason. All mystics universally testify to the joy and sweetness of these experiences. "In religious experience the co-ordination and systematization of the impulses reach the farthest limits. Here sets of impulses which, in ordinary, non-religious experience would be inhibited to give unarrested scope to others, are blended and reconciled with one another, and, where all rivalry or conflict is dissolved, man feels that his contact with actuality has increased. Along with a new vitality the mystic develops a sense of immutability and all-inclusiveness of his experience, bestowing a feeling of freedom, of relief and sanity."[54] Further, mysticism's "hold upon mankind lies rather in its practical efficiency in soothing troubled emotions, in steadying the will, and in conserving what has already been approved."[55]

Thus far we have tried to elucidate the diverse effects ensuing from spontaneous and cultivated religious experiences. We now take a look at two remarks made by Selbie and Greelay, which will further focalize the field of effects of religious experiences. According to Selbie a religious experience "must be judged not by its psychological origins, but by the degree of religious assurance which it brings, and by the many and great contributions which it has made to religious life and service."[56] From this is evident the social impact of religious experiences. But, from Greelay's suggestion that "we must also examine the possibility that in the proper context and under the proper circumstances, ecstatic experiences can be extra-ordinarily functional for human personality development and mental health",[57] it becomes apparent that religious experiences are, in a way, agents that mould and reshape human personality. There is, quite obviously a correlation between religious experiences and positive psychic health. "Far from being "some kind of nut" it may be possible the ecstatic is among the healthiest and most "normal" of humans. It may even be—as the religions of the East have insisted—that under some sets of circumstances ecstasy can be induced with the precise purpose of facilitating personality development."[58] This raises the basic question—Do religious experiences make a difference? In answering this question we will have to take into account both the individual and social fields of effects.

It has been seen how religious experiences effect human personality. But, can the effects be limited to individuals alone, not to reach out to the community or society? Most enduring, historical religious traditions find their roots in the religious experience and insight of charismatic individuals who have served as founders; the sharing of their experience among disciples and followers leads to the establishment of a religious community. The social dimension of religious experiences is a primary fact, finding expression in the formation of specifically religious groups distinct from any other kind of groups. Such religious communities serve to preserve and interpret their traditions or the body of doctrines, practices and liturgical forms through which religious experience comes to be expressed. They further play a significant role in the shaping of religious experience and in determining its meaning for the individual through the structure of worship and liturgy.

Through the media of individuals the message of religious experiences reach out to, and leave their impressions on, social and community life, which actually gives birth to beliefs and dogmas within every social system. "The mystic has a direct vision of God communicated to himself alone, and in virtue of it he is able to mediate the things of God to others in a way that sets him apart from common men."[59] "It is plain that this ... has considerable plausibility .... Certain persons of religious genius, such as some of the Hebrew prophets and founders of Christianity and of Buddhism, do seem to have introduced new ethico-religious concepts and beliefs which have won wide acceptance, just as certain men of scientific genius, such as Galileo, Newton, and Einstein, have done in the sphere of science."[60] It is appropriate to point out in this context the remark that "every turning point in the history of Christianity is marked by the emergence of a man to whom had come some individual vision of God's truth and who could speak to the world or to the Church in the authentic personal tones of a prophet. These men stand out like light houses over the dull waters of convention and religious routine."[61] Although a mystic is primarily an individualist, one does see oneself as the spokesman for the divine to the community, or all of human kind, and regards one's own experience as a message that enables one to interpret the past and future in the light of the divine will.

Religious experiences are pointers to eternal values, like Truth, Beauty and Goodness, as absolute, which transcend any human values. From religious experiences ensue renewed faith, beliefs and stability on the whole. They bring peace, joy, insight, love and confidence. The mystic energes with new serenity and confidence in everyday life. As religious experienccs are truth revealing, new doctrines come to humankind. The practical and ethical standards and methods of institutionalised religions are fortified or altered in this way. A subjective experience thus attains significance by dint of its objective applicability. Also, religious experiences may fortify and give birth to personal religion independent of institutionalised religion. They were invariably mocked, derided, and persecuted and had to sometimes give their lives for publicising the truth as they saw it. Through all this "they indicated for all time the right of the individual to a religious experience of his own, and they left as a legacy to mankind not merely the right but the duty of private judgement in the things of faith .... they have been the chief factors in religious progress, and the chief mediators of God's word to man. In case of many of them their teaching was accepted, and what began with them as heresy became the orthodoxy of a later time."[62] In spite of their value and function, in that they afford the way to the deepest apprehension of religious truth, religious experiences at times tend to become one-sided, and in their extreme form acquire pathological symptoms.

It will be observed that the resultants of religious experience dealt with so far fall into two distinct categories : some of them describe the experience itself, they are intrinsic to it ; others are its fruits. The intrinsic traits may be summed up in the words, suddenness, unexpectedness, passivity, illumination or revelation, and ineffability. Its fruits surface in the form of peace, tranquility, insight, serenity, hope, confidence, love, etc. And it is our contention that the fruits of religious experiences have some effect on personality and may even transform it. "Existential thinkers, such as Soren Kierkegaard, Gabriel Marcel, and Paul Tillich, have seen God manifested in experience in the form of power that overcomes estrangement and enables man to fulfil himself as an integrated personality."[63]

Some Reflections

This chapter on the psychological bases of religious experiences has brought us closer to religious experiences and the psychological factors that encourage and facilitate them. Discussions herein have elicited some suggestions pertaining to human personality; how it develops into what it is in adulthood, how past experiences and encounters determine choice and preference, how personality is itself an important element that promotes the realisation of religious experiences, and how, again, religious experiences influence personality. Some of the important psychological factors that act as motivating factors of religious experiences have emerged—not only this, as a corollary to the main findings of the preceding sections the existing two-way relation between personality and religious experiences is seen clearly. The last section sheds light on the therapeutic aspect of religious experiences.

The discussion of the environmental and psychic factors, in the second section, clearly shows how personality is moulded by the influences of the many relations, needs—whether fulfilled or unfulfilled—objects and persons encountered, religious training and environment, general set up and personal mental and physical constitution. This leads to the realisation how deep set reiigion is in the life of any person. The important factor in any voluntary religious experience, as has been emphasised in Chapter II, is one's desire for the religious encounter—the craving, as it were. And, this desire grows or does not grow, in an individual, depending on the various factors discussed in this chapter. With these general remarks, we are now in a position to take up for evaluation some of the questions that may arise from the study so far.

The facts revealed in the section on 'Religious Experience And Integration of Personality' warrant the following conclusions :

1. Religious experiences come with power and authority, and produce a deeper and more lasting impression than natural words/sensory experiences.

2. They produce peace; worry, doubt, discouragement, etc., vanish, and are replaced by joy and happiness or by a pain free from any distressing implication.

3. They stimulate progress in the virtues; in particular, they incline to obedience, humility, and the praise of God; and they increase faith in the teachings of the Church.

4. They also encourage development of the subjective opinion with regard to religious matters, thereby diminishing the degree of attachment to, and influence of, traditional religious teachings and beliefs.

5. The favourable impact on the individual following these experiences is not merely beneficial to the individual, but through the individual society is also benefited.

6. They have no undesirable physiological effects. In this way, religious experiences are certainly both religiously and morally desirable.

Though the positive role of religious experiences in integrating personality cannot be denied, one of its other aspects arouses intriguing questions regarding the relationship of some of their manifestations to the symptoms of mental disorder that they elicit.

It has already been hinted that in extreme cases mystics seem to develop pathological conditions to the extent of what appears to be mental imbalance. With the general factors discussed are mingled, in many instances, influential circumstances of the individual's own psycho-physical constitution or incidental condition Nervous instability, whether inherited or induced, non-fulfilment of needs and drives, as we have seen, favour the occurrence of religious experiences. When these traits are excessive in any individual, can one be called unstable? Also can the experience have so intense an impact as to affect mental imbalance? Pointing out both possibilities it is suggested that a close relation may be found to exist, in individual cases, though not generally, between mystical religion and hysteria, epilepsy, delusional insanity or neurotic condition.[64]

The symptoms of hysteria are often parallelled to incidents in the life of Catherine of Genoa, particularly in her last illness. Anaesthesia, with loss of skin sensitivity over parts of the body, is a typical hysterical symptom, and it is recorded of Catherine of Genoa that she would press thorny rose-twigs in both her hands, and this without any pain. Examples of this kind cannot conclusively establish that religious experiences can be parallelled to hysteria in every case, because in the Indian tradition it is a common feature among yogis to lie down on a bed of thorns without feeling any pain. Of course, in the case of a yogi such practice is the outcome of severe discipline and self-control. It is believed that self-mortification is an effective means of self-elevation and is largely practised in the Sufi tradition too.

However, having been made aware of this relation between religions experience and mental disorders at various levels, it would be inappropriate to make any hasty remark about it. Usually, during an intense religious experience the subject is in the so-called trance state which implies—a) experiences loosing their usual meanings; b) experiences having special meanings which result from their isolation from the totality of general experiences; and c) special orientations that function temporarily as the only possible reality for the subject as a result of one's break from the totality of general sense experience. So, in the mystic state there is suspension of generalised reality-orientation and a shift to some special orientation which becomes the only one of worth. Such experiences involve the annihilation of one's awareness of separate existence—there is self-obliteration which is the perception of oneself as a dimly apprehended instrument of a more universal influence rather than as a separately functioning personality. Self-surrender is sought for in most religions, e.g., the practice of Yoga encourages the devotee to lose one's individuality in merging with the universal spirit. Involvement in the new orientation that ensues from the experience, and break from the subject's empirical orientation, is, in all likelihood, responsible for the imbalanced behaviour of mystics and religious persons. When these intense experiences become a regular feature in the mystic life, their impact may take some permanent form by becoming part of personality. Usually the impact is not lasting but more a temporary phase of mystic life.

In a study of creativeness[65] it was found that innovative and independent people are not only unconventional, politically radical and disposed to prefer change over routine, but also more overtly anxious, frequently lacking in a sense of security or optimism regarding the future, and more generally distrustful of others and the world. Creativity and first-hand religious experiences as visions, mystical beliefs and superstitions and a sense of oneness with the universe are associated. The crucial variable in distinguishing the mentally ill person, who also reports such experiences, and the creative person, is the ability of the latter to return to a high degree of rationality and to integrate one's inner experiences into a wider reality context. The mentally ill cannot at any cost come out and rationalise, and this is the greatest difference between mystics and the mentally ill.

All neurotic states are manifestations of insecurity, and what is a sense of insecurity but perceiving oneself as unpleasantly separated from God, and fellow beings and also from the world one lives in ? States of severe depression are experienced by mystics during the period of spiritual dryness which may explain their indifference to logic and their tendency to indulge in self accusation.

Moreover, hysterics show none of the steadfastness and dedication which characterises the mystic. The mystic lives in one's experience of reality and one's efforts are enriched by it. The cure of any neurosis is slow and even then the patient is prone to relapses. But the mystic's passage into calm waters, after the experience, is comparatively rapid with remote chances of relapse. Thirdly, hysterics are highly suggestible; most symptoms resulting from suggestion, while a mystic is least of all suggestible to human influences. In the mystic state there is no confusion—conviction of truth is implicit. It is characteristic that nothing can shake the mystic's belief in the reality of the experience. It may be argued that the delusional patient's unshakeable belief in one's delusions is held on to with equal tenacity In such cases the person is almost always impeded or even paralysed as a functioning unit –no logic appeals. Contrasted to this, the potentialities of the mystic are enhanced by the experience one has undergone.

Of course, there's no denying that in particular cases the mystic may show symptoms akin to insanity, but that condition is largely dependent upon the various personal factors in play. Therefore, "There seems no sufficient ground for supposing that mysticism is merely hysteria misunderstood by a superstitious and wonder-loving age, but there can be little doubt that certain forms of mysticism and hysteria are on their psycho-physical side closely related. Possibly the extent of their connection is that both are characterised by a dissociation of personality, and that the symptoms they have in common are the symptoms of their dissociation."[66]

Rather, as evinced by the personal life histories or mystics, religious experiences can be deemed to have therapeutic value. After the culmination of religious striving and experience, a person takes sorrow and joy alike, is established and integrated in the self, awards equal value to everything, receives both pleasant and unpleasant in the same spirit.

samaduḥkhasukhaḥ savasthaḥ
samaloṣṭāsmakāncanaḥ
tulyapriyāpriyo dhīras
tulyanindātmasamstutiḥ [67]

After the religious experience mystics emerge as elevated, balanced and composed beings. This aspect of religious experiences has received some recognition by psychologists. Uday Shankar in his *Personality Development* devotes a chapter to 'Development through Religious Experience', wherein he discusses the various ways in which religious experiences influence and modify the personality. " ... in spite of the psychopathic temperament, crankiness, emotional instability or neurotic trends or symptoms depicted by some of the truly religious persons ... whose ideas are accepted by their age or by all ages: it is they who count and who really possess inner happiness, religious happiness or trance. Their serenity, unique humanity, love and compassion, their forgetfulness and self-absorption, their sagacity, depth and grace in walking are simply enchanting and emulating and people just follow them blindly."[68]

Apart from this, religious experience proves the human capacity to rise above the conditioning factors of nature, nurture, and society and to transform collective life, though this remains a controversial issue. We wish to differ in our opinion on the stand that mystics owe no special responsibility. It is true that in the search for reality it is necessary for mystics to spend long hours in solitary contemplation, but this is no mark of their being shut off from the world. Once the mystic has experienced the conviction of the peace of God-realisation one very often resumes earlier and non-contemplative habits of life but with the difference that, whereas formerly one functioned as a separate entity, one now does so as an instrument of something higher, wider and deeper than oneself.

Religious experiences usually treated as ego-centric, abnormal escapist activity, is in fact an escape from the ego and an encounter with the totality or experiences of Reality. They mark self-realisation and one is no longer fostering misconceptions about the individual self. If society could accept it, mystics as elevated and integrated indviduals could help a lot in bettering the human conditions and life in general. From mystics society could learn to rectify its inadequate world view effective in individual life. Mystics as enlightened beings could correct the fallacies and limitations of the technique of violent revolution and our obsession with matter and physical force as the only weapon of social change. It is our contention, therefore, that a survey of mysticism, honestly carried out, is likely to provide us with hope and understanding regarding ourselves and our lives.

So, it is not fair to presuppose that religious experiences can only lead to or culminate in mental derangement. As long as psychologists are content to compare it with pathological mental states, we will never make much progress in acquiring empirically validated theories to explain (so far as a social science can explain anything) religious experiences. If the human mind is seen as nothing more than a nervous system, religious experience can be explained physiologically and nothing more need be said. The oft-present neuroses in mystics are explained by the difficulty they face in combining a grip on the everyday world and their dazzling experiences. Therefore, in a normally functioning personality, an ecstatic interlude, while it may be temporarily disorienting, probably has a positive function for emotional development; yet if a personality is not reasonably healthy, a mystical experience may be enough to unhinge it completely.

Though much of what has been said in this enquiry has been derived from psychology, it raises an intriguing question regarding the merits and demerits of this science, so far as religious experiences is concerned.

We have seen how the psychological approach to religious experiences does bring to light many facts about the human being, one's life and ways: which are invaluable in any study on the genesis and motivating factors of religious experiences. It has been suggested in this chapter, the possibility of distinguishing a number of probable factors in the development of a religious attitude which is one among the important prerequisites for the voluntary realisation of religious experiences. Approaching the issue from the point of view of psychology it transpires that on the psychological front such factors as the influence of social environment and the activity of vague unverbalized feelings are generally recognised as parts of the foundation of the religious attitude which are likely to precede any kind of religious experience.

Everything described, discussed and analysed in this chapter, impels us to express indebtedness to psychology, which provides extension in the limits of our knowledge about religious experiences. Whatever may be the shortcomings of individual psychological theories or approaches, our understanding of religious experiences has not only been facilitated but greatly enhanced by them. However, speaking of the shortcoming of psychological systems call for a deeper look into the matter.

Though a dispassionate approach is favoured care must be taken not to stretch it beyond limits while making a psychological enquiry of religious experiences because it may lead to undesirable consequences. Rational criticisms of religious experiences are sometimes based on the rather naive assumption that since the critic has had no similar experience as the kind reported one feels justified in referring to such persons as self-deceived, a charleton or a sentimentalist.

In dealing with the psychological approach to religious experiences—in applying psychology to the study of religion, we are under no obligation to embrace one of its systems or theories and to use only that because we owe no loyalty to any particular thinking. We shall probably stand a better chance of achieving psychological understanding of religious behaviour, attitude and experience, if we are willing to use a variety of the alternatives, in the form of psychological theories, that are at our disposal.

Casual observation may convince or suggest that women show a higher level of religious conformity in comparison to men, and it is empirical research which can afford us the details as to how much higher this level is, whether it is found in all religious bodies, whether it is correlated with some more general personality difference between the sexes and similar matters. M. Argyle in his *Religious Behaviour*[69] has quoted Cavan who carried out quantitative investigations on the question of relation between age and positive attitude towards religion. Cavan studied a sample of 1200 people in the age group of 60 to 100, which showed a clear tendency for acceptance of the gradual increase in religious belief in this age group, while acceptance of the reality of an after-life rose to cent precent after the age of 90. In the same book Argyle quotes the finding of Goren that the religious activity of the single is somewhat greater than that of the married, while that of the widowed is considerably greater than either. This finding is consistent with the hypothesis that religious activity is inversely corelated with the degree of satisfaction of the sex instinct which is what would be expected if sexual deprivation were one factor in the drive behind the religious behaviour.

As we shall see in the next chapter, there has been an encouraging interest in matters concerning the states of mind and human behaviour. The changed states of consciousness produced by drugs and meditational practices have increasingly engaged the attention of psychologists. This concern with problems of consciousness opens the way to a wider use of psychology in the task of understanding the problem of religious experience and religion.

Whatever may be the advantages offered by psychology to a psychological approach in studying religious experiences, one thing must not escape attention. All individuals have certain psychological functions in common, but individually we are not all of one type. As has been discussed in this chapter, people of different temperaments have different spiritual abilities. It is not possible to fit any individual in one of the available classifications of personality types because none of the classified types are all-embracing—an individual may have some of the traits that come within a particular classification and still have others outside it. It would be sheer shortsightedness if wc were to treat an individual under such rigid conditions, without leaving room for what is additional in each individual apart from what the type suggests.

Most studies have been concerned with the validity and objectivity of these experiences. But, by delving into the depths of psychology it is possible to see that the objectivity or validity is not the only important aspect of these, because it points out thc significance and contribution of the subjective element in the occurrence of religious experiences. Not only in the induced or created type of religious experiences is the subjective element operative, but also in the spontaneous kind of experiences.

A clear and vivid grasp of what is meant by the subjective element is available to us from the various personality theories and typologies. From these it is evident that persons with particular personality (and sometimes physical) traits are liable to indulge in specific activities and adopt specific modes of expression, i.e., some knowledge about personality traits enables us to judge who is likely to encounter religious experiences. Though it has been attempted to enlist a few personality types and then draw upon them to arrive at some generalisation of propensities, in human beings, that encourage the occurrence of religious experiences, it cannot be claimed that the list is exhaustive. Neither can we attribute to any specific combination of traits the responsibility of producing religious experiences. Even so, these personality classifications do suggest some of the crucial tendencies that may facilitate religious experiences, and we may also expect to find these in mystics and persons who have encountered the divine. No personality classification is absolute because there is overlapping of traits, and no person is absolutely what is included in a particular classification—it may be that majority of the traits that come within a particular personality type may be pronounced in someone.

REFERENCES

1. W.H. Clark, *The Psychology of Religion*, New York, 1958. pp. 55-56.
2. W.P. Montague, *The Ways of Knowing*, London, 1962. p. 54.
3. F.C. Happold, *Religious Faith and Twentieth Century Man*, Penguin Books, 1966. p. 37.

4. David L. Sills (ed), *International Encyclopaedia of the Social Sciences*, Volume XIII, The Macmillan Co. & the Free Press. p. 415
5. Paul E. Johnson, *Psychology of Religion*, New York, 1945. p. 13.
6. W.H. Clark, *The Psychology of Religion*, *op. cit.* p. 267.
7. L.W. Grensted, *The Psychology of Religion*, London, 1952. p. 25.
8. W.H. Clark, *The Psychology of Religion*, *op. cit.* p. 266.
9. Frits Staal, *Exploring Mysticism*, Penguin Books, 1975, p. 106.
10. *Ibid.*
11. Andrew M. Greelay, *Ecstasy a Way of Knowing*, New Jersey, 1974. p. 63.
12. F.C. Happold, *Mysticism a Study and an Anthology*, Baltimore, 1963. p. 235.
13. J.H. Leuba, *The Psychology of Religious Mysticism*, New York, 1925. p. 67.
14. *Ibid.* p. 75.
15. *Ibid.* p. 155.
16. R H. Thouless, *An Introduction to the Psychology of Religion*, London, 1971. *p.* 17.
17. C.A. Bennet, *A Philosophical Study of Mysticism, An Essay*, New Haven, 1923. pp. 24-25.
18. First Staal, *Exploring Mysticism*, *op. cit.* p. 103.
19. Kamakhya Prasad Singh Choudhary, *Modern Indian Mysticism*, Delhi, 1981. p. 86.
20. D.M. Edwards, *The Philesophy of Religion*, Calcutta, 1968. p. 154.
21. *Ibid.* p. 18.
22. G.A. Coe, *The Psychology of Religion*, Chicago, 1916. p. 279.
23. Andrew M. Greelay, *Ecstasy A Way of Knowing*, *op. cit.* p. 58-86. Source : American Priests, NORC Report, National Opinion Research Centre at the University of Chicago, March, 1971.
24. C.D. Broad, *Religion, Philosophy and Psychical Research, Selected Essays*, London, 1953. p. 191.
25. R.H. Thouless, *An Introduction to the Psychology of Religion*, Third Edition, *op. cit.* p. 20.

26. Michael Argyle, *Religious Behaviour*, London, 1958. p. 39. According to Wright, "If his childhood and early adolescence are passed in religious surroundings, an individual is likely to learn to seek the conservation of the values attached to all the impulses ... through the objects of the religious sentiment .... The religious sentiment has its origin in childhood, in the simple teachings of home and Sunday school. It receives considerable enlargement during adolescence, as an outcome of modifications that come in part subconsciously. Later the youth experiences a religious awakening, and enters into the conscious possession of this enlarged sentiment". W.K. Wright, *A Student's Philosophy of Religion, op. cit.* p. 223.
He also points out how "Professor Starbuck believes that conditions are rendered more favorable for continuous religious growth if children are kept reasonably free from dogmas which they are incapable of understanding, if their doubts and other needs are wisely and sympathetically met whenever they arise, and if they have been brought up so as to have a certain healthy mixture of faith and doubt." *Ibid.* p. 248.
27. *Ibid.* p. 41.
28. R.N. Haber, A.H. Fried, *An Introduction to Psychology*, New York, 1975. p. 536.
29. *Ibid.* pp. 540-542.
30. Michael Argyle, *Religious Behaviour*, *op. cit.* p. 69.
31. *Ibid.* p. 78.
32. Geddes Macgregor, *Introduction to Religious Philosophy*, London, 1960. p. 182.
33 Robert E. Ornstein, *The Psychology of Consciousness*, London, 1975. pp. 51-52.
34 Michael Argyle and Benjamin Beit-Hallahmi, *The Social Psychology of Religion*, London, 1975. p. 183.
35. Robert E. Ornstein, *The Psychology of Consciousness, op. cit.* pp. 57-58.
36. G.S. Spinks *Psychology and Religion* ; *An Introduction to Contemporary Views, op. cit.* p. 154.
37. William James, *The Varieties of Religious Experience, A Study in Human Nature*, New York, 1961. p. 85.
38. Aldous Huxley, *The Perennial Philosophy*, London, 1946. p. 142.
39. *Ibid.*

40. G.S. Spinks, *Psychology and Religion* ; *An Introduction to Contemporary Views, op. cit.* p. 157.

41. Evelyn Underhill, *Mysticism*, London, 1911. pp. 108-109.

42. H.P. Owen, 'Our Experience of God'—Review article, *Religious Studies*, Vol. 7, Cambridge, 1971. p. 178.

43. Evelyn Underhill, *Mysticism, op. cit.* p. 204.

44. G.A. Coe, *The Psychology of Religion, op. cit.* p. 281.

45. Radhakamal Mukherjee, *The Theory and Art of Mysticism*, New Delhi, 1960. p. xiv.

46. W.H. Clark, *The Psychology of Religion, op. cit.* p. 191.

47. G.A. Coe, *The Psychology of Religion, op. cit.* p. 153.

48. W.K. Wright, *A Student's Philosophy of Religion*, New York, 1958. p. 242.

49. *Ibid* p. 247.
According to Thouless "Starbuck ... describes the stage preceding conversion as : a sense of incompleteness and imperfectinn ; brooding, depression, introspection, and a sense of sin ; anxiety about the future life, and distress over doubts. These are followed after conversion by a happy relief, a sense of pardon, and of certainty." R.H. Thouless, *An Introduction to the Psychology of Religion* (Second Edition, reprint 1956) *op. cit.* p. 65.

50. W.B. Selbie, *The Psychology of Religion*, Oxford, 1926. pp. 188—189.

51. J.R. Puri, 'Experimental Approach to the Study of Religion', Harbans Singh (ed.), *Approaches to the Study of Religion*, Seminar Papers, Punjabi University, Patiala. p. 108.

52. Joseph Havens (ed.), *Psychology and Religion : A Contemporary Dialogue*, New York, 1968. p. 70.

53. W.B. Selbie, *The Psychology of Religion, op. cit.* pp. 142-43.
Speaking in similar vein Coe remarks that "Mysticism fascinates men partly because it produces, more largely because it promises, this exquisitely satisfying sense of individual selfhood." According to him religious experiences produce the 'Now I know for myself' feeling—a feeling extremely satisfying for the individual who has it. G.A. Coe, *The Psychology of Religion, op. cit.* p. 280.

54. Radhakamal Mukherjee, *The Theory and Art of Mysticsm, op. cit* p. 37.

55. G.A. Coe, *The Psychology of Religion*, *op. cit.* p. 282.
56. W.B. Selbie, *The Psychology of Religion*, *op. cit.* p. 263.
57. Andrew M. Greelay *Ecstasy a Way of Knowing*, *op. cit.* p. 87.
58. *Ibid.* p. 88.
59. W.B. Selbie, *The Psychology of Religion*, *op. cit.* p. 142.
60. C.D. Broad, *Religion. Philosophy and Psychical Research, Selected Essays*, *op. cit.* p. 201.
61. W.B. Selbie, *The Psychology of Religion*, *op. cit.* p. 140.
62. *Ibid.*
63 *Encyclopaedia Britannica*, Macropaedia, Vol. 15. p. 647.
64. Leuba has pointed out that "The condition of the entranced mystic is in certain respects ... similar to that of a hypnotized person under the sway of ideas that have been suggested to him ; with the difference, however, that the mysttc is his own hypnotizer ; or, if one prefers to put it that way, that God (as present to his consciousness) is the hypnotizer." J.H. Leuba, *The Psychology of Religious Mysticism*, *op. cit.* p. 158.

    Judging from the external manifestations of religious experiences Spinks says that "It cannot, however, be denied that some of these psycho-physical phenomena are in fact results of morbidity, some are signs of incipient insanity and all have borrowed something from the temperamental peculiarities of the persons to whom such phenomena have occurred." G.S. Spinks, *Psychology and Religion, An Introduction to Contemporary Views*, *op. cit.* p. 161.
65. Joseph Havens (ed.), *Psychology and Religion, A Contemporary Dialogue*, *op. cit* p. 123.
66, Robert H. Thouless, *An Introduction to the Psychology of Religion (2nd. Edition)*, *op. cit.* pp. 239-240.
67. *Bhagavad Gīta* XIV-25.
68. Uday Shankar, *Personality Development*, Delhi, 1981. p. 181.
69. Michael Argyle, *Religious Behaviour*, *op. cit.*

4

Psychological Bases of Religious Experience II Freud and Jung

The 'body' part of the 'mind-body' complex—human beings—had received greater attention till Freud gave the 'mind' due recgnition and placed it on a pedestal of importance. The controversies about its exact nature, mode and scope of operation, that ensued, pale out when contrasted to the fact that humankind has been made aware of that vital domain which silently determines their lives. Mind as an active part of human beings suggests different states or levels of being. This is apparent from the consciousness altering drugs which when experimented with demonstrate how ordinary consciousness is not the only way in which consciousness can operate. Normal waking consciousness, as we call it, is but a special type of consciousness, and there are forms of consciousness different from it.

"In defining consciousness Davis (1962) lists three things we must be aware of in order to be considered conscious :

1. Self-Recognition of self as distinguished from the environment.

2. Time-Recognition of now as opposed to the past and the future.

3. Location of space. A sense of where we are located in the external world."[1]

As per Davis's marks of consciousness, it can be said that absence of any of the characteristics implies the possible existence of some mind state other than the conscious. Psychology and the medical sciences say that the degree of consciousness range from coma, which occur in situations of severe bodily injury, through dreaming, which we all experience, to wakefulness, alertness, full activity and creative thinking and hyperactivity. One further aspect of consciousness concerns an activity that goes on within us during most of our waking and sleeping hours. There are the subconscious and unconscious beyond the conscious. The mind is in a subconscious state when the defining marks of consciousness are partially present in an individual, whereas their total abeyance implies the unconscious state. It is an observed fact that stimuli and processes that are not consciously perceived or experienced have exerted their influence on overt behaviour. This has, rightly, led psychologists to posit the existence of mind-states as dynamic forces underlying behaviour. The unconscious, is the foundational conception which psychoanalysis rests.

Uprushes from the unconscious and subconscious are often quite unaccountable, but they have real influence on conscious life —all the evidence goes to show that they are active in religious life. In fact, the unconscious "is a factor in religious experience which has to be taken account of and provides an explanation of phenomena not otherwise easily explicable."[2] However, we are only exploring possibilities and not contending that the subconscious or unconscious is the exclusive ground for the occurrence of the said religious phenomena, but guided by the evidence available, are compelled to hypothesise the mind states to be actively involved in the eventuality of religious experiences.

Taking the individual to be a bundle of active feelings, emotions, urges and capacities in certain states of being—conscious, subconscious, unconscious—some are of the opinion that what appears as supernormal is actually over-activity in these domains. Parapsychology undertakes to examine the empirically incomprehensible experiences from which has evolved the possibility of ESP (extra-sensory perception); i.e., a mode of perception other than the proven five sense organs. Accordong to parapsychologists it is the unconscious region of the psyche that is, in all probability, especially subject to religious experiences—the channel which opens up the unseen world. As yet we lack psychological evidence for ascertaining its role and field of operation, leaving it undecided whether it can be considered the repository of religious experiences.

As our chapters on the psychological scrutiny of religious experiences attempt at comprehending the underlying psychological mechanisms, it is incumbent upon any such venture to include a search into mind states within the limits of its inquiry. As the previous chapter has dealt with the influence of almost all but the states of mind as motivating factors of religious experiences, the course of enquiry herein focuses on the states of mind and the degree to which they influence the production of religious experiences. "The evidence is overwhelming, ... all psychologists now concede, that *neural* processes go in the brain and other nerve centers that are unattended by consciousness at the time, but which either then or later may affect the contents of consciousness.'"[3] Freud and Jung having pioneered any serious study of the levels of consciousness constitute major portions of the discussions in the pages that follow, with some focus on the findings of para psychology (ESP).

Religion and Religious Experience in the Light of Freud

Freud along with Jung pioneered the notion that there are levels of consciousness and sometimes we derive our behaviour and personality traits from them. They also looked at various other aspects of human life and also the forces that work within and influence one's behaviour and mould personality. Based on these basic tenets they sought to explain religion and the need for it. But both of them have differed in many of their approaches and explanations of issues which make it necessary to take a look at each of their submissions separately. This will not merely facilitate a holistic understanding of religious experiences in the light of Freud and Jung but also enable us to derive psychological forces that underlie the promulgation of these experiences.

Psychoanalysis throws new light upon human life—its motives, its needs and its overall possibilities. Father of the psychoanalytic school, Sigmund Freud, being trained in medicine had great interest in neurology. His interest, in neurotic disorders and his actual dealings with cases of this sort helped him gradually to work out the practice and theory of psychoanalysis. Originally of value in therapeutics, it was later found to have bearings on almost every aspect of life and existence Although Freud has not dealt with religious experiences as a separate issue, his writings on the states of mind, psychoanalysis and religion have far reaching implications for a study of the genesis of religious experiences.

On analysis Freud found that the symptoms of hysteria could be attributed to incidents in earlier life. These incidents could lead to emotional disturbances which were prevented from expressing themselves. Not finding their outlets they sought other channels and expressed themselves as symptoms. "The discovery that an incident, unconscious and long forgotten, was nevertheless the source of marked disturbances in behaviour not only called attention to the role of the unconscious, but suggested that the unconscious is strongly dynamic."[4] For the treatment of such cases Freud used the method of 'catharsis', which is a release of pent-up emotion brought about by a patient's recall and reproduction of the experience that lay at the root of one's trouble, under hypnosis.

Psychoanalysis "is the method developed for reaching down into the hidden depths of the individual to bring to light the underlying motives and determinants of his symptoms and attitudes, and to reveal the unconscious tendencies which lie behind action and reactions and which influence development and determine the relations of life itself."[5]

While trying to use the talking method—in which a patient is made to talk in waking state—as the therapeutic means for neurosis, Freud encountered resistance from the patients. There was this tendency to hold back or repress whatever was pain evoking or led to unpleasant feelings. Repression is the "means by which we keep a painful or anxiety-producing idea out of the consciousness. Repression is the most extreme form of "taking our mind off things"."[6] A repressed experience is one charged with emotion and desire, tending to be impulsive, seeking to express itself, but being held back by force.

"Repression operates in a threefold manner: (1) it prevents unconscious elements from entering consciousness and is itself the result of early social training exerted upon the infantile mind by the convention and moral standards of society; (2) it opposes attempts aimed at investigating the contents of consciousness; (3) it is a dynamic barrier which functions as a censor to these mental events which seek to appear in consciousness. The censor is not always active, and when relaxed certain unconscious elements appear as in dreams."[7] As the repressed complexes go on perpetually striving to surface and they are held back, there ensue conflicts which become evident in behaviour patterns. Thereby. repression is an indication of conflict between ego and unconscious desires. In spite of the warfare between the conscious and the unconscious, in the level beneath consciousness, the desires live on, and though frustrated, strive with all their might and cunning to circumvent the prohibitions of the ego. Repression is the means by which the disturbing influence of unadjusted tendencies is excluded from consciousness and becomes unconscious. This explains how the human tendency has been to push to the background the undesirable. The repository for this has been the unconscious or the subconscious and again these have tried to express but not having succeeded show up in some form of behaviour.

The unconscious became an existential truth which Freud conceived as active, striving and powerful. "In the psychoanalytic sense the term Unconscious is fully mental and the categories, such as ideas, purposes, resolutions and so forth can be applied to it. The unconscious is effective in influencing the experience and behaviour of an individual without his being aware of its presenee."[8] The unconscious is the source of certain concealed forces that constitute the real driving power behind human actions. An in-between state of mind is the preconscious, which merges gradually with both the conscious and the unconscious, but bears characteristic resemblance with the conscious. It does not consist of material that has been actively discarded and repressed; consequently its contents can be summoned by the ordinary process of association.[9]

By way of summing up we may say—"What the individual is aware of is conscious; what he is not aware of but may become so at any time is preconscious; what he cannot become aware of without definite effort or cannot become aware of at all is unconscious."[10]

It may therefore be said that the human mind has desires, instinctively produced, which are dealt with by the mind in three ways.

1. There may be action in accordance with them (i.e. they may be manifested or at least attempts made for their fulfilment) ;
2. because of the conflict of these desires with other desires (inherent conflict of desires) they may be relegated to a subordinate place and not acted upon ; in which case apparently they die or are cast out harmlessly;
3. the desire may be ignored: it may be suppressed as the desire by dint of its very nature is contrary to social norms or values, because of which the individual seeks to suppress it. In this case the desire continues to live and retains its dynamic character.

From his stand regarding the mind states, Freud goes on to dreams, the basic human instincts and other social phenomena. According to him the unconscious plays a very significant role in motivation and this applies to events of everyday life. "Errors, slips of the tongue, and dreams are evidence of unconscious wishes "breaking through" into consciousness, when we mishear or misread a word, forget something or "accidentally" destroy something, unconscious motivation are liable to be at work."[11] Through the imagery of dreams such unconscious wishes and impulses find expression as they would be extremely painful and cause anxiety if they were revealed in conscious waking state.

The permanent contributions of Freud may be briefly enlisted as —(*i*) Psychic processes are strictly determined. (*ii*) Actions, feelings and thoughts or ideas, may be determined by unconscious motivations which would astonish the individual when and if 'conscious mind' comprehends them. (*iii*) Our motivations are emotional forces. These are the basic tenets on which are structured the Freudian theories of infantile sex, Oedipus and Erata Complex, *Id*, ego, superego, dreams, etc. The implications of these have been traced in human social life, religious urge, creative arts, etc.

Though Freud in his works *Totem And Taboo* and *The Future Of An Illusion* has mainly dwelt upon the question of the origin of the religious urge, one can see the underlying implication this has on the subject of study, viz., religious experiences. This together with his well defind thoughts on the conscious, preconscious and unconscious should enable us to define the place of religious experiences in the Freudian context and explain the phenomena in comprehensive terms.

Religion, Freud contends, is another expression of wish fulfilment, arising out of human confrontation with powerful objects and phenomena, and one's subsequent failure to overcome or withstands such confrontation, resulting in one's subordination. Religion, according to Freud, is a socio-psychological phenomenon and religious feeling is a craving for protection and power. "There are the elements, which seem to mock at all human control: the earth, which quakes, is rent asunder, and buries man and all his works; the water which in tumult floods and submerges all things; the storm, which drives all before it; there are the diseases, which we have only lately recognized as the attacks of other living creatures; and finally there is the painful riddle of death, for which no remedy at all has yet been found, nor probably ever will be. With these forces nature rises up before us, sublime, pitiless, inexorable; thus she brings again to mind our weakness and helplessness, of which we thought the work of civilization had rid us." It is a struggle for "the preservation of mankind against the supremacy of nature".[12] This threat from nature plus the natural propensity to seek protection motivates one to look for solace in religion. Freud starts with the notion that life on earth is a burden and "Man is the continual victim of natural disasters and of a destiny over which he has no control. On earth he is a helpless being and because of his helplessness he is in need of a father, God .... Freud maintains that the idea of God develops and is maintained through remembrance of the situation of childhood years. God protects man against the perils of nature, the perils of destiny and the perils of society."[13] God is, then, the outcome of one's innate feeling of insecurity and consequential desire for protection. The origin of religion and the God-idea has its roots in human helplessness. When confronted with uncontrollable forces within and without oneself, one "remembers, as it were, and regresses to an experience he had as a child, when he felt protected by a father who he thought to be of superior wisdom and strength, and whose love and protection he could win by obeying his commands and avoiding transgression of his prohibitions.

Thus religion, according to Freud, is a repetition of the experience of the child. Man copes with threatening forces in the same manner in which, as a child, he learned to cope with his own insecurity by relying on and admiring and fearing his father."[14] Human helplessness is perceived to persist till adulthood, and with it father-longing and god. Gods, Freud mentioned, have threefold task: "they must exercise the terrors of nature, they must reconcile one to the cruelty of fate, particularly as shown in death, and they must make ammends for the sufferings and privations that the communal life of culture has imposed on man.[15] Religion is a phenomenon belonging to the years of childhood which persists into maturity.

Religion is an illusion because through it human beings find satisfaction in difficult and unpleasant situations. This is possible because religion provides all those things desired by humankind, which to a great extent reduces the feeling of insecurity. According to Freud religion "is marked by the tension between the pleasure principle and the reality principle. Man would prefer to follow his desires, but reality forbids him to do so; consequently he has to learn to accept it ... accordingly, religion is merely the—unreal—attempt to come to terms with the problem of reality. By means of religion man tries to solve the riddle of reality and to reconcile himself to it, in its aspect of suffering. According to Freud this attempt is unsuccessful, for religion is an illusion, a wish fulfilment. It might perhaps be said that religion *could* under certain circumstances be true, but in the form in which it actually appears, it is fed by wishes which carry no power of conviction; for they are the wishes of a helpless child who is incapable of coming to terms with reality."[16] Religion is an illusion because like most illusions it is also derived from hidden wishes. Quite clearly religion fulfils psychic needs.

Having discussed Freud's views, we are in a position to evaluate his contributions in the realm of religious thought. Freud's contributions may be briefly put as—

1. Religion is an illusion arising as a result of wish fulfilment.
2. There are specific grounds in the process of personality development from which religion grows.
3. The influence of the unconscious must be taken account of.

Freud's efforts, then, have a twofold bearing in later understanding of religious experience.

1. The same laws of behaviour governing all human behaviour and experience are found to be operative in the case of religious experiences. Freud's works have brought to light many factors actively involved in the growth and development of personality.
2. A prominent place has been awarded to the unconscious state of mind. Freud emphasises the indubitable role and significance of the mind states,

which not only determine adult personality but also suggest the possibility of religious experiences.

Freud has sought to "unify under a few basic principles of explanation phenomena from diverse fields of experience."[17] The consistency of his system is evident from his revelations about the influences of childhood days and sex (*Eros*) and the destructive (*Thanatos*) instincts on personality, and how the superego as the restraining or forbidding element controls them. The converging of all these basic principles and their interaction reveal that "the essential character of religion is determined by its origin in man's wish for a supreme father-protector. Just as the infant is weak and needs his father's protection, so also is adult man weak in the face of nature and society and needs, or wishes for, a supra-human protector."[18] This makes religion an illusion. On analysis, the Freudian concept of religion and God may be summed up thus: "religion appeared as an illusory rationalization of unconscious wishes, as a projection to compensate for an infantlie sense of helplessness. God was a projection of the infantile father-image, a fantasy-substitute for an actual, and not altogether satisfactory, father."[19] In this light it is apt to emphasise that the findings of psychoanalysis leave no scope for accepting religious ideas as true. But the system's greater contribution lies in its explanation how false ideas, in the context of religion, come to be accepted and defended. Freud falsifies religious ideas on the basis of their essential similarity to neurotic conditions. He noticed something which pertains not only to pathological but also to normal ideas, and not only to neurotics, patients and analysts, but also to others – a fact of which he was undoubtedly aware and which provided a firm foundation for his works.

In the context of religion, Freud's views are at times considered ambiguous as they are not clearly spelt out. Falsification of religious ideas leaves it unclear whether Freud basically intends to limit his discussion to psychological meaning or whether he was inclined to determine the ontological meaning of religion. Freud calls religion " 'mass obsession', 'delusion', 'illusory' and 'potentially infantile'. Now as a psychoanalyst Freud could have only analysed and discovered the unconscious factors involved in religion, but he has also additionally assumed the role of a theologian and a philosopher in as much as he evaluates religion in terms of infantilism, illusoriness, etc."[20] Owing to this confusion, theologians have tended to react violently to Freudian opinions, thereby forgoing the system's rich psychological insight. Freud "has tended to rationalize the religious instinct in man and to attribute it to causes which could be explained in materialistic terms."[21]

The second aspect of Freud's psychology pertains to the activity of the unconscious. "The unconscious seems to be a level of activity which is complementary and compensatory to our ordinary conscious life. It is both a deposit for discarded or repressed ideas and a creative treasury from which images and ideas emerge of a highly significant value. Psycho-analysis by the rise of special techniques has been able to bring into consciousness experiences forgotton by the subject, techniques which have not only contributed to the relief of emotional conflicts but also have provided evidence that mental activities can and do operate outside consciousness"[22] The unconscious is not the mere repository of elements which have been forgotten but also those instinctual energies which have never been in consciousness. This latter fact – that the unconscious contains instinctual energies—is noteworthy for our study, because it enables us to explain the not so common or frequent religious phenomena that some people are likely to experience. An individual is endowed with a large number of instincts and capabilities, all of which are neither similarly nor equally pronounced in all individuals. The uneven occurrence of religious experiences naturally means, in Freudian terms, that some people, be it by dint of their characteristics, interests, environment or any other factors, are more susceptible to have these experiences.

Apart from the direct influence of the unconscious we must not overlook its constant play in the conscious. The former's hidden, primordial energies are found to be influential in all or most of conscious life. "This amounted to a new form of epi-phenomenalism : the idea that consciousness is a by-product of other aspects of the total person, influenced by, but exerting no influence upon, those other aspects."[23]

In spite of his great contributions Freud has left room for shortcomings and lapses. "It is the limitation of the Freudian approach to religion that it has no place for religious experience and none for supernatural revelation ; that in its emphasis upon the determinism of the father-son relationship it overlooks the need which man has had at every level of culture for explanations and interpretations of life itself. Man has a deep craving for some kind of metaphysical belief."[24] Moreover, the psychologist for whom religion is a proved illusion, the phenomena are explicable in terms of analyseable mental processes, is liable to find oneself in a awkward predicament. On similar grounds the objective reality of the world around us can be denied. Also, "To reduce religious ideas to symbols of subconscious desires is not to prove them illusory, for it leaves the question still open whether the universe does or does not correspond with our desires. To trace the psychological history of a belief does not dispense with the question of its truth or falsity ....The question of validity must not be confused with that of origin [25]

Jung's Approach to Religion and Religious Experience

Following his initial affiliation with Freud, Jung set off his own way. This break meant a set of independent ideas which later became the pillars of Jung's system. Their differences rest on the probable fact that they were temperamentally opposites – Freud the "empiricist and scientist, with an obviously positivist strain .... Jung ... much more speculative and romantic."[26] Regarding his approach Jung has stated it to be "exclusively phenomenological".[27] His standpoint is phenomenological in so far as "it is concerned with occurrences, events, experiences, in a word, with facts. Its truth is a fact and not a judgment."[28] In this context Jung claims that : "I restrict myself to the observation of phenomena and I refrain from any application of metaphysical or philosophial considerations."[29]

Like Freud, Jung also stresses the significance of the unconscious in overt behaviour. Jung was also a psychoanalyst who was keenly involved with the structure and activity of the unconscious, in which connection he devoted a fair amount of attention to recording dreams and subsequently studying the different phenomena belonging to the 'collective' unconscious. Jungian psychoanalysis is founded on the conviction that "there is a tension in man between the conscious and the unconscious life of the psyche. Where this tension leads to a neurosis, healing can only be expected if a successful attempt is made to lift the unconscious into the consciousness."[30] This bringing of the unconscious into the consciousness Freud would call the 'id' becoming 'ego' but Jung works out additional points as a result of which views are often in contradiction to those of Freud's.

For Jung the psychic is as real as the physical though it is not comprehensible in explicit terms but by special means of expression. The psyche consists of two spheres—the conscious and the unconscious—the one supplementing the other, but opposed in their properties. The psyche is the totality of all conscious and unconscious psychological processes. Relatively speaking the conscious constitutes a very small part of the whole psyche. It is the function or activity which maintains the relation of the psychic contents to the ego. It works towards adjustment with the environment.

The psyche is made up of four components with the ego as central. Our ego is surrounded by and rests on consciousness, representing the side of the psyche which is concerned with adjustment to external reality. Next comes the sphere surrounded by the unconscious. Regarding the unconscious Jung argued that there are two kinds of unconscious material: the personal unconscious, which, as Freud proposed, contains memories, sensory impressions, and repressed wishes; and the collective unconscious which contains elements of personality that are inherited from ancestors. The contents of the collective unconscious are the "archetypes", and Jung emphasised their universality at least within a single culture, and sought to establish their existence by means of an exhaustive study of myths, folklore, and literature from many cultures. More about archetypes later. "Jung agrees with Freud in recognizing that the unconscious comes into existence with the growth of the individual, but holds that in addition to the 'personal' unconscious there is an unconscious which is inborn and not due to repressive process. Jung, therefore, places greater emphasis upon the hereditary aspect of the unconscious."[31]

In the personal unconscious, then, are those contents which have been put aside but which can be raised again at any time into consciousness – i.e. they are the ones we repress because they are disagreeable. The personal unconscious is the repository of the forgotton, repressed, subliminally perceived, thought, and felt matter of every kind. The collective part of the unconscious does not include contents that are specific for our individual ego, resulting from personal acquisitions, but such that result from the inherited possibility of psychical functioning in general, namely from the inherited brain structure. This inheritance is common to all humanity and forms the basis of every individual psyche. Jung points out that a part of the collective unconscious includes those contents which can never be raised into consciousness. A figure in Jacobi's

The Psychology of C.G. Jung, gives a schematic representation of both layers of the unconscious.

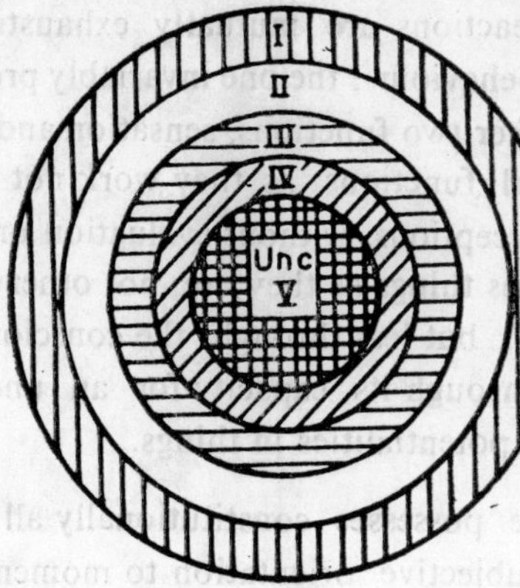

Fig. 1*

Sphere of the Unconscious

I Memories	Personal Unconscious
II Repressed Material	Personal Unconscious
III Emotions	

IV Irruptions from the deepest part of the Unconscious

V That part of the Unconscious that can never be made conscious.

IV & V Collective Unconscious.

Jung differentiates between four psychological functions that are constitutionally present in every individual—thinking, feeling, intuition and sensation. Psychological functions are certain forms of psychic activity that remain theoretically the same under varying circumstances and are completely independent of their momentary contents. Feeling and thinking have

* Jolande Jacobi, *The Psychology of C.G. Jung*, *An Introduction with Illustrations*, 1942. p. 30.

been characterised as rational because they work with values—the latter evaluates by means of cognition from the view point 'true-false', and the former in terms of 'agreeable-disagreeable'. These forms of reactions are mutually exhaustive as practical determinants of behaviour ; the one invariably predominates over the other. The other two functions, sensation and intuition, Jung calls the irrational functions as they work not with judgments but with mere perceptions, without evaluation or interpretation. Sensation perceives things as they are, not otherwise. Intuition perceives likewise, but less through the conscious apparatus of the senses than through its capacity for an unconscious inner perception of the potentialities in things.

Although one possesses constitutionally all four functions, which facilitate subjective orientation to momentary situations, experience shows that it is always only one of these functions with the support of which one orients and adjusts oneself to reality. This makes it the dominant function for adjustment, it gives the conscious attitude its direction and quality, and stands constantly at the disposal of the individual's conscious will. It is therefore named the 'superior function', which determines the individual's type. Besides the principal function, a person generally makes partial use of a second function—the 'auxiliary function'. The third function is only seldom available for the ordinary person's use, while the fourth or the inferior one, is entirely beyond [the disposal of the will. Jung differentiates these four functions from one another because they are neither mutually relateable nor reducible, and further because they exhaust all possibilities. If all the four functions could be raised into consciousness, we would speak of a complete human being.

The complementary or compensatory relation of the functions to each other is a law inherent in the psyche. The specific form of the general psychic behaviour of an individual with respect to the external world has been called by Jung the

'Persona'. "*The persona is a compromise between the individual and society ....*" (Two Essays on Analytical Psychology, p. 165 Translated by H.G. and C.F. Baynes, London: Bailliere, Trindall and Cox, 1928) A compromise, that is, between the demands of the environment and the necessities of the individual's inner constitution."[32] In a person well adjusted to both one's external and internal world the persona assures one a natural, well-ordered and easy contact with one's environment. But it poses a danger when the real nature is concealed behind such habitual means like adjustment—in such an instance the individual runs the risk of neither being what one is, nor being that which one seeks to be. Therefore, a well-fitting and functioning persona is an essential condition for psychic health and is of great importance if the demands of the environment are to be met successfully.

In addition to the general psychological attitude or an individual's way of reacting to what confronts one from without or within, Jung determines two attitudes – Extraversion and Introversion. They represent orientations that essentially condition all psychic processes. According to Jung, "they govern external behaviour on the one hand, and on the other mould specific experience."[33] Extraversion is characterised by a positive relation to the object, while introversion by a negative. The extrovert follows in one's adjustment and responses patterns more the external, collectively valid norms, the ideals of the time. The introvert's reaction, however, is mainly determined by subjective factors, which account for one's often unsuccessful adjustment to the external world. "The extravert "thinks, feels and acts in reference to the object"; he displaces his interest from the subject *out upon* the object, he orientates himself predominantly by what lies outside him. With the introvert the subject is the starting-point of his orientation and the object is accorded at most a secondary indirect value .... If consciousness is extraverted, the unconscious is introverted, and conversely."[34] The conscious and unconscious stand in compensatory relation to each other.

In the preceding chapter it was concluded that personality is an important motivating factor of religious experiences. In this context Jung's personality types had been discussed and now after having gone through his fourfold division of psychological functions and the two basic attitudes, the foundation on which his theory of personality types rests, becomes explicit. Both of them afford explanations for variations in personality which again goes a long way in accounting for the emergence of religious experiences. Apart from this, we have been immensely benefited by Jung's explorations in the realm of neuroses and their causes. The reasons that cause neuroses, according to him, illuminate us about the question of personality and religious experiences. In the examples, with specific reference to the life and personality of some mystics, cited in the previous chapter, an inherent strain or conflict was observed to persist in the person concerned, which ensued from the failure to reconcile the subjective internal and the external world.

We are now in a position to discuss the relevance of Jungian concepts and theories to religious experiences. Jung has painstakingly included religious experiences within the framework of this thought system. He does not, however, deal with their ontological status, but does ascribe psychological authenticity to them. Before proceeding further, we must first try to understand the Jungian concept of religion. In defining religion Jung is greatly influenced by Rudolf Otto's views as expressed in *The Idea Of The Holy*. Otto analyses religious experience as 'the feeling of the numinous' which implies the experience of the divine as fascinating and awesome mystery. For Jung religion "is a careful and scrupulous observation of what Rudolf Otto aptly termed the 'numinosum', that is, a dynamic existence or effect, not caused by an arbitrary act of will. On the contrary, it seizes and controls the human subject which is always rather its victim than its creator."[35]

From his definition of religion it necessarily follows that "religious experience is characterized by a specific kind of emotional experience : surrender to a higher power, whether this higher power is called God or the unconscious."[36] This characterisation holds good for a certain type of religious experience—in Christian religions—while it contrasts with others like Buddhism. Elsewhere he is noted to have viewed religious experiences from another perspective—"Creeds are codified and dogmatized forms of original religious experience. The contents of the experience have become sanctified and usually concealed in a rigid, often elaborate structure. The practice and the reproduction of the original experience have become ritual and an unchangeable institution .... it can become the form of religious experience for ages of time and for millions of people without there being any vital necessity for alterations."[37]

Having granted the essence of religious experiences to be submission to powers higher than ourselves, Jung proceeds to interpret the concept of the unconscious as being areligious one. H.G. Baynes, in the translator's preface to Jung's Psychological Types has said—" 'the lungs of the new born infant know how to breathe, the heart knows how to beat, the whole co-ordinated organic system knows how to function, only because the infant's body is the product of inherited functional experience'."[38] If functional inheritance is acceptable in the case of the physical organism, can we not say the same of human psychical aspect ? Arguing along these lines Jung promulgated the concept of a racial or collective consciousness common to and inherited by all "The means whereby instinctual energy (libido in a generalized sense) produces this 'currency' of significant images are the archetypes proper. Archetypes are 'dominants' which, operating within the collective unconscious, 'create' those symbolic patterns by which man expresses his reactions to the numinous and the mysterious."[39] Archetypes are used in two senses—(*i*) as denoting dominants or proceses within the collective unconscious, and (*ii*) as an adjective to qualify imagery produced by these dominants. The chief characteristics of archetypal images are that they are archaic, non-personal, unconscious in origin, and common to all races and all times. They are the means of expressing psychologically the significance of situations whose rational counterparts appear less vividly or less satisfactorily in the form of dogmas and doctrines.[40] Archetype is like the concept of the electron, a concept for a centre of energy, which cannot be observed in itself but can be only known by its effects. The archetype of the collective uncouscious are known through the symbols which are the manifestatations of their creative enery.

Knowledge of the contents of the collective unconscious has been made possible by comparing the mythological patterns of various religions with the complexes and dream symbolisms collected from many sources. That which is unknown to consciousness is maintained to be determinable through their effects or indirect manifestations such as symptoms or complexes, images or symbols that are encountered in dreams, fantasies and visions. The latter are related to dreams, and occur in states of diminished consciousness. For all practical purposes, they are the visible links in a chain of unconscious events. However, the most effective way of acquainting oneself with the mechanisms and contents of the unconscious is via the dream whose material consists of conscious and unconscious, familiar and unfamiliar elements.

Both Freud and Jung acknowledge the significance of dreams as they are deemed to be reflections of unconscious psychic processes. Unlike Freud, for Jung a dream is not only disguised wish-fulfiment but along with its symbols is both concealment and revelation. Dreams, he maintains, are more than the products of repressed desires because they reveal in veiled form truths not known. In dreams the unconscious ego speaks, expressing itself in symbols, which derive both from the personal and collective unconscious. Jung is known to have remarked—"It is certainly true that there are dreams which embody suppressed wishes and fears, but what is there which the dream cannot on occasion embody ? Dreams may give expression to ineluctable truths, to philosophical pronouncements, illusions, wild fantasies, memories, plans, anticipations, irrational experiences, even telepathic visions, and heaven knows what besides."[41] Stressing their revelation aspect Jung "sees in the dream an attempt from the side of the unconscious to 'say' something in a disguised way, something which the person needs in the process of individuation but which has not yet penetrated to his consciousness."[42]

Jung conceives the unconscious, apart from being a storehouse of memories, repressed material and emotions, as intelligent, active and purposeful. Here it must be mentioned that his fundamental idea of one's growing into consciousness is a process of individuation. What is individuation ? In the framework of Jung's system psychotherapy is a help in one's coming to selfhood and this process of becoming in Jungian terminology is individuation. In the course of psychotherapeutic work Jung concluded that the healing of a neurotic patient is nothing but one's psychic movement in the direction of acquiring selfhood. The crux of the concept is represented by the striving of the ego, the soul towards becoming self. The unconscious is endowed with a restless striving for something higher and better, which accounts for the process of individuation and finally the religious attitude and experience.

Individuation is essentially a religious process "Because in this process the person is confronted with the numinous content of his unconscious, which strives towards illumination out of primitive darkness ... "[43] In calling the human process of individuation "essentially a divine one" Faber finds the point at which Jung the therapist and Jung the believer are united. About the religious significance of individuation Spinks grants that "Individuation as a psychological process appears in religion as the desire for re-birth; it is not only one of the main incentives in the life of the individual, it is also one of the main engagements of religion. It is that craving for completeness which, whether it be described as 'man's essential quest' or as the desire 'for union with the Other', is the telos of all religious activity."[44]

Jung claims to see in all happening the play of opposites and derives from this conception his idea of psychic energy. The total psychic system is in continuous dynamic movement, and the psychic energy which is analogous to 'energy' in physics Jung terms libido. The distribution of psychic energy determines the relations between the various psychic data, and all disturbances therein lead to pathological phenomena. Till some time Freud took sexuality to be the only psychic driving power. For him libido had this limited meaning, but Jung refers to it as energy which operates in all psychical processes. For Jung libido is not only sex instinct, it is the source and origin of all and every instinct. It is a kind of cosmic urge, a life force which expresses itself in all sorts of human activities and interests. However, "Jung does not deny that many expressions of libidinal energy are intimately related to sexual activitities, but he holds that as man in the course of his evolution extended the range of his interests so his libidinal energy was diverted from its primary sexual expression to objectives largely desexualized. In situations described as religious or numinous libido presents man's reactions in terms of primordial symptoms."[45] "The libido or psychic energy, as Jung conceives it, is the foundation and regulation of all psychic existence. This concept serves for the correct description of the actual processes in the psyche and of their relations."[46] Thus, according to Jung desexualized libido is that supply of energy by which humankind has produced the whole range of activities that conglomerate to make civilization.

Our exposition of the Jungian system, thus far, gives the impression that Jung is drawn to admit the fact that the unconscious mind is capable at times of assuming an intelligence and purposiveness which are superior to the conscious. Also, it seems to be a necessary consequence of his definition of religion and the unconscious that Jung arrives at the conclusion that, in view of the nature of the unconscious mind, the influence of the unconscious upon us "is a basic religious phenomenon."[47] Jung was inclined to ascribe religious significance to most concepts. In his opinion dreams also contain much collective material, fixed themes, for example, archetypes—a concept holding a prominent place in Jung. In this context he discusses the number four, which often occurs in dreams and which he thinks also had a great importance in fixed forms in Christian iconography and in mystical speculation. Drawing upon the similarity in the symbolism of dreams and religion, Jung said " ... I attribute a positive value to all religions. In their symbolism I recognize those figures which I have met with in the dreams and fantasies of my patients."[48]

Jung considers it a regrettable mistake to interpret his observations as some sort of proof for the existence of God. His observations, he contends, prove only the existence of an archetypal image of the Deity. And this, in his opinion, is all that can be asserted about God from the psychological perspective. "The development of the human consciousness demands a withdrawal of all attainable projections, and thus according to Jung no doctrine of God, in the sense of a non-psychological existence, can be maintained any longer" whereby "the integration of man now seems to take the place of God."[49] This resolves Jung's double-edged opinion about religion. He holds that "Religion is in the theological sense 'the consciousness of the numinous' but psychologically it is 'a relationship to oneself' and in both systems of co-ordinates also 'a relationship to the archetype God who is present in the unconscious'."[50] So we see how Jung avoids God as an ontological fact, but does award the concept psychological validity.

One knows God not as a theological concept but as an experience from which concepts may subsequently be formulated. That is why Jung refers to God as the God-imago or God-symbol since a symbol by its very nature is able to reveal 'reality' in a way no other medium can. By promulgating this view Jung has not reduced 'God' to a mere psychic event within the unconscious. He has accepted that something existing in the psyche exists in reality.[51] God is 'psychologically real' but cannot be 'absolute' because the Absolute cannot be known experimentally. "The God that is in the soul (God-imago) is that reality which we meet in religious experience, while the Godhead is that which is beyond our experience and beyond all human comprehension."[52] Regarding this psychology is not competent to say anything. In his views on religion and God is evident a leaning towards humanism. This tendency is explained—God is a function of the unconscious, namely the manifestation of a split-off sum of libido which has activated the God-imago. The traditional view that God is absolute implies a complete severance from the unconscious, which means, psychologically, a complete unawareness of the fact that the divine effect springs from one's inner self.

Jung's views have perplexed later thinkers, particularly theologians. According to Jung it is only through the psyche that we can establish that God acts upon us. Post Jungian thinkers are unable to distinguish whether these actions emanate from God or from the unconscious. It is difficult to tell whether God and the unconscious are two different entities. Even though Jung's concepts are consistent within the framework of his system, they are not totally free of shortcomings.

As far as religious experiences are concerned, they are psychological facts and Jung refrains from commenting on their ontological status. Jung is aware that "there are certain religions which .... insist ... upon the essential identity of God and man, either in the form of an apriori identity, or of a goal to be attained by certain practices or initiations, as we know them ... from ... certain yoga methods."[53] God-imago is deemed to be a very important and influential archetype, its most noteworthy feature being its relatively frequent occurrences. Since the experience of it has the quality of numinosity, often to a high degree, it ranks among religious experiences.

Jung has made certain positive remarks about religious experience in his *Psychology and Religion.* "Religious experience is absolute. It is indisputable. You can only say that you have never had such an experience, and your opponent will say: "Sorry, I have". And there your discussion will come to an end. No matter what the world thinks about religious experience, the one who has it possesses the great treasure of a thing that has provided him with a source of life, meaning and beauty and that has given a new splendor to the world and to mankind. He has pistis and peace. Where is the criterium by which you could say that such a life is not legitimate, that such experience is not valid and that such pistis is mere illusion? Is there ... any better truth about ultimate things than the one that helps you to live?"[54] Apart from his favourable stand on religious experiences; Jung considered the "feeling of dependence and powerlessness the core of religious experience."[55] This is immanently suggestive of the factors that promote religious experiences. Regarding the motivating elements of religious experiences Jung maintained that "a man who is defenseless against God and is no longer shielded by walls or communities, he has the unique spiritual chance of immediate religious experience."[56]

Owing to the support he rendered to mystic and religious experiences, Jung's system is called 'mysticism' which means a break from the scientific. Jung is very much aware of this and has his own points of defence. He does not hold himself "responsible for the fact that man has, everywhere and always, spontaneously developed religious forms of expression, and that the human psyche, from time immemorial, has been shot through with religious feelings and ideas. Whoever cannot see this aspect of the human psyche is blind, and whoever chooses to explain it away, or to "enlighten" it away, has no sense of reality."[57] Jung is critical of Freud's inability to understand religious experiences, in his book : *The Future of an Illusion.* He on his part prefers "to look at man in the light of what in him is healthy and sound, and to free the sick man from that point of view which colours every page Freud has written. Freud's teaching is definitely one-sided in that it generalizes from facts that are relevant only to neurotic states of mind ..."[58]

Some Reflections

The writings of Freud and Jung reveal how great has been their contribution in understanding the phenomena of religion. Their theories on personality and its process of crystallisation have far reaching implications. The various factors they take to be determinants in personality development clearly show that a person's very psychic constitution is instrumental in promoting religious experiences. "Freud and Jung are agreed that the influence of the past is of very great importance. To Freud this influence is to be found largely in a return to the repressed", while Jung "maintained that racial archetypes play an extremely important role in religious beliefs and account for the remarkable similarities of dogma and symbolism found in the different parts of the world."[59] Apart from this, assertion of the unconscious as an active element with a wide range of effectivity in human behaviour has explained many phenomena previously revelling in mystery. They have extended the evidence which goes to show the extent to which intellectual and behavioural operations are influenced by unconscious processes, specially when concerned with personal matters. These are, of course, contributions, speaking in very general terms as there are minute differences in the details of almost every theory and concept. As the domain of concern is the 'religious' a few lines will be devoted to assessing both the views of Freud and Jung in this context and an attempt to evaluate them on a comparative plane will be made.

Freud's approach in comparison to Jung's is rather limited and this is mainly because he failed to apply his findings, from the therapeutic application of psychoanalysis, to normal man. Further, Freud's evaluation of religion has been considered by various exponenents of religion not merely as unauthorised but also one sided. He was so involved with the abnormal that in every normal act he could trace abnormality. And in doing so, he drew further away from the inherent humane features of human beings. The picture of humankind that is derivable from Freudian observations would be that of a being overpowered by the sex instinct.

Jung did recognise the vital role of the sex instinct but did not consider it to be the only operative factor. In Jung it is obvious that his collective unconscious alongwith the archetypes are very important as they explain the religious in human beings. He has worked out a system which is consistent and one thing is made to follow the other—the basis of everything is the twofold division of the psyche into conscious and unconscious. Moreover, his endeavours in medicine brought forth findings which he utilised to study individuals as they are, and this has revealed a treasury of facts unknown and unheard of.

Freud's opinion that religion is an illussion because it is a means for wish-fulfilment shows his hastiness in assessing human beings. Contrary to his views, Jung exhibited grasp of certain subtle traits that are inevitably found in any person. According to Jung religion is not a matter limited to creedal acceptances. Religion may be a term designating the attitude peculiar to a consciousness which has been altered by the experience of the numinosum.[60] Religion, in this way, is a matter of experience—one knows or believes in God not as a theological concept but as an experience from which concepts may consequently be formulated. In Freud there is no room for religious experience, yet it is a fact encountered by human beings. That the validity of these experiences is questionable because they do not submit to verification cannot prove them non-existent —this vital point was given due respect by Jung, and he did not indulge in discussing these experiences beyond their relevance in psychology. He is of the opinion that religious experiences are crystallisations of the archetypes present in the collective unconscious. In this way, "Dogma, creed, and ritual are crystallized forms of original religious experience, worked over and refined, sometimes for centuries until they reached the form in which we know them."[61] For him the collective unconscious was, emotionally speaking, a womb pregnant with images.

Jung has often been accused of being mystical in approach rather than being scientific in his outlook on account of his using the terms 'spirit' and 'faith'. To this Jung had protested that it could be unscientific to ignore the fact that mystical idea is enforced by the natural tendencies of the unconscious mind. Jung's religion tends to be mystical and in it he recognised the signs of supra-personal forces which wield a fate-like power over our lives—these are the forces of the subconscious. The important thing is that Jung regards religion or the religious attitude to be an element in psychic life while Freud contends religion to be the externalisation of human unconscious conflicts and their rising to the cosmic level. Freud was concerned about the truth of religion while Jung was not so concerned—he is generally considered more sympathetic to religion than Freud. It is the opinion of Thomas Mcpherson that "Neither Freud nor Jung ... in putting forward his ideas about religion, is advancing theories capable of being consclusively demonstrated by empirical evidence ... The best way of regarding them both is as imaginative writers who have thrown new light on a fundamentally important aspect of life much as a great novelist might do."[62]

The function of psychoanalysis lies in analysing religious experience with a view to describing the unconscious motivation which lies at its roots. This kind of psychoanalytic knowledge will be helpful in the control, prediction and guidance of the religious development of the individual, and negatively would help us in avoiding neurotic forms of religion. The essential postulate of psychoanalysis is the existence of something which is at one and the same time consciousness and not consciousness : sometimes designated as the subconscious and sometimes as the unconscious mind.[63] So, apart from their direct contributions, the works of Freud and Jung suggest the active influence of the unconscious and subconscious realm in all behaviour. It is not unjustified that W.K. Wright uses the word subconscious to imply "those brain or other neural processes which are not attended by consciousness, but which modify the contents of consciousness. If these neural processes *had* been attended by consciousness while they were taking place, they would be typical instances of perception, imagination, memory, reasoning, etc. but they were ***not*** so attended, and so they are styled subconscious."[64] It transpires that "Our personal consciousness, then, cannot fully represent the external world or even our internal world, but mostly consist of an extremely small fraction of the entire "reality"."[65] So, from Freud and Jung it is quite evident that consciousness is extended into areas beyond those usually included within the rubric of psychology.

Whatever may be their individual opinions both Freud and Jung are basically agreed that overt human behaviour is determined by those unknown realms as subconscious and unconscious. Jung, in fact, feels compelled to "admit the fact that the unconscious mind is capable at times of assuming an intelligence and purposiveness which are superior to conscious insight. There is hardly any doubt that this fact is a basic religious phenomennon ... "[66]

It is Mukherjee's opinion that "Jung's insight has been truer than Freud's when he regards the unconscious as a perennial source of revelation of the highest and the noblest, symbolised as god, angels, sages and other "archetypes". In the concrete religious experience of mankind the unconscious is, however, the reservoir of both the worst and the best in man, in the impulses, emotions and thoughts which he can delve into."[67] To Faber "It appears that Freud was afraid of occultism – of everything that philosophy, religion and parapsychology had learnt to say about the psyche; it was this that was for Jung the really important thing. He even interpreted this as meaning that Freud obviously felt himself to be threatened by an eruption of unconscious religious factors."[68] Unconsciousness by itself does not lead to religious experience, but Jung, we have seen, held the transcendental elements of religious experience to come through the unconscious.

Displacement of the cerebral consciousness, i.e., of the normal self-awareness functioning through the brain, results in inhibition of the sense organs, implying a slackening in their normal power of reaction to sensory stimuli. By making the brain artificially inactive, by completely suppressing sensory intake as well as motor output, consciousness is displaced. In this condition it is likely that the consciousness of the subject be activised in the parapsychic way, to result in what may be called awakening of the subliminal or subconscious self. "The intuitions of creative imagination as expressed in the cosmic revelations of the philosophic and religious mystics, and even in the less generic vision of the great poets, owe their grandeur and uniqueness to the fact that in them the subconscious functions more spontaneously, more nearly as a unified whole."[69]

This seems to be in support of the possibility that states of mind are potent guides of human 'action' behaviour and experience. There seems to be no doubt that the unconscious or subconscious is a storehouse of impressions and experiences by which the conscious life is unquestionably affected under certain conditions. However, it must be borne in mind that religious experiences are not the product of the unconscious and subconscious exclusively. "To relegate religious experience to the subconscious realm exclusively is to deprive religion both of rationality and of motive power. If man is to respond to the voice of God with any effect he must do so as a conscious, free and intelligent being."[70]

Therefore, psychoanalysis which is simply a special branch of psychology tries to find out the unconscious factors underlying any mental phenomenon. It endeavours to show the repressed, infantile complexes underlying religious experiences. Its emphasis on the continued helplessness of individuals throughout life, and on the parental imago by way of insurance against all the unknown dangers which life may bring forth is an important contribution in understanding religious experiences.

Freud explained the religious urge in human beings as an illusory rationalization of unconscious wishes, as a projection to compensate the infantile sense of helplessness. God is the projection of the father-image, a fantasy substitute for an actual and not altogether satisfactory father. This being his stand, the referent of a religious experience is reduced to mere projection. From his projective point of view one can no longer reconcile the belief that religious experience is the immediate certainty of the uncertain, that religion, is the immediate assurance of power, love, salvation, etc. All this, because religion is nothing more than the psychological outcome of defensive behaviour. Leuba, though no psychoanalyst, keeping within close proximity of Freudian views, expounds the view, that religion deals with illusory reality.

Jung on the other hand exhibits a good amount of tolerance towards religion and tends to support religious experiences. God is explained as lying in the collective unconscious, as the archetype God-imago. For Jung, God is in the unconscious as the archetype God, and one has only to realise this. In this way, any religious experience, with God as its referent, at least awards it phenomenological authenticity. Of course, Jung has avoided the question of God's ontological validity, though he asserts that what exists in the psyche is existent in reality.

As a consequence of Freudian studies could sex be acknowledged as one of the major triggers of religious experience? Here we have to understand the meaning of sex as used by Freud, and its non-Freudian meaning. According to the former sex is the suppression of the sexual desire or its non-fulfilment, and its resulting expressions, while the latter is the gratification from sex life. How far negative sex (as used by Freud) can be deemed a trigger of religious experience in every instance is doubtful, because suppression or excess of any need tends to disbalance both physical and mental homeostasis. But when usual sexual activity ushers in religious experience, it is the resultant of normal human ativity. Just as the various means as discussed in Chapter II, still the mind and bring it to a state of high receptivity, sexual gratification may also still the mind and body in similar fashion. Laski presents a table of the percentage distribution of "triggers"; the precondition that apparently bring ecstatic interlude, and sexual love is one among the 11 triggers mentioned.[71] The resulting feelings following physical love have been recorded by Greelay as—"Suddenly, a new and very different kind of pleasure takes possession of her. She smiles first and then laughs; her entire body takes on a peculiarly delightful glow. This new pleasure makes intercourse seem mild in comparison. The whole of the universe has somehow flooded her being."[72]

A notable aspect of Jung is his gentle hint at the significance of parapsychology. His theory of 'synchronicity' provides a theoretical approach to ESP. According to Alan Gauld, "Jung holds that ESP and kindred phenomena demonstrate the existence in the universe of a form of order not hitherto explicitly recognised, a form of order which is totally different from the causal order in which scientists and philosophers of science have commonly traded."[73] Jung's key notion is that of coincidences which somehow 'make sense' or are 'meaningful'. Such coincidences include all spontaneous and experimental examples of ESP and they are too numerous to be attributed to the chance harmonising of independent causal sequences. These meaningful coincidences show that there is in the universe a way of knowing other than that what is captured by the senses. The existence of some other sense organ apart from the five we know of is a debatable issue. Although some psychologists believe that the evidence for the existence of certain forms of ESP is now incontrovertible most remain unconvinced. Those convinced, contend on the basis of their experimental findings that one's "relation with his environment need not be soley dependent on the sensorimotor system ; an independent mode of interaction has been discovered that is reversible in operation ... "[74] as evinced in the experiences of telepathy and clairvoyance. Much of what is hesitantly put forward as hypothetical statements or suggestions, in the context of religion and religious experiences, may stand proved once the existence of ESP is established.

We know that according to Jung there lies in our unconscious minds certain basic ways of thought or inherited propensities, ones which are common to the whole human race and these are the archetypes. They find expresston in consciousness through archetypal images which symbolise our instinctual attitudes to recurrent human situations. Synchronistic events occur when there emerges from the unconscious an image which either directly represents or symbolises an event whose distant occurence or whose impending occurence is already known to the unconscious mind. There is no causal relationship between the image and the event which fulfils it. However, we must take note of Alan Gauld's remark which represents the opinion of a section of psychologists to the Jungian synchronism. He says, "Many psychologists, (and I am one of them) would be tempted to say that Jung's doctrines about the archetype are part and parcel of a psychological theory which has dramatic unity rather than logical coherence, and which can therefore accommodate any conceivable turn, which the facts may take."[75]

REFERENCES

1. Ralph Norman Haber, Aharon H. Fried, *An Introduction to Psychology*, New York, 1975. p. 403.
2. W.B. Selbie, *The Psychology of Religion*, Oxford, 1926. p. 83.
3. W.K. Wright, *A Student's Philosophy of Religion*, New York, 1958. p. 216.
4. Edna Heidbreder, *Seven Psychologies*, Ludhiana, 1961. p. 378.
5. C.G. Jung, *Psychology of the Unconscious*, (Authorised translation, with Introduction, by Beatrice Hinkle), London, 1951. p. viii.
6. Ralph Norman Haber, Aharon H. Fried, *An Introduction to Psychology, op. cit.* pp. 407-408.
7. G.S. Spinks, *Psychology and Religion* ; *An Introduction to Contemporary Views*, London, 1963. p. 53.
8. Y. Masih, *Freudianism and Religion*, Calcutta, 1964. p. 69. Beatrice M. Hinkle remarks : "To say that an idea or feeling is

unconscious merely means to indicate that the individual is unaware at that time of its existence, or that all the material of which he is unaware at a given time is unconscious." C.G. Jung, *Psychology of the Unconscious*, op. cit. p. xi.

9. According to Wolman "The preconscious is what is unconscious at a given time but can easily become conscious; it is latent or temporarily unconscious." Benjamin B. Wolman, *Contemporary Theories and Systems in Psychology*, New York/Tokyo. 1960, p. 216. He further points out that, "The preconscious contains thoughts, memories, and so on that can be made conscious by an effort of attention, while the unconscious contains psychic events that are actively buried from consciousness and can only be made conscious with considerable effort." Ralph Norman Haber, Aharon H. Fried, *An Introduction to Psychology, op. cit.* p. 407.

10. Benjamin B. Wolman, *Contemporary Theories and Systems in Psychology, op. cit.* p. 216.

11. Ralph Norman Haber, Aharon H. Fried, *An Introduction to Psychology, op. cit.* p. 408.

12. Sigmund Freud, *The Future of an Illusion*, (Translated by W.D. Robson-Scott), London, 1943. pp. 26-27.

13. Heije Faber, *Psychology of Religion*, Translated by Margaret Kohl, London, 1976. p. 15.

14. Erich Fromm, *Psychoanalysis and Religion*, New Haven, 1977. pp. 11-12.

15. Sigmund Freud, *The Future of an Illusion, op. cit.* p. 30.

16. Heije Faber, *Psychology of Religion, op. cit.* p. 16.

17. Fred Berthold, Jr., 'The Meaning of Religious Experience', *The Journal of Religion*, Vol 32, 1952. p. 267.

18. *Ibid.*

19. F.C. Happold, *Religious Faith and Twentieth- Century Man*, Penguin Books, 1966. p. 66.

20. Y. Masih, *Freudianism and Religion, op. cit.* p. 283.

21. F.C. Happold, *Religious Faith and Twentieth-Century Man, op. cit.* p. 65.

22. G.S. Spinks, *Psychology and Religion*; *An Introduction to Contemporary Views*, London, 1963. p. 52.

23. Anthony Quinton, 'Freud and Philosophy', in Jonathan Miller (ed.), ***Freud the Man, His World, His Influence***, London, 1972. p. 75.

24. G.S. Spinks, ***Psychology and Religion***, *An Introduction to Contemporary Views*, *op. cit. p. 89.*

25. D.M. Edwards, ***The Philosophy of Religion***, Calcutta, 1968. p. 236.

26. Heije Faber, ***Psychology of Religion***, *op. cit.* p. 37.

27. C.G. Jung, *Psychology and Religion*, New Haven, 1960. p. 4.

28. Erich Fromm, ***Psychoanalysis and Religion***, *op. cit.* p. 15.

29. C.G. Jung, *Psychology and Religion*, *op, cit.* p. 2.

30. Heije Faber, *Psychology of Religion*, *op. cit.* p. 39.

31. G.S. Spinks, *Psychology and Religion*; *An Introduction to Contemporary Views*, *op. cit.* p. 53.

32. Jolande Jacobi, *The Psychology of C.G. Jung*, *An Introduction with Illustrations*, *1642*. p. 19.

33. C.G. Jung, *Modern Man in Search of a Soul*, London, 1962. p. 99.

34. Joland Jacobi, *The Psychology of C.G. Jung*, *op. cit.* p. 22.

35. C.G. Jung, *Psychology and Religion*, *op. cit.* p. 4. It is his further contention that "Religion is the term that designates the attitude peculiar to a consciousness which has been altered by experience of the numinosum." *Ibid.* p. 6.

36. Erich Fromm, ***Psychoanalysis and Religion***, op. cit. p. 19.

37. C.G. Jung, ***Psychology and Religion***, op. cit. p.6.

38. G.S. Spinks, ***Psychology and Religion***, *An Introduction to* ***Contemporary Views***, op. cit. p. 54.

39. *Ibid* p. 63.

40. *Ibid.* p. 64. "The archetypes are something like the organs of the pre-rational psyche. They are eternally inherited identical forms and ideas, at first without specific content. The specific content appears during the individual life span when personal experience is absorbed in just these forms." Jolande Jacobi (ed.) ***C.G. Jung Psychological Reflections***, New York, 1961. p. 36. XXXII, 26.

41. Jolande Jacobi (ed.), *C.G. Jung Psychological Reflections, op. cit.* p. 53 XXVII 81 (J, 12f)

42. Heije, Faber *Psychology of Religion, op. cit.* p. 42.

43. *Ibid.* p. 47.

44. G.S. Spinks, *Psychology of Religion, An Introduction to Contemporaty Views, op. cit.* pp. 60-61.

45. *Ibid.* p. 55.

46. *Jolande Jacobi, The Psychology of C.G. Jung, An Introduction with Illustrations, op. cit.* p. 58.

47. C.G. Jung, *Psychology and Religion, op. cit.* p. 46.

48. C.G. Jung, *Modern Man in Search of a Soul*, Londan, 1962. p. 137.

49. Heije Faber, *Psychology of Religion, op. cit.* p. 46.

50. *Ibid.*

It is Jung's further contention that one can "rediscover God through the archetype God in his own unconscious—that is to say, he can only find him, in a certain sense, 'immanently' ". *Ibid.* p. 48.

51. G.S. Spinks, *Psychology and Religion, An Introduction to Contemporary Views, op. cit.* p. 97.

52. *Ibid.*

53. C.G. Jung, *Psychology and Religion, op. cit.* p. 72.

54. *Ibid.* pp. 113-114.

55. Erich Fromm, *Psychoanalysis and Religion, op. cit.* p. 14.

56. C.G. Jung, *Psychology and Religion, op. cit.* p. 62.

57. C.G. Jung, 'Freud and Jung', *Modern Man In Search of a Soul, op. cit.* p. 140.

He further feels that, "if such experience helps to make your life healthier, more beautiful, more complete and more satisfactory to yourself and to those you love you may safely say : "This was the grace of God"." C.G. Jung, *Psychology and Religlon, op. cit.* p. 114.

58. C.G. Jung, 'Freud and Jung', *Modern Man in Search of a Soul, op. cit.* p. 135.

59. S.M. Tripathi, *Psycho-Analytic Concept of Religion*, Delhi, 1979. p. 254.

60. C.G. Jung, *Psychology of Religion : West and East*, Collected Works, Vol II, 1953. p. 7.
61. S.M. Tripathi, *Psycho- Analytic Concept of Religion, op. cit.* p. 360.
62. Thomas McPherson, *The Philosophy of Religion*, London, 1971. pp. 166-167.
63. Y. Masih, *Freudianism and Religion, op. cit.* pp. 281-282.
64. W.K. Wright, *A Student's Philosophy of Religion, op. cit.* pp. 216-217.
65. Robert E. Ornstein, *The Psychology of Consciousness, op. cit.* p. 17.
66. C.G. Jung, *Psychology and Religion, op. cit.* pp. 45-46.
67. Radhakamal Mukherjee, *The Theory and Art of Mysticism*, New Delhi, 1960. pp. 12-13.
68. Heije Faber, *Psychology of Religion, op. cit.* p. 56.
69. W.P. Montague, *The Ways of Knowing*, London, 1962. p. 57.
70. W.B. Selbie, *The Psychology of Religion, op. cit.* p. 85.
71. Andrew M. Greelay, *Ecstasy A Way of Knowing, op. cit.* p. 22.
72. *Ibid.* pp. 1-2.
73. Alan Gauld, 'ESP and Attempts to Explain It', Shivesh C. Thakur (ed.), *Philosophy And Psychical Research*, New, York, 1976. p. 34.
74. Sidney Hook (ed.), *Dimensions of Mind*, New York, 1961. p. 74.
75. Alan Gauld, 'ESP and Attempts to Explain It', Shivesh C. Thakur (ed.), *Philosopyhy and Psychical Research, op. cit.* p. 36.

5

Religious Potentialities of Psychedelic Drugs

Drugs : Their Nature and Extent of Operation

Apparent similarities in the effects of drug intake and religious experiences bring into focus the probability of their identity of quality and content. "It seems difficult to deny that there are numerous parallels and similarities between mystical and drug induced states."[1] Though Huxley was first among contemporary thinkers to argue for a positive connection between drugs and religious experiences, the idea is gaining widespread acceptance. Drugs, owing to their power of altering and modifying states of consciousness, have long associations with religion. "The claim has been made that the experience facilitated by psychedelic (or mind-opening) drugs such as LSD, psilocybin and mescaline can be similar or identical to the experience described by the mystics of all ages, cultures and religions."[2] One of the most important questions raised by psychedelic drugs is whether authentic religious and mystical experiences actually occur among the drung subjects.

Reference to the religious use of drugs are scattered throughout the history of religions, and there is no doubt that the practice is ancient. G.A. Coe has traced the roots of contemporary spiritual practices in olden times. When primitive beings experienced loss of self-control through drug intoxication or through any of the trance inducing processes, the only possible interpretation that made sense was 'possession'—that some external force was controlling the muscles and thoughts of the subject. Occurrences of visions and auditions were taken to be actual seeing and hearing. From such mental and bodily automations grew spiritualistic practices—methods that occasion visions and auditions. Herein lies the roots of present time spiritism which lives and moves within the same general sphere.[3] "A Yogic writer, Patanjali, speaks of the use of *ausadhi* (medicinal herb) as a means to Yogic experience, and the Vedas and Tantras (Hindu Occultic writings) refer to wine as a part of worship and the initiatory rites. The Greek Mysteries (religion of salvation) sometimes used sedatives and stimulants."[4] In many cases the plant sources of these drugs have been worshipped as gods, and those persons who employed the drugs as means for acquiring 'supernatural' powers and visions have been recognised as priests, prophets or pioneers of various religious cults.

The abundance of evidence to this effect is indicative of the use, role and importance of mind-changing drugs in religions from early times. The use of drugs with a religious or spiritual purpose cannot be restricted to any particular religion. From recorded evidence it is known that religions of Siberia, the Greeks, the Eastern Mediterranian islands, the Sumerians, Zoroastrianism and Hinduism all used drugs for enhancing spiritual pursuits. It is therefore, appropriate to say that, "In a number of cults drugs are regularly used at religious rituals, not as a result of psychological research but since it was found that certain substances enhanced religious experiences."[5] "... the dried heads of the peyote cactus, whose chief active ingredient is mescaline, were used by the Aztecs at least as early as 300 B.C. and are currently being employed by over 50,000 Indians of the North American Church as a vital part of their religious ceremonies."[6] Ololiuqui, a variety of morning-glory seed, and teonanacatl (kind of Mexican mushroom) were used by Aztecs for divinatory and religious purposes. These practices have continued to the present among remote Indian tribes in the mountains of Oaxaca Province in Mexico. The active chemical in mushroom is psilocybin and several compounds closely related to LSD in the case of ololiuqui.

In the Indian traditions drugs like opium and cannabis (a form of hemp) always found the patronage of ascetics. G. M. Carstairs, reporting on the use of *Bhang* in India, quotes a Brahmin as saying, "It gives good bhakti .... you get a very good bhakti with bhang ... "[7] Drugs like these were consumed to elevate the level of consciousness and do away with the feeling of 'I-ness'. As per the report of the Indian Hemp Commission, Volume I, 1893-4, pp. 160, 161, 165, "Reference to the almost universal use of hemp drugs by fakirs, yogis, sanyasis, and ascetics of all classes, and more particularly of those devoted to the worship of Siva, will be found in the paragraphs of this report dealing with the classes of people who consume the drugs."[8] Moreover, evidence of the cultic use of opium in the eastern Mediterranean islands, Greece, and among the Sumeri ans points to dates as early as 3000 B.C.

The drugs employed by diversified cults for their psychedelic effects were incorporated into the cults for explicit and implicit religious functions and purposes. Drug effects reportedly enhance religious experiences in a manner similar to those that occur in religious ceremonies or acts practised among those not dependent on drugs. The loftiest aim of the cultic utility of drugs is the pure delight in what drug users describe as a direct experience of God, ultimate reality, the spirits that preside over one's destiny, or whatever the worshipper may conceive as the object of worship.

The question is whether communion with God is in fact facilitated by the use of drugs and alcohol or is it merely a notion of some kind ? Thus arises the need for a thorough study of the aspects of the human-drug relation It is one thing to induce psycho-physical effects such as are commonly associated with religious experiences, and another to have an actual religious experience.

Those who indulge in drug ingestion in a frank search for 'kicks', or maybe to escape a sometimes barely tolerable reality, raise doubts regarding the religious authenticity of drug induced experiences. Moreover, it goes without saying that the sudden popularity of drugs cannot be attributed cent percent to the subject's intention of attaining religious experience. Aurthur Guiraham brilliantly reveals the root of contention when he says, "Certainly man has used alcohol since the beginning of civilization .... Over the centuries alcohol has been the most readily available means enabling him to dissipate his sense of himself as a separate and isolated entity."[9] The role of alcohol as a panacea for one's mental disturbances is a decided fact, as the alcoholic or one who consumes alcohol experiences dissolution of individual existence. To surpass the bounds of individuality is a requisite both for attainment of religious experiences as well as for easing and forgetting turbulent emotional states. So also, mind-changing drugs dissolve the boundaries of selfhood. From all this it is possible to deduce three categories of persons who are likely drug users : (*i*) those who indulge in the practice just for 'kicks', (*ii*) those who soothe or drive out undesirable mind-content, and (*iii*) those who are genuine aspirants of religious experiences. Given this categorisation, it is no wonder that the psychedelic drugs have resulted in a proliferation of 'fun' mystics and armchair pilgrims who hardly claim mystical mandates for experiences that are basically nothing beyond routine instances of conscious alteration.

Therefore, the reason for indulging in drug ingestion is a matter of personal preference. Owing to alternatives, skeptical views regarding the capacities of drugs have surfaced. Added to this, the popularity claimed by drugs is held responsible for criticisms against its own capacity to facilitate religious experiences.

It is not surprising that the religious use of drugs has not met with the approval of the religious establishment. Formal religion by nature is dogmatic and moralistic, with a tendency to derive its dogmas and moral content from scriptures and prophetic writings. On the whole its liturgical character makes little room for religious experiences, which clearly explains the lack of tolerance towards drug induced experiences.

The claim posited by drug users that drug can produce genuine mystical insight is summararily rejected by moralists and religious orthodoxy in general. They are of the opinion that, mere ingestion of drugs can hardly be considered meritorious, and therefore, such an act of ingestion cannot possibly lead to exalted states of mystical insight. On moral grounds they attach greater merit to the performance of difficult actions than to that of an easy one, as the former is deemed more deserving. They argue thus – how can the authenticity of two experiences, one acquired after adherence to moral codes etc., and the other is acquired by drug ingestion, be taken at par? "Many persons concerned with religion are distrurbed by drug-facilitated mystical experiences because of their apparent ease of production, with the implication that they are 'unearned', and therefore 'undeserved'. Perhaps the Puritan and Calvinistic element of our Western culture—especially in the United States, where most of the controversy about psychedelic drugs has centered—may be a factor in this uneasiness. Although a drug experience might seem unearned when compared with the rigorous discipline which many mystics describe as necessary, our evidence has suggested that careful preparation and expectation play an important part, not only in the type of experience attained but in later fruits for life. Positive mystical experience with psychedelic drugs is by no means automatic."[10]

A more serious allegation is that, frequent intake of drugs may result in addiction, whose ill effects hardly require elaboration. This negative aspect of drugs has disuaded many from accepting the religious potentialities of drugs. Swami Akhilananda argues that, "drugs do not produce any actual knowledge of the Reality nor do they integrate the personality. On the contrary, the drug addict gradually becomes less than what is normal. On the other hand, religion brings out the finest qualities in man ; it brings out his divine nature ; it makes him aware of what he really is."[11] Talking about the risks involved Greelay warns, "Those using drugs to resolve religious or personal problems should know that they are taking serious risks and would be better advised to concentrate on the ascetical practices of the Orient if they feel the need for ecstatic experience."[12] Researches have corroborated the fact that growing dependence on hallucinogenic drugs is both physically and psychologically dangerous for the human constitution.

An insight into the nature of drugs and the factors involved in their action on the human physiology will certainly be of immense help for our study. Research conducted to study the reaction of drugs on human affairs reveals that "the term drug refers mainly to substances that affect psychological or behavioral functions or lead to varying degrees of dependence or addiction."[13] The primary basis of drug action is an interaction between a drug molecule and some specific cellular component, which is called a receptor or receptive substance. Functional changes produced by a drug on various organs (e.g., heart, lung, kidney) are termed effects. Most drugs are selective in their activity ; i. e., a main action may be associated with some primary effect.

Drugs of different categories are classified in accordance with their actions on specific organs. First come the 'Anesthetics' which are drugs affecting the central nervous system, used to prevent sensation of pain during surgery. Then we have another set of drugs affecting the autonomic nervous system. Important for our purposes, however, is the next category of drugs —the Hallucinogenic drugs. These drugs have a diverse range of effects on the human physiology, making it impossible to attach to them a suitable generic name. "Abnormal behaviour as profound as the swings in mood, disturbances in thinking, perceptual distortions, delusions, and feelings of strangeness that sometimes occur with these drugs is usually indicative of a major mental disorder."[14] Altered mode of perception is the distinctive feature of this drug reaction. However, even under the influence of these drugs, subjects are aware that their perceptions have no basis in reality. This makes the drugs better known as psychedelic drugs, because they are definitely mind-manifesting. Here occurs a shift from the medicinal or therapeutic aspect to the educational or mystical-religious aspect of drug experiences. A simultaneous shift involves an expansion of consciousness.

The psychedelic substances that have aroused interest and controversy, as far as the question of their religious import is concerned, are the LSD type drugs that produce marked abberations of behaviour. Important among these are—(*i*) d-lysergic acid diethylamide, commonly known as LSD-25, a derivative of the ergot fungus, (*ii*) mescaline, the active principle of the peyote cactus, and (*iii*) psilocybin and psilocin which are derived from Mexican mushrooms. Though cannabis, obtained from the leaves and tops of the hemp plant, is not included among psychedelic drugs, it too has signficance in the history of religions, particularly in India.

"The psychedelic drugs have somewhat different effects. For example, mescaline makes ordinary objects appear abnormally clear, while LSD produces visual hallucinations. However, the effects experienced are very much a function of the beliefs and expectations of the drug taken, in turn a function of the preparation and social setting."[15] "All drugs .... have multiple effects, none of which are completely reliable or predictable. They vary from person to person and from time to time for the same person."[16] From this it becomes clear that the quality and degree of the effects of a drug are influenced and facilitated by factors that are divided into three classes. (*i*) Those factors concerned with the drug itself—the dose, route of administration, absorption, distribution in the body, metabolism, and rate of excretion. (*ii*) Those factors concerning the features of the subject on whom the drug is used—age, weight, sex, hereditory factors, physiological variability and associated disease states. Morever, influences and bias on the part of patient and physician can significantly modify drug respones, thus interfering with the interpretation of the therapeutic efficacy of a drug. (*iii*) Thirdly, we have drug combinations—effect of drug combinations may be totally different from the individual effect of the component drugs.

Experiments and investigations with drugs have revealed that the resultant effects are either physiological or psychological In view of the facts about drugs and their connected circumstances, the effects of drugs may be discussed under the two heads already mentioned. The former group includes frequent decline in the pulse rate, in concentration of blood lacate and in the respiratory rate, and an increase in the concentration of carbon dioxide in the blood. It is also possible that drugs may increase the respiratory rate, or produce an alteration of states in which the respiratory rates are increased or decreased. Sometimes body tremour and perspiration result. The psychological effects are marked by an insensitivity to outside stimuli which would normally induce sharp reaction from the subject, and introversion and trance like behaviour.

Without prior knowledge of the identifying features, subjects are unable to distinguish the reaction of LSD, mescaline and psilocybin. On the physiological side, they induce responses consistent with the kind of effects expected of a central-nervous-sytem stimulant. As a matter of course, there is a rise in the systolic blood pressure, dilation of the pupils, along with occasional facilitation of the spinal reflexes and excitation of the sympathetic nervous system and brain. Two marked reactions seem to be invariable as understood from the accounts of drug users – the effect of being 'flooded' with visual experience and the change in feelings and awareness of the self. Speaking in specific terms, "The use of LSD-25 can promote two varieties of psychedelic experience and experience of mystical consciousness, and a non-mystical form of altered consciousness. The major phenomena of LSD-induced states of consciousness are vivid perceptual distortions or hallucinations, including changed spatial relationships ; apparent flexibility of solid masses ; intensification of color ; sharpening of contours ; synesthesia, in which sound, usually music, is accompanied by rich visual imagery."[17]

These drugs are potent psycho-chemicals that temporarily alter and expand the human consciousness. Even the briefest summation of the effects of these drugs would have to include the following ; changes in visual, auditory, tactile, olfactory, gustatory, and kinesthetic perception. Hallucinations appear and there are vivid images – eidetic images—when the eyes are shut, which are of a blinding brightness and highly coloured, symmetrical and usually take the form of lattices, cobwebs and spirals. Perception is changed in various ways : ordinary objects become more vivid, contrasts are emphasised, objects move about and are misinterpreted fantastically. Emotions, feelings, and thoughts well-up to end in frequent fluctuations of mood, heightened suggestibility, and enhanced memory.[18] Drugs seem to exercise a direct stimulating effect upon certain tendencies and emotions. Thought processes are considerably impaired : there is a fall of efficiency in performance at tasks, there is flight of thought with blocking of deliberate thinking, while imagination is no longer restricted to rational channels or checked by the sense of the irrelevant, the improper or the grotesque, but rather moves into the domain of infinite possibility.

"Some evidence suggests that LSD blocks the activity of certain nerve cells that form serotonin, a transmitter substance in the brain. On the other hand, other evidence indicates that LSD can "fool" nerve cells into accepting it in the place of serotonin. Certainly the chemical structure of LSD and several other "hallucinogens" or "psychedelics" - mescaline, peyote, psilocybin, psilocin—is very similar to that of serotonin. However LSD cannot transmit messages in the same way that serotonin can, as a result the message becomes 'garbled' as it crosses the synapse between two nerve cells. This may explain the widely exaggerated sensations that one experiences on a "trip". In addition LSD may over stimulate the reticular formation, which in turn alerts the cortex more than it usually does ; this may account for the "heightened awareness" that LSD users often report."[19] Dissolution of the ego, and an awareness of the internal organs and processes of the body, known as depersonalisation, results in detachment and dissociation. The experience is wholly incommunicable, except as a bare statement, and in this respect utterrances of drug users remain inadequate as representations of their experiences, though the experient is absolutely certain of the experience and its contents. Under the influence of drugs music may evoke visual impressions and light may give the impression of sound. "Mescalin and a number of other drugs reduce the amount of glucose in the blood that passess over the brain, with the result that the phenomenal world appears to be different to the person in whose blood stream the drug has been introduced. The ego is no longer troubled about the world of space and time ; it is interested instead in a realm of intense colour and light, and has a feeling of identity with a world in which *being* is felt to be identified with the All."[20]

Briefly then, hashish, marijuana and bhang lead to the immediate reaction of altered state of perceptions, breakdown of inhibitions and relaxation, and their long term effects take the form of fatigue and psychosis. Similarly, LSD and mescaline produce hallucination, anxiety, psychosis, and panic as immediate reaction, while increased delusion stays on as their long term effect.[21] A vivid and first-hand account of the disastrous implications of drug intake, as experienced by a a drug addict, is available in Ravindra Singh's *I Was A Drug Addict*.[22].

Drugs in the Context of Religious Experiences

Our discussion so far has been a pointer towards revealing the parallels between drug-induced experiences in the laboratory or otherwise and religious experiences. The similarity that is being established indicates that drugs are effective stimulants so far as the inducement of religious experiences is coneerned. That is, states of being that ensue from drug ingestion are suggestive of contextual similarity between the two experiences under scrutiny. It is interesting, the frequency with which drug subjects have fallen back on religio-mystical modes of linguistic expression in formulating, describing and communicating their experiences. Such usage of religio-mystical vocabulary is a clear hint that drug experiences have religious significance. For ascertaining this one needs only to turn to the characteristics of religious experiences enlisted in Chapter I of this work, and also the definitive features of mystical experiences as presented by scholars like Pahnke, Stace, Greelay, Maslow and Ludwig. This will be compared to the characteristics of drug experiences as suggested in the present chapter. A presentation of the typologies and the charaeteristics of drug experiences alongside each other will enable us to draw out the common elements that mark both categories of experiences. This will sufficiently determine the religious content of drug experiences.

The following table facilitates a test of the similarities between the drug-provoked experiences and naturally acquired religious experiences, based on the characteristics of religious experiences as summarized by different people. Any parallels alone would be sufficient to establish the religious content of drug experiences. The table contains lists of the characteristics of religious experiences, altered states of consciousness (ASC). mystical experience, peak experiences and drug experiences. The characteristics of ASC provided by Ludwig[23] seem to suggest mystic or religious experiences.

From Greelay's [24] Appendix A—Varieties and Description of Religious Experiences containing questions asked in a national survey along with the responses in percentages, consisting of 1467 subjects, the description of mystical experiences have been taken. Pahnke's [25] typology of mysticism has been formulated out of W.T. Stace's typology as presented in his *Mysticism and Philosophy*, setting it as the standard while conducting his research with psilocybin. The opening section of Maslow's[26] appendix has been devoted to the religious aspects of Peak-Experiences. Alan Watts observed that. "In the course of two experiments I was amazed and somewhat embarrassed to find myself going through states of consciousness which correspond precisely with every description of major mystical experiences that I had over read .... Through subsequent experimentation with LSD-25 and the other chemicals ... I found I could move with ease into the state of "cosmic consciousness", and in due course became less and less dependent on the chemicals themselves for "turning-in" to this particular wave length of experience."[27]

TABLE I

In terms of the typologies referred to in the table above, it stands decided that drug induced experiences demonstrate the phenomena of all the typologies in a maximal way. Thus, there seems to be ample ground for accepting that drugs are endowed with religious potentialities.

At this point we must refer to a few of the researches carried out on psychedelic drugs, in the recent past, as they have left the evidence that seems to support the contention that an authentic religious experience may occur within the context of the psychedelic drug-state. Dr. Walter Pahnke conducted his well known 'The Miracle of Marsh Chapel' experiment on Good Friday, 1962, in order to test the hypothesis that persons who were given psilocybin would have experiences resembling those reported by spontaneous mystics. He designed his experiment to test a typology of mysticism, based on the categories of mystical experience summarized by W.T. Stace, on subjects who were given psilocybin in a religious setting. Twenty students, majority belonging to middle-class Protestant background, having no prior acquaintance with drugs, and ten guides with considerable psychedelic experience were used as subjects. The students were divided into five groups of four each, with two guides assigned per group. In each group two students received 30 mg of psilocybin—a fairly strong dose of the drug—and one guide 15 mg of it, while the other two students and guide received a placebo containing 200 mg of nicotinic acid which causes transient feelings of warmth and a tingling sensation, but produces no psychedelic effects. During the three hours that followed the participants attended a Good Friday service in a chapel, which included organ music. It should be noted that psilocybin was registered in a double-blind framework—neither subjects (students or guides) nor the experimenter knew who got psilocybin and who got the placebos.

Prior to conducting the experiment, the participants underwent five hours of various preparation and screening procedures, which included psychological tests, medical history, physical examination, questionnaire evaluation of previous religious experience, intensive interview and group interaction. The guides met with their groups to encourage trust, confidence, group support and fear reduction. The method of reaction to the experience was emphasised (*i.e.*, to relax and cooperate with the effects of the drug). Throughout the preparation, it was avoided, with caution, to acquaint the participants with the test typology devised.

Data were collected during the experiment and at various times up to six months afterwards. Subsequently, the reports the subjects wrote of their experiences were rated by three college-graduate housewives, uninformed about any details, as strong, moderate, slight or none. This was done in accordance with which descriptive (strong, moderate, slight or none) was best applicable to individual reports in view of the test typology provided by Pahnke. To Pahnke, the statistical results of these ratings indicated that "those subjects who received psilocybin experienced phenomena which were indistinguishable from, if not identical with ... the categories defined by our typology of mysticism."[28] There are other studies which attest the findings of Pahnke. Timothy Leary and his associates experimented with 69 full-time religious professionals who took psilocybin in a supportive setting. The experimenter wanted to explore the revelatory potentialities of the human nervous system. Leary reported that over seventy five percent of the subjects claimed to have experienced "intense mystico-religious reactions, and considerably more than half claim that they have had the deepest spiritual experience of their life."[29]

Supportive evidence may be found in the experiments of Oscar Janiger and William McGlothlin who reported on a study of 194 LSD subjects in a non-religious setting. In spite of the negative setting, ten months later, 24 percent of the subjects continued to refer to their experiences of having been 'religious'.[30] Ditman and Hayman reported remarkable percentages of their LSD subjects, claim that they had a religious type of experience in a supportive environment.[31] Savage carried out the same experiment in a setting both supportive and structured to provide religious stimuli, which resulted in higher percentages of subjects reporting religious experiences.[32] Masters and Houston conclude that, "In the five studies just cited between thirty-two and seventy-five percent of psychedelic subjects will report religious-type experiences if the setting is supportive ; and in a setting providing religious stimuli, from seventy-five to ninety percent report experiences of a religious or even mystical nature."[33]

From our discussion thus far, it transpires that subjective idiosyncracies, orientation, attitude to life, and environmental conditions are most important in facilitating the fullest actualisation of the potentials of drugs. The experiments, referred to, all stress the varying impact, with variances in setting, in which drugs were registered to the subjects. The proportion of people reporting religious experiences after a drug session is much higher in the case of a religious setting. As an example of this finding we may refer to the table given below (Ditman, Hayman ; and Savage).[34]

TABLE II

	Ditman & Hayman (Supportive environment) N=74 percent	Savage (Supportive environmental and some religious stimuli) N=96 percent
Feel it (LSD) was the greatest thing that ever happened to me	49	95
A religious experience	32	83
A greater awareness of God or a Higher Power, or an Ultimate Reality	40	90

Moreover, "There is some evidence ... that a person's experience under drugs are affected by the beliefs he already possesses. As Zaehner observes, Huxley was steeped in Eastern thought, which may explain why he had pantheistic experiences."[35] In the context of setting in drug experiences, Zaehner remarks, "Throughout the average LSD session the greatest use is made of sensory aids—visual, auditory and tactile. Almost invariably music is played. This is in sharp contrast to the practice of religious contemplatives for whom the suppression of all sensory impressions is the first step on the mystic path."[36]

Thus it is sufficiently clear that the right atmosphere along with other favourable conditions make drugs issue forth in religious experiences. The drugs do not merely secrete some experiences—there is no such thing as the drug experience *per se*. "Every experience is a mix of three ingrediants : drug, set (the psychological make-up of the individual), and setting (the social and physical environment in which it is taken).

But given the right set and setting, the drugs can induce religious experiences indistinguishable from experiences that occur spontaneously. Nor need set and setting be exceptional. The way the statistics are currently running, it looks as if one-fourth to one-third of the general population will have religious experiences if they take the drugs under naturalistic conditions, meaning by this, conditions in which the researcher supports the subject but does not try to influence the direction his experience will take. Among subjects who have strong religious inclinations to begin with, the proportions of those having religious experiences jumps to three-fourths. If they take the drugs in settings that are religious, the ratio soars to nine in ten."[37] Zaehner too is in agreement with this, and has said, "By now it has become a commonplace to observe that no beneficial effect can be expected from psychedelic drugs unless the 'set and setting' are right, the atmosphere relaxed and friendly, and the session directed by an experienced 'guide'."[38] In this context Zaehner refers to Dr. Leary who insists that psychedelic experience "is essentially religious, and it *can* be induced by LSD, given the right, 'set and setting', that is, a friendly environment, sympathetic company, and a qualified and experienced 'guide' to see you through the psychedelic game of snakes and ladders."[39]

An ordinary drug experience would probably be devoid of the usual content that marks a religious experience. Of course, there have been instances when drug experiences have been spontaneously described as 'religious' by the drug subject. This is exceptional and in most instances drugs lead to hallucinations, sensory disorientation and mental depression. This being the case, the content of drug experiences is far from being 'religious'. So, the referent of religious experiences and drug induced experiences cannot be paralleled because the contents of the latter tend to be 'nonsensical', *i.e.*, incoherent with normal spatio-temporal orientations. But drug ingestion supported by desire for religious experience may change the entire picture. Supported by the contemplative mood and urge for religious experience the aspirant who takes drugs may be assured of the desired experience. When drugs, in this way, help in promoting religious experiences their referent is akin to that of any spontaneous religious experience. The referent comes in the form of what is contemplated. This answers all doubts regarding the difference in referent in the two types of experiences.

In considering the religious potentials of the emotional experiences induced by, or enhanced by, certain drugs, one must not lose sight of the fact that habitual dependence on drugs for emotional stimulation can lead to addiction and to physiological and psychological deterioration. Drugs do produce temporary relaxation of both body and mind, along with feeling of elation and freedom. All this, however, is deceptive and far from the actual. That is why drugs are taken recourse to, to soothe the disturbed mind. Drugs, by dint of their organic connection with the human physiology, modify the functions of individual organs and the nervous system. In the case of drugs it is a case of functionary modification while the methods suggested for attaining religious experiences aim at stilling or at least limiting the function of the senses and organs and not distorting their functions. Whatever may be the apparent impact on the functional plane, by way of modifications and alterations in sensory-motor operation, the drug experience when backed by supportive 'set' and 'setting' should culminate in religious experiences. 'Set' covers the subjective factors like religiosity, temperament, background, personality type, childhood experiences and so on, while 'setting' accounts for the environment or conditions under which the drug is consumed—*e.g.*, favourable conditions would be a religious environment, a tension-free and relaxed atmosphere, etc. Under these conditions the impact of the drug subject is positive and desirable. This is because the subject experiences satisfaction of having attained what one aspired for and also the wonder and awe at confronting the supreme being. With reference to the Peyote cult of the Native American Church it is said that "Its fruits ... include not only a rapturous enlightenment, but also the lasting achievement of such virtues as humility, temperance and loving kindness."[40]

Here crops up the question of 'means' and 'end'. It is expected that people in search of religious experiences have the same intensity of love for God, compassion towards humankind and respect for moral and ethical principles, as any recognised religious person or mystic. It is only that their means for attaining the desired experience may be different and unconventional—especially in patronising the use of psychedelic drugs for attaining religious experiences. "It is the quality of the result that is to be judged and not the physical or psychological processes by which it is obtained. We may, therefore, adopt a suggestion made by Evelyn Underhill (See Evelyn Underhill : Mysticism, 15th edn., 1945, pp. 272 ff.) that what are often described as 'mystical automations' are 'the *media* by which the self receives spiritual stimulus' ; so it may be argued that drug-induced or ascetically induced experiences can be the means by which the human personality is laid open to the suggestion of the unconscious through whose primordial imagery the deeper activities of the soul emerge as conscious recognition of the transcendental."[41] Apart from this an addict's personality is marked by 'hopelessness' whereas the mark of a genuine seeker is 'hope'.

From the above it transpires that once the end is achieved, the means no longer make any difference. As Stace explains—if X has an alleged mystical experience P_1 and Y has one P_2, and if the phenomenological characteristics of P_1 and P_2 resemble each other, the two experiences cannot be regarded as being of two different kinds—for example, it cannot be said that one is a 'genuine' mystical experience while the other is not—merely because they arise from dissimilar causal conditions. This principle says that *if* the phenomenological descriptions of the two experiences are indistinguishable, so far as can be ascertained, it cannot be denied that if one is a genuine mystical experience the other is also.[42] From our study it seems that religious experiences and drug-induced experiences have symptomatic similarity in their overt manifestation and this tempts us to deduce that drugs can effectively facilitate religious experiences even though drugs may be placed in the group of 'catalytic agents'.

Therefore, the end, being the important thing, once reached does not leave any room for according merit or demerit to different means. Any means that lead to the end is approvable provided no harm to self or other individuals results from it.

"Huxley, Leary, and Masters and Houston have all claimed that LSD and similar drugs cause chemical changes in the body closely akin to those produced by ascetic practices."[43] This fact would explain how and why drugs may produce similar results as ascetic practices. When the Yogic practices and other techniques of self-mortification transform the body chemistry such as to usher in religious experiences, drugs too may be credited with this capacity because drugs have been proved to alter the physico-mental being in similar direction as the former.

So far, a distinction between three classes of drug users has been pointed out and our discussion is restricted to the context of the third class—those who are genuine aspirants of religious experiences. However, despite the scrutiny of drugs as religious stimulants, we are aware of the host of questions awaiting answers ! All the questions will be automatically answered once it is understood that the religious efficacy of psychedelic drugs is much dependent on the 'set' and 'setting' in which the subject consumes the drug. Of greater importance is the 'set' because it happens to be the only determinant which decides the religious and non-religious content of drug induced experiences.

One time drug addict. Ravindra Singh, during the period of rehabilitation, assessed the drug-scene in India, and divided drug-users into the following groups —

1. Those who take drugs out of sheer curiosity and fancy for experiment.
2. Those who take drugs as a recreation—just for "kicks".
3. Those who go for drugs to overcome some emotional problem arising out of confusion about sex, loneliness, or other problems of growing up.
4. There are hashish or ganja smokers or opium eaters from low income social groups. There are cases where parents are perhaps themselves addicts, with neither the means nor inclination to do anything about it.
5. There are those who use drugs on account of some deep underlying personality problems.[44]

To all this, a stiff resistance has been offered by R.C. Zaehner himself, who refuses to concede that drug experiences can be religious. Huston Smith, on examination attributes three causes for Zaehner's rigidity —

1. Zaehner's mescaline experience was rather trivial.
2. According to him, the theistic kind of religious experiences cannot be induced by drug ingestion.
3. Being a Roman Catholic, for him, religious experiences are gifts of grace and irreducible to human control.

Zaehner indulged in experimenting with mescaline just to verify Huxley's statements about his own mescaline experiences. However, prior to partaking the experiment Zaehner was firmly convinced that drugs did not have religious importance.

For Zaehner this experiment was of vital importance as it would decide on evidential basis whether Huxley's thesis can be rejected—which in theory he had already rejected and only sought the practical evidence to assert his own thesis. In a way he was resisting and fighting the drug effects, instead of co-operating with them. Pahnke had taken care to eliminate this element of individual resistance, because he realised the implications.

Zaehner's second objection that drugs cannot induce mystical experiences of a theistic kind but only of the lower kind—natural and monistic—may be attacked from two perspectives. The heirarchy ascribed to three kinds of mysticism is questionable. Besides this, the well known peyote rituals of the Native American Church have been overlooked by him. "James Slatkin, an anthropologist, has noted that the Indians during these ceremonials "see visions which may be Christ Himself. Sometimes they hear the voice of the great Spirit. Sometimes they become aware of the presence of God and of those personal shortcomings which must be corrected if they are to do His will." (Slatkin .... had observed the Indians' rites and been a participant in them)."[45] It stands proved that personal beliefs and peculiarities determine the content of an experience.

Next we take up a scrutiny of the moralists' disapproval of drug provoked experiences. The objection raised by moralists is largely a moral one as their difficulty lies in ascribing equal status to experiences acquired by 'easy' and 'difficult' methods. The issue being a moral one, implies that the resulting mystical and corresponding brain states need not be different. For a clear explanation of this we will make use of the following :

α—Method I, easy

β—Method II, difficult

C—The Mystical State

A & B—The elements of personal or subjective conditions that affect the production of mystical state C

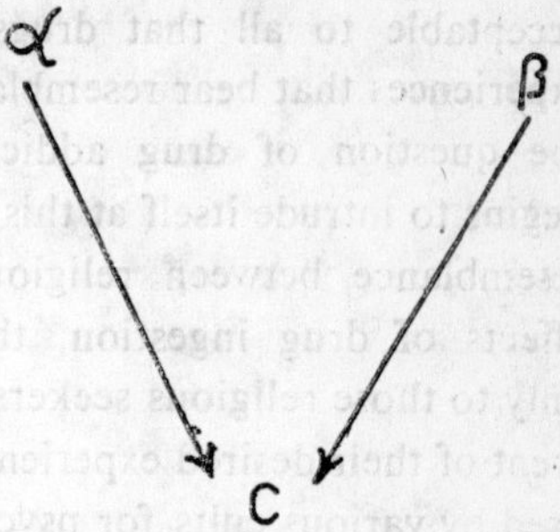

Consider two methods α and β, the former easy and the latter difficult. Both induce an identical brain state C, corresponding to certain mystical experiences. The subjective experiences, however, besides being of C, will also reflect the precedents of the methods α and β. From different conditions A and B, the different results of α and β will be located in the brain. Mystical experiences will correspond to a condition of the brain which incorporates (*i*) A and C, and (*ii*) B and C. The resulting state which incorporates A and C or B and C, may present itself as a unified experience. But one should be able to distinguish A and C or B and C. A and B reflect past experiences, expectations, degree of satisfaction, confirmation of existing beliefs, etc., and on the other hand C which reflects the mystical state itself.

"Minimally, one can say that ecstasy-producing drugs are the functional equivalents of the natural triggers of the ascetical practices which predispose a person towards an ecstatic interlude. They either clear away the distractions of ordinary life by helping or forcing us to "tune out", or they reveal to us beauties, goodness, and truths of the universe to which we had only dimly paid attention before."[46] It thus seems proved that the ordinary person could by the mere swallowing of a pill attain to those states of exalted consciousness which a lifetime of spiritual exercises does not guarantee to the most ardent and adept seeker of mystical enlightenment, the desired experience. In this way, humanity may avail itself of psychedelic drugs as a surrogate for religion, when they are adequately supported by favourable conditions.

Before concluding this chapter, some clarifications must be submitted for the sake of those accustomed to established ecclesiastical norms and practices. It would generally be acceptable to all that drugs enable individuals to have such experiences that bear resemblance to religious experience. But the question of drug addicts and genuine religious persons begins to intrude itself at this point. When referring to any resemblance between religious experiences and the ensuing effects of drug ingestion, the reference is not to addicts, but only to those religious seekers who turn to drugs for enhancement of their desired experience. It is well known that "drugs used by various cults for psychedelic effects were incorporated into the cults for explicit and implicit religious functions, and purposes. The effects of the drugs were and are reported to enhance religious experiences similar to those that occur in religious ceremonies or acts practiced among those who do not use drugs."[47] Further, "The most lofty aim of the cultic use of drugs is the pure delight in what drug users describe as a direct experience of God, ultimate reality, the spirits that preside over one's destiny, or whatever the worshipper may conceive as his object of worship."[48]

As a final word of warning we submit that though drugs are found to act as helping agents or catalytic agents in producing religious experiences we do not say that a *pure* drug-experience has religious import. Also, purification of mind or *antahkaran* is lacking in a *pure* drug experience, while it is a necessary prerequisite of genuine religious experiences. Another difference, and a more important one, is that religious experience is supposed to have some extra-mental referent. There is no such referent in drug-induced experiences. A genuine religious experience is subjective as well as objective and leaves some permanent mark on personality. It brings about the moral and spiritual transformation of psyche, not for a few moments or hours but, permanently, and *pure* drug-experiences do not leave any such impact on the psyche.

However, a person in pursuit of the experience may be fruitfully assisted by the moderate ingestion of drugs. So, a religion-oriented background is the essential requirement which coupled with drugs can result in religious experiences. This we have deduced from the following :

(a) A *pure* drug-experience does not necessarily have a religious referent. It will depend solely on the person's subjective framework.

(b) The three distinct purposes for which drugs are taken make our point clear that only those with religious mental tuning can expect to acquire religious experiences by drug intake.

REFERENCES

1. Frits Staal, *Exploring Mysticism*, Penguin Books, 1975. p. 148.
2. W.N. Pahnke, 'Drugs and Mysticism' in L.B. Brown (ed) *Psychology and Religion Selected Readings*, Middlesex, 1973. p. 301.
   "Whether the 'doors of perception' are opened by more traditional means or by LSD and other psychedelic drugs, the results is the same, and the result is, according to Leary, direct *religious* experience of the eternal being that pervades all that is ephemeral and transient."
   R.C. Zaehner, Drugs, *Mysticism, and Make Believe*, London, 1972. p.76.
3. G.A. Coe, *The Psychology of Religion*, Chicago, 1916. p. 265.
4. *Encyclopaedia Britannica*, Macropaedia, Volume XII, 15th Edition, 1974. p. 788.
5. Michael Argyle and Benjamin Beit-Hallahmi, *The Social Psychology of Religion*, London, 1975. p. 46.
6. W.H. Pahnke, 'Drugs and Mysticism, *op. cit.* p. 301.
7. Huston Smith, 'Do Drugs have Religious Import', *The Journal of Philosophy*, Vol. LXI, No. 18, October, 1964. p. 522. Quoted in 'Daru and Bhang', G.M. Carstairs, Quarterly Journal of the Study of Alcohol, 15, 1954, p. 229.

8. J.H. Leuba, *The Psychology of Religious Mysticism*, New York. 1925. p. 10.
   It has further been said in this regard that, "In India, various types of hemp derivatives, yielding visions. heightened concentration, and other psychedelic effects, have been in use for hundreds possibly thousands of years as aids to spiritual development and sources of occult power. Presently an estimate ninety percent of Indian holymen use hemp, often along with other drugs..."
   R.E.L. Masters & Jean Houston, *The Varieties of Psychedelic Experience*, London, 1966. p. 37.
9. Aurthur Guirdham, *Christ and Freud : A Study of Religious Experience and Observance*, London, 1959. pp. 35-36.
10. W.N. Pahnke, 'Drugs and Mysticism', *op. cit.* p. 314-315.
11. Swami Akhilananda, *Mental Health and Hindu Psychology*, London, 1952. p. 200.
12. Andrew M. Greelay, *Ecstasy A Way of Knowing*, New Jersey, 1974. p. 71.
    "The intense subjective pleasure and enjoyment of the experience for its own sake could lead to escapism and withdrawal from the world. An experience which is capable of changing motivation and values might cut the nerve of achievement. Widespread apathy toward productive work and acomplishment could cripple a society. Another possible danger might be suicide or prolonged psychosis in very unstable or depressed individuals who are not ready for the intense emotional discharge." W.N. Pahnke, 'Drugs and Mysticism', *op. cit.* p. 316.
13. *Encyclopaedia Britannica*, Macropaedia, Volume V, *op. cit.* p. 1042.
14. *Ibid*, Volume XIV, p. 1054.
15. Michael Argyle and Benjamin Beit-Hallahmi, *The Social Psychology of Religion, op. cit.* p. 47.
16. Ralph N. Haber, Aharon H. Fried, *An Introduction to Psychology*, New York, 1975. p. 434.
17. *Ibid.* pp. 435-436.
18. R.E.L. Masters & Jean Houston, *The Varieties of Psychedelic Experience, op. cit.* p. 5.
19. W. Donald Hudson, *A Philosophical Approach to Religion*, London, 1974. p. 300.

20. G.S. Spinks, *Psychology and Religion, An Introduction to Contemporary Views*, London, 1963. pp. 170-171.

21. Ayesha Kagal, 'The Story of the Drug Addict', *The Times of India*, Sunday Review, New Delhi, June 27, 1982. p. 1.

22. Ravindra Singh, *I Was A Drug Addict*, New Delhi, 1979.

23. Andrew M. Greelay, *Ecstasy a Way Of Knowing*, (Quoted from Arnold M. Ludwig, "Altered States Of Consciousness", *Arch. Gem. Psychiat.*, Vol. 15, 1966, pp. 227-234), *op. cit.* p. 42.

24. *Ibid.*

25. W.N. Pahnke, 'Drugs and Mysticism', L.B. Brown (ed.), *Psychology and Religion, Selected Readings, op. cit.* pp. 301-319.

26. Abraham H. Maslow, *Religions, Values and Peak Experiences*, New York, 1970. pp. 59-68.

27. Donald K. Cutler (ed.), *The World Year Book of Religion*, The Religious Situation Vol. 2, Alan W. Watts, 'Psychedelics and Religious Experience', London, 1969. p. 617.

28. Huston Smith, 'Do Drugs Have Religious Import ?' *The Journal of Philosophy*, Vol. LXI, No. 18, October 1, 1964. p. 522. Quoted from W.N. Pahnke, "Drugs and Mysticism : An Analysis of the Relationship Between Psychedelic Drugs and the Mystical Consciousness", a thesis presented to the Committee on Higher Degrees in History and Philosophy of Religion, Harvard University, June, 1963.

29. R.E.L. Masters & Jean Houston, *The Varieties of Psychedelic Experience, op. cit.* p. 254. Quoted from T. Leary, "The Religious Experience ; Its Production and Interpretation", *Psychedelic Review*, Vol. 1, No. 3 (1964), p. 325.

30. *Ibid.*, pp. 254-255. McGlothlin, 'Long Lasting Effects of LSD on Certain Attitudes in Normals'. Printed for private distribution by the RANA Corporation, May, 1962.

31. *Ibid.*, p. 255. K.S. Ditman, R. Hoyman and J.R.B., Whittlesay, and 'Nature Frequency of Claims Following L.S.D., *Journal of Nervous and Mental Disease*, Vol. 134, 1962, pp. 336-352.

32. *Ibid.*, p. 255. C. Savage, W.W. Harman, J. Fadiman and E. Savage, 'A Follow-up Note on the Psychedelic Experience' Paper delivered at a meeting of the American Psychiatric Association, St. Louis, Missouri, May, 1963.

33. *Ibid.*

34. *Ibid.*
35. Michel Argyle, *Religious Behaviour*, London, 1958. 115.
36. R.C. Zaehner, *Drugs, Mysticism and Make-Believe, op. cit.* p. 99.
37. Huston Smith, 'Do Drugs have Religious Import ?' *op. cit.* p. 520.
38. R.C. Zaehner, *Drugs, Mysticism and Make-Believe, op. cit*, p. 99.
39. *Ibid.* p. 83.
40. R.H. Thouless, *An Introduction to the Psychology of Religion*, 3rd. Edition, Cambridge, 1971. p. 49.
41. G.S. Spinks, *Psychology and Religion ; An Introduction to Contemporary Views, op. cit.* p. 173.
42 W.T. Stace, *Mysticism and Philosophy*, London, 1961. pp. 29-30.
43. R.C. Zaehner, *Drugs, Mysticism aud Make-Believe, op. cit.* p. 245.
44. Ravindra Singh, *I Was a Drug Addict, op, cit.* pp. 169-173.
45. R.E.L. Masters & Jean Houston, *Varieties of Psychedelic Experience, op. cit.* p. 257.
46. Andrew M. Greelay, *Ecstasy A Way of Knowing, op. cit.* p. 70.
47. *Encyclopaedia Britannica*, Macropaedia, Vol. XIV, *op. cit.* p. 201.
48. *Ibid.*

6

Music as a Religious Stimulant

Understanding Music in its Relation to the Psyche

After an exposition and analysis of psychedelic drugs as religious stimulants the focus of our inquiry shifts to the religious potentials of music. Certain sorts of phenomenon like nature and music apparently have special powers to trigger religious experiences. This relationship between music and religion has been subject to scrutiny in this chapter on the basis of the former's ability to create religious experience. It must be mentioned at the outset that the study will be restricted to Hindustani Classical Music, as it would surpass the scope of this chapter to deal with music in the broader sense—i.e., music of various ages and nations.

The discussion of Hindustani Classical Music as related to religious experiences in the light of the latter's genesis, brings some vital facts to the level of awareness. In spite of the fact that music had a prominent place in most religions, it has not received the kind of academic attention drawn by drugs in recent years. The discussion of Hindustani Classical Music may make clear how music, in general, can affect the being of an individual as it is closely connected to their psychic set up. Though this exposition is restricted to Hindustani Classical Music, it is not deemed to be the exclusive prerogative of Hindustani Classical Music alone to stimulate religious experiences. Rather, this study is a pointer towards the possibility of finding in all forms of music this inherent ability to rouse the religious in human beings. For instance, Carnatic Music of Southern India is also endowed with this capacity.

When we speak of music in this context, we must pay heed to the fact that the psychic and emotional bases of every kind of music may not be as well worked out as Hindustani Classical Music, nor have such a rich spiritual background as the latter. Even so, on the strength of its aesthetic appeal music can incite the religious in man.

Apart from these remarks abcut music in general, it is found that music has been put to use for specific purposes. And in such varied use, the emotional ability is operative. That is, specific musical patterns and combinations are found to elicit specific feelings and emotions, and this fact provides the basis which explains the flexibility of music. In the religious context we have church music and other forms of devotional music which are the specially created forms of music ingested with religious ability.

Evidently then, in attributing religious potentialities to music we are understanding music on two planes—pure music and devotional music. The latter is specially designed and composed, such that it stills the mind with awe and wonder, and rouses the religious feeling, which is but the analogue to formal religious experience. Our concern, here, is more with pure music, which, in our opinion, when rendered, understood and enjoyed in the true sense, produces religious experiences.

History reveals that since earliest times humankind has been aware of a greater power than itself, and amidst sorrow and sufferings the hope of peace and solace led one to pour out one's inmost self to this 'power'. This 'pouring out' is essentially praise, petition, adoration, devotion and so on, sometimes presented in musical form. Little wonder that religious ideas are detectable in Vedic songs. "Along with the sacrificial offerings lays and songs were sung in rhythm and music was considered part and parcel of the rites and sacrifices. The songs were accompanied by various musical instruments..."[1] The Vedic period marked a profuse culture of music which came to be known as *aranyegeya-gana* (also known as *rahasya-gana* or mystic songs) and *grameyagaya-gana* or secular songs. *Ganas* like *uha* and *uhya* are mystic ones, which accompanied the performances of Vedic rites and sacrifices.

In support of the affinity between music and religious experiences one needs only turn to religious discourses and sermons set to tune and rhythm, along with instrumental accompaniment. These testify the deep set capacity of music to still and direct the human mind and concentration, to the extent of ushering in moods and feelings (a state of mind) appropriate for religious experiences. Or else, why do religions like Christianity resort to church music, and Hinduism to *Bhajans*, *kirtans* (devotional songs) and narration and enactment of the epics, like Ramayana, in musical form ? The *Vaishnavites*, in particular, are greatly stimulated by rhythm, and the best example is provided by Chaitanya Mahaprabhu. The Krishna Consciousness people, who sing in the praise of Lord Krishna in tune and rhythm, and rhythmic gesticulations, follow the path shown by Chaitanya Mahaprabhu. Certainly there is a close relation between music and religious practice—one of dependence for expression by religions—as evinced by historical facts. It transpires, thus, that music is an art which probably elevates one to deep moral and religious levels, free from worldly frivolity and carnal desires.

One outcome of this association between music and religion is the creation of *bhakti sangeet* (devotional music). The element of *bhakti* is ingrained in such music wherein it is accorded the place of importance above the musical content. Contrary to this, Hindustani Classical Music has the potentials of working as a religious stimulant. It is aimed to explore how music in this form is also a means of God realisation without having religious qualities of *bhakti sangeet*. For a musician, music is the ultimate goal (*Nād Brahman*) whereas *bhakti sangeet* is a means of God realisation.

In the course of our discussion we will dwell upon the following issues—(*i*) relation of human emotions and Hindustani Classical Music, (*ii*) Hindustani Classical Music as a mode of expression, (*iii*) the factors involved in fully exploiting Hindustani Classical Music as a media of expression, and (*iv*) Hindustani Classical Music as a means of spiritual attainment. By an analysis of facts we aim to explore whether Hindustani Classical Music can rightly be deemed a media for union with, and experience of, the divine. While undertaking this task, we will also touch upon views that do not concede to music the powers of producing religious experiences (or any extra musical powers).

With the purpose of facilitating a firm grasp of the relation between Hindustani Classical Music and religious experiences, we begin with an elucidation of the principles on which it is based and nurtured. Music, as we know, is essentially certain tones in their harmonic and rhythmic relations. Though all music is the outcome of certain notes (*svaras*) in combination set to rhythm, the visualisation and presentation varies in time and tradition. Indian music, vocal or instrumental, is characteristically linear, i.e., sound follow one another expressing an emotional state and an aesthetic unity. "Different materials of music are systematically blended with one another, and they together create the form as well as beauty of music."[2] In other words, the finesse of Hindustani Classical Music, as we shall see, has grown out of emotional and human considerations.

In Hindustani Classical Music *rāgas* or modes are of prime significance—"*rāgas* are the prime things or lives (prāna)"[3]—because they constitute the framework on which the system of music stands. *Rāgas* possess certain characteristics and tempers. "A particular arrangement of sound characterized by musical notes and adorned by their varied movements having the quality to delight the heart of humans, came to be called a Raga."[4]

A *rāga* is a conglomeration of *svaras* (notes). This conglomeration is a definite, disciplined, well-balanced, planned and organised conglomeration, effusive of emotions, and not any arbitrary conglomeration of *svaras*. The *svaras* that make a *rāga* are its alphabet, and every *rāga* has its own alphabet of notes which it neither exceeds nor reduces. This is how a *rāga* becomes a special aesthetic scheme having an individuality. Broadly, then, a *rāga* is a melodic scheme characterised by a definite scale or notes, order of sequence of these notes, melodic phrases, pauses and stresses, and tonal graces. To this, a rider is invariably suffixed—a *rāga* must be pleasing, must have both emotional and aesthetic appeal. Thus, Hindustani Classical Music "has to adopt the melodic law and order of the chosen rāgı and then must make suitable arrangements and combinations of tone and rhythm so as to re-create the essence of the emotion associated with the chosen Rāgas."[5]

One of the features of a *rāga* is the ascent (*Arohana*) and descent (*Avaroha*) - i.e., the group of notes in sequence in ascent and descent that remain fixed. Based on these fixed groups of notes, all rendering is a manifestation through expansion and visualisation within that framework"...*rāgas* are born of the combinations and permutations of notes or tones and as they produce sweet and soft impressions (*sainskaras*) in the minds of man ... they are termed as *rāgas*..."[6] A *rāga* then is defined by certain indispensable factors like definite scale, arranged in particular order of sequence (*chalan*) in the ascent and descent, specific melodic phrases, apart from the techniques that beautify. Certain ways of presenting and tackling notes are of great significance in retaining the form and and temper of *rāgas*.

Every *rāga* has a dominant note (*vādi svara*) which is a note distinct from the others of the *rāga*, rendered more often and is always accentuated, having long pauses. The *rāga* is so developed that the *vādi-svara* stands out in striking prominence, as its distinguishing mark. Then comes the *samvādi svara* or a note which a relation of fourth or fifth to the *vādi*, providing a musical reflection or balance to it. Other notes of the *rāga* called *anuvādi* (assonant) and the notes alien to it are called *vivādi* (dissonant). Sometimes *vivādi svaras* are used for increasing the aesthetic and emotional appeal of a *rāga*, but care must be taken that such use does not alter or distort its temper, spirit or mood. So also in the case of *rāgas* identical in their *svara* content, utmost care has to be taken to preserve their individual character intact. Thus, *rāgas* made up of the same *svaras* are individually different by dint of the fact that each *rāga* has its own personality representing specific moods.

The emotional content of a *rāga* is brought out by considering *rāgas* with same *svaras*, e.g. *rāgas Bhoopali* and *Deskar* both have the same set of *svaras*, *Sa*, *Ri*, *Ga*, *Pa*, *Dha*. But the former moves such that *Ga* gets emphasis and the latter makes prominent *Dha*. Thus, the same scale forms different *rāgas* with distinct moods by this simple change in *vādi* For its emotional content a *rāga* has to be accented and intoned, which is possible by attacking and releasing the sounds in different ways — by gliding, surging, etc. "Technical skill is in fact not the art at all, but the condition that removes the impediments of clumsiness which might prevent the work of art from coming into being."[7] Usha Gupta, agreeing that notes in a *rāga* are instrumental in evoking feeling and atmosphere which produce the corresponding *rasa*, also indicates that the way notes are tackled determine the *rasa* that is produced.[8]

The strange phenomenon by which co-ordinated sounds have the power to evoke feelings or images, is accepted simply as a fact. Hindustani Classical Music has offered some basis on which is grounded the *svara*-emotion relation, though much of it may be scientifically questionable, not because it is invalid, but simply becaus science has not yet discovered the truths we have inherited. How is it possible for sounds in combination to express and evoke sentiments and moods ? As far as Hindustani Classical Music is concerned, we can understand this *svara*-emotion relationship once we take a look at the *rasa* theory and time theory, both having determined the emotional and aesthetic details of each *rāga* and its rendering.

"The aesthetics of music in India are embedded in her spiritual and philosophical traditions. The philosophy of music was also conceived and developed against the background of the Vedānta and the Upanishads. The Absolute is called the "Brahman"....Brahman is self-revealed as *Sat* (being), *Chiti* (consiousness), *Anand* (bliss)—the satchitananda. For the cardinal substance which is the basis for Ananda, the Upanishads use the word "Rasa" (essence). It is the attainment of *Rasa* that leads to blissfulness. Thus *Rasa* and *Ananda* are the fundamental principles of Indian aesthetics and music is part of it."[9] The ultimate state of bliss, '*Ananda*', attained after rendering or listening to a good piece of Hindustani Classical Music, is always defined as 'Brahmanand Sahadara' which means it is similar to the experience (*ananda*) one has on attaining Brahman or God.

The Indian concept of emotions associated with art appreciation, the theory of *rasa*, based on, what is sometimes termed,

Hindu is psychology. Like Jung, for whom the collective unconscious is a formative force in human life, this psychology also recognises the role of the unconscious and racial memory (instincts), for which it uses the comprehensive terms *vāsana* and *samskāra*. Though these forces constitute the core and motivation of human behaviour, they are not only racial memory but memory of the individual attained through innumerable cycles of births. The individual collective memory is not merely unconscious but also the guide to one's feelings and actions at all levels of psychic life. At birth an individual is under the influence of *vāsanas* and *samskāras* ; but one's gradual acquaintance with the environment results in ego development with its various modes of affective activities at the conscious plane—what is called emotional behaviour.

The factors that make up the constituents of emotional behaviour in Indian psychology are—

1. *Vibhāvas* (the determinants) : they are the causes of emotional responses—in modern terminology, the stimuli. *Vibhāvas* are of two categories—*Ālambana* (the person or object which acts as the stimulus) and *Uddeepana* (the situation which is the context for such behaviour).

2 *Anubhāvas* (the consequents) : these form the responsive reactions.

3. *Sattvabhāvas* (involuntary responses) : They are bodily signs of emotions in which are included both external and internal responses to *vibhāvas*.

4. *Bhāvas* : They are states of mind referred to as emotions. *Bhāvas* are considered to be of two kinds, (a) *Sthāyi Bhāvas* are the permanent emotions, and (b) *Sanchari Bhāvas* the transient moods. The essential difference between the two seems to be that the former are more lasting and common to all human beings, while the latter are more fleeting, moulded and charaterised by personal idiosyncracies.

"Though *rasa* itself is identified with emotion in most of the current literature, it is both emotional behaviour and more ; *it is an awareness of the totality of the emotional situation.* "The experience of *rasa* is absolute and is known only by empathy.... by entering into feeling that permanent motive." "Delightful or disgusting, exalted or lonely, obscene or refined, actual or imagery, there is no subject that cannot evoke *rasa* in man." While finally *rasa* is a contemplative state of mind, there are said to be nine *rasas* corresponding to nine emotional conditions: *sringara* (erotic), *hasya* (humorous), *karuṅa* (pathetic), *raudra* (furious), *veera* (valorous), *bhayanaka* (fearful), *beebhatsa* (odious), *adbhuta* (wonderous) and *santa* (peaceful)."[10]

Constituents of emotional behaviour (*bhāva, vibhāva, anubhāva, sattvabhāva*) are divisible into two categories – the first group (*vibhāvas – alambana* and *uddeepana*) providing details of the matter and situation to which the listener reacts, while the second group (*anubhāva, sattvabhāva, bhāva*) exposes the minute details (human and circumstantial) of the reactions of a listener. *Alambana*—the person or object acting as the stimulus—includes factors like the nature of tonal quality of a singer, whether the rendering is vocal or intrumental, if vocal, whether male or female voice, if instrumental, the rendering varies with different instruments, and the *tāla* (rhythm) and *laya* (tempo) to which a rendering is set. *Uddeepana*, on the other hand, covers the seasons and specific times during which particular *rāgas* are to be rendered. From the second set of factors we may derive the responses and the two—*sthāyi bhāvas* and *sanchāri bhāvas* – forms of impressions that are found in human beings. From this it becomes apparent how closely and systematically the Indian *rasa* theory and Hindustani Classical Music are linked, to the extent that the former explains the metaphysical aspect of the latter.

Thus far, the emphasis has been on the melodic aspect of Hindustani Classical Music, with little reference to its rhythmic component. *Rāgas* are rendered both free from rhythmic bindings (*ālāpa*) and in rhythm—rhythm being in tempo—slow (*vilambit*), medium-fast (*madhyalaya*) and fast (*drut*). These characteristic features of *tāla* contribute extensively in the expression and realization of the *rasa* of the *rāga*. "A *rāga* or *tala* is, therefore, the externalization of an inner consciousness. It is a concept or a mood unfolding itself."[11]

Some scholars are of the opinion that different *tālas* when endered in different tempos are evocative of different *rasas*. It is also true that every *tāla* (regardless of the tempo) does not match the spirit and mood of each *rāga*. A reference may be made here to to the example cited by Dr. Lalmani Misra. He has taken the *rāga Bhairav*—a *rāga* of the sombre and pathetic kind—and made a composition set to *keherwā tāla* in *drut laya*, which, he says, would produce erotic feelings. In the same way, use of techniques like variations in octave, pitch and rhythmic tempo, could make pathetic *rāgas* like *Bhairavi* and *Todi* evoke valour, while *rāgas Desh* and *Bageshree*, of the pathetic kind, could produce erotic feelings.[12] From this perspective a *tāla* is more of a catalyst in producing religious experiences.

It must be noted that the school or style of training is largely responsible for the inclination to produce a particular *rasa*. For example, the *Dhrupad* style cannot be associated with production of *sringār rasa*—rather it produces feelings of valour, peace, devotion and ferocity. On the other hand, the *Dhamār*, *Khayāl* and *Thumri* styles arouse the erotic feelings ; but again, for an effective rendering in these styles there are specific *rāgas* and *tālas*. *Tarānās* and *Tappās* are always rendered in the medium-fast and fast tempos, which evoke *adbhuta* (wonderous) *rasa*.

Further, every *svara* is a repository of some feeling or emotion, but the actual from or full expression of *rasa* can be had in the combination of the different *svaras*. Every *rāga* is associated with particular feelings because each *rāga* is created by the combination of specific *svaras*, and specific *svaras* are endowed with the inherent capacity to rouse specific feelings.[13]

This brings us to the end of our discussion of *ālambana* and we are now in a position to begin with *uddeepana*. Time and season are factors determining the emotional quality of *rāgas* – i.e., there are times and seasons appropriately suited for rendering particular *rāgas*. *Rāgas* are in subtle relation to seasons as compared to diurnal variations. The relation of *rāgas* with diurnal variations is more definite ; there is more order here. We have the monsoon *rāgas*, *Megh*, and all the forms of *Malhar*, and spring is marked by *Basant* and *Bahar*. The time season distribution has been made on the basis of human psychological considerations.

Though the musical qualities which determine the time for rendering *rāgas* have not been satisfactorily examined, Bhatkhande had attempted to establish some empirical rules for this psychological aspect.

Svaras and time are so associated that we are able to categorise the *rāgas* of Hindustani Classical Music into three – according to their time of rendering. Such categorisation is made on the basis of the use and the place of flat (*komal*) and sharp (*teevra*) notes.

1. These are the *sandhīprakash rāgas*, i.e., *rāgas* using *Re* flat and *Dha* flat. By *sandhīprakash* is understood that period of the day when night and day merge – i.e., in the morning a few hours prior to sunrise (*prabhatkāleen*) and the evening a few hours prior to sunset (*sayankāleen*). In this way, *sandhīprakāsh rāgas* are distinguishable into two. The *svara madhyama* (*Ma*) plays a very significant role in *sandhiprakāsh rāgas*. In the twilight watch or *prabhtkāleen sandhīprakāsh rāgas Ma* is natural while *Ma* sharp is used in *sandhīptakāsh*

rāgas of the evening. Thus, *Ma* natural is indicative of *prabhatkālaen sandhīprakāsh rāgas*, and *Ma* sharp indicates the *sayankāleen sandaīprakāash rāgas*.

2. *Rāgas* with *Re-Dha* natural belonging to the second category in the time cycle, follow the *sandhīprakāsh rāgas*. In this category of *rāgas* it is necessary that *Ga* natural be used. Yet one more identifying mark of these *rāgas* is the unfailing prominence of *Ma* natural i.e., flat, in them.

3. Next come the *rāgas* which use *Ga-Ni* flat. Their distinctive mark lies in their use of *Ga* flat regardless of whether *Re-Dha* are natural or flat.

According to Bhatkhande, the following generally determine the watch of the day for a *rāga* : (*i*) Tonal quality : whether the notes in the *rāga* are natural, flat or sharp. *Rāgas* with *Re* flat, *Ga* natural, *Dha* flat, *Ni* natural, are of twilight and dusk (*sandhīprakāsh*). Those *rāgas* using *Re* natural, *Ga* natural, *Dha* natural, *Ni* natural, belong to the first two watches of the day or night after twilight. *Rāgas* with *Ga* and *Ni* flat are rendered during the third and fourth watches of the day or night (12 noon to 6 p.m. or 12 midnight to 6 a.m.). In all this, the role of the *svara madhyama or Ma* cannot be over looked. With variation in the use of *Ma* natural, flat or sharp, the difference in *rāgas* become apparent. When *Ma* flat in the morning *rāga Bilawal* is replaced by *Ma* sharp it is transformed into *rāga Yaman* which is rendered at night. This is why it is said that at the instance of the *svara Ma*, day and night of the scholars in music is determined.[14] (*ii*) Tonal level : By this is meant the position of a note in the octave – the octave being divided into two sect ions – *angas* (the tetrachords). The lower tetrachord or *Poorvanga* is from *Sa* to *Pa*; the upper section or *Uttaranga* extends from

Ma to *Sa*. *Rāgas* with the *vādi* in the lower section are called *Poorva-rāgas*, and the *rāgas* with the *vādi* in the upper tetrachord are *Uttara-rāgas*. Conventionally, *Poorva-rāgas* are to be performed between midday and midnight, and *Uttara-rāgas* are limited to the period from midnight to midday. Use of *Ma* sharp indicates the passing of twilight *rāgas* into the later ones.

It is maintained that *rāgas* rendered in their stipulated time make it possible to understand and enjoy them effortlessly. To realise the significance of time, let us take the Tajmahal, a monument beautiful in itself, which provides aesthetic enjoyment to spectators. But, for an experience of its beauty in full glory, the Taj should be visited on a full moon night. Experience tells us that the impact of the full moon certainly adds to the beauty of the already beautiful Taj. So is the case with *rāgas* and time. A *rāga* is inherently beautiful but its personality unfolds in its actual form when rendered in the appropriate time. Thus, "The aesthetic potentialities of a Rāga are further extended by assigning to it particular combinations of the principal notes of the chosen scale, certain embellishments, ascending or descending, conjunct or disjunct forms of melodic motion, and the hour of the day appropriate to the mood or aesthetic stamp given by the Vādi and Samvādi of the Rāga."[15]

In spite of all this, lack of scientific evidence makes it difficult to accept a close knit relation between *rāgas* and time. There has been no systematic investigation into this very interesting psychological aspect of Hindustani Classical Music. Without any established results it is awkward to contest opinions that take the *rāga*-time relation as mere traditional conditioning. Morever, "how does one reconcile patterns of mixed *rāgas*, when such an admixture is of those melodies of different times of the day. As an instance there is a *rāga* called *Bhairav-Bahar*; this is a combination of *Bhairava* (early hours of the morning) and *Bahara* (late night). Now what could be the time for such a fused *rāga* ?"[16]

The Religious Ability of Hindustani Classical Music

Understanding the emotional and Psychological aspects of Hindustani Classical Music would remain incomplete if the role of the renderer (artist) and the listener is not taken into account. An artistic process may be broken up into the following : (*i*) the artist (*ii*) the work of art, (*iii*) the audience. "The artistic process begins with the artist who produces the work. This work is in turn presented to an audience, perhaps for their enjoyment .... Artist and audience are linked by work of art itself."[17] However, the credit for the original creation of *rāgas* and *bandishes* or *gats* must go to those who created them. But they have been relegated to the background as many of the *rāgas* themselves have undergone various transformations and nothing can be said with certainty about their original forms. But the fact remains that a piece of Hindustani Classical Music provides a link between the artist and listener and it is possible for the religious sentiment to be aroused in both.

With the work of art the act of artistic enjoyment begins. In Hindustani Classical music a *rāga* is the original creation. But *rāga* having been constructed does not mark the end of creativity. This is a peculiar feature of the type of music under scrutiny. Any rendering of a *rāga* involves creation, imagination, improvisation and application of technique, all of which assist in maintaining the mood and character of the *rāga* by adhering to its basic feature like *chalan*, *vādi*, etc. This explains why no two renderings of the same *rāga* are identical; each rendering is a manifestation of individual capacities of musical creation. Further, the glides, the turns and twists and rise and fall of music serve as a true index of the mood or subjective experience of the renderer.

The act of musical appreciation involves "the application of the practical activity of one mind to the practical activity of another mind, in such a way that they seem to coincide or become "as one", so causing the peculiar delight of the emphatic experience. It seems to be possible, however, for one mind genuinely to delight in the mind of another person without the response of the other."[18] The demand which a work of art makes upon the spectator for artistic appreciation and enjoyment requires that the spectator both submit to the object (i.e., neither pass it by nor critically reject it before it is understood) and cooperate with it. "Thus...the act of aesthetic appreciation is a re-creation of the artist's creative act."[19] A work of art is an expression of the artist's creative activity, born out of emotional states, which, if successful, can be communicated to the public or at least becomes capable of communication for those prepared to respond to it. The spectator must be empathetic in the fullest sense, such that one mind does not merely hold or passively receive the delight of another in it, but is active as is the other within at least the certain area, and there the two activities coincide.

Sound and its ingenious combinations are but the material and medium of expression by which the renderer represents various emotional states. "The innumerable varieties of emotion constitute the idea which, on being translated into sound, assumes the form of a musical composition."[20] By entering into an empathetic relation with the artist a listener is able to grasp the feel of a musical composition by a sort of re-expression of the original expression.

One is aware that the materials and sometime the very subject of an artistic creation is derived from or inspired by nature – art is an artificial and human made product. Different view have been offered by Aristotle and Plato regarding the creative process in art. According to the Aristotelean view, art is the imposition of form upon matter for which technique is required, i.e., the artist must have great skill and mastery of the art—the particular virtue of the artist lies in one's intellect. This suggests that the artist's control of the medium is at the service of one's intellectual vision, which, along with personal feelings, finds expression in a kind of artistic knowledge. Contrasted to the intellectual view of Aristotle, Plato visualises art as the expression of some inspiration. The artist creates because one is inspired and possessed, and one cannot really know wherefrom one's creation comes. The theory of creation through emotion is thus opposed to the doctrine of artistic creation as an imposition of idea upon matter.

These seemingly opposed views, however, operate in step in Hindustani Classical Music. Here, the artistic creation is both inspired and also an imposition of form upon matter. The *rāgas* are unchanging facts constituting matter, and artistic creation is a new way of visualising and presenting them. In this process, the artist, by inspiration, may impose form upon some material already existing. The creation of new *rāgas* may occur as an act of inspiration or as an intellectual process. Thus, in Hindustani Classical Music we cannot sharply distinguish the two – Aristotelcan and Platonic – views of artistic creation as both are operative at one and the same time.

The very act of artistic creation, especially the inspired ones, may be traced to some experience of closeness to divinity. An experience of oneness, unity, peace and tranquility often result in the spontaneous outflow of musical compositions. This spontaneous act the artist fails to explain because, at the time of creation he was possessed by, and was under the spell of some great inspiration. It is as if a whole world of fantasies is at the disposal of the artist transporting one into a state of trance when one creates. During the state of creativity the artist rises above all worldly affairs and knows no sorrow or happiness.

We may here refer to the circumstances that resulted in Tagore's *Balākā*, a masterpiece in literature. "I quote the poet's account of its composition. "I was in Allahabad, at my nephew's house. I used to have a very quiet time there, in the evening sitting on the terrace. One day, I felt the restlessness of the scene, and everything arouud me. It was a dark evening, and suddenly there came to me the feeling, there is flowing rushing all round me — that invisible rush of creation — the stars flecks of foam. I could feel the flow of that dark evening, with all the stars shining and that current of eternity touched me very deeply. I felt in the heart of it. So I began to write. And when I start writing, one thing leads to the next. That was the beginning of *Balākā* — the sweep of this impalpable and invisible stream." "[21]

Therefore, "The artistic-creative process is, quite simply, one in which the deeper level of "knowing" is permitted to become conscious and "do its own thing". Yet the power and ingenuity of the preconscious intellect is so great that it is not surprising that one frequently has the feeling of being "taken possession of" by some outside force .... When some of these levels become conscious one has the experience of being "taken possession of" by an outside power."[22] Further, "In many of the experiences .... especially .... the creative one, a tendency has appeared to identify oneself with the object, a tendency to mysticism. Through art, the poet or musician, at least during his creative periods participates in the beauty he envisages and tries to express "[23] This association between the artist or composer and religious experiences is easily detectable in Hindustani Classical Music. Swami Haridas created music from mystic sources. "More than anything else his music and language were inspired by the mystic experience of *bhaktī* ... "[24]

But, what of the listener ? Can the listener acquire religious experiences by wholehearted participation and entering into empathy with the artist and the rendering ? It is said that the listener's satisfaction is analogons to the satisfaction that comes from solving a complex intellectual problem or the enjoyment that comes from reading or writing a great poem. The listener, no doubt, holds a very important position in Hindustani Classical Music.

The role of listener and artist in aesthetic experience has received attention since the time Bharata wrote his *Nātya Shāstra*. Scholars have tried to develop the *rasa* theory by interpreting Bharata's text and trying to establish a view of the role of audience and artist. In the beginning *Bhaṭṭa Lollata* considered *rasa* as the permanent mental state (anger, fear, etc. , unfolded by the combined operation of the determinants, consequents and transitory mental states. For him *rasa* lies both in the represented personage and in the imitating actor, who feels the different *bhāvas* and *rasas* as though they belonged to him. *Śaṅkuka* disagrees with this view. *Rasa*, according to him, is an imitated mental state. The successful imitation by the actor is no doubt artificial, but is not realised to be so by the spectators who inferentially experience the mental state of the characters themselves. According to *Bhaṭṭa Nāyaka* the aesthetic state of consciousness is seen and lived independently of any individual interest–i.e., the experience of objects or persons appear in a generalised from. *Rasa* is not noetic in character, nor a perception, but an experience, a fruition (*bhoga*). "This fruition is characterized by a state of lysis (*laya*), of rest into our own consciousness, the pervasion of consciousness by bliss and light : it belongs to the same order as the enjoyment of the supreme *brahman*."[25]

Abhinavagupta's view is an admixture of the views of previous thinkers. The ultimate outcome of his efforts stressed on the importance of the spectator in realising *rasa* and the artist in evoking *rasa*. Ae arrived at this from the following :

1. *rasa* experience is possible in audience.

2. *sthāyi bhāvas* are permanently present in spectators in the from of *vāsanas* or *saṁskāras*.

3. manifestation of *sthāyi bhāvas* is made possible by means of generalised *vibhāvas—ālambana, uddeepana*.

4. to facilitate manifestation of *sthāyi bhāvas* in their pure form the mind (*citta*) of the spectator must be concentrated (*ekāgraha*) such that it is dead to all other sensations. *Rasa* experience under these conditions is like *brahmānanda*.

5. *rasa* experience is brought about by the co-ordination of whnt the artist is trying to express and the spectator's wholehearted effort to understand it.

In Hindustani Classical Music feelings or emotions are the substance of musical sounds, and the renderer (artist) tries to express the specific *rasa* and the music is tinged with affective life, and the listener is the one who shares in it. The *rāgas* are embodiments of emotional states. And a musician is expected to create this affective state and the audience to participate in this creation. "That is why, a listener, of really fine sensitivity is a *rasika* and a *sahridaya*—a person who can attain to a state of *rasa* and one who attains the condition of empathy."[26]

Hindustani Classical Music as understood so far, provides the scope for acquiring religious experiences by the renderer and the listener. This is probably because "Music cannot be understood entirely through the laws of physics and its impact is more than physical and biological. It has profound effect on the psyche and its spiritual value cannot be brushed aside. Great music induces the rapture of the body and the mind, and brings tears to the eyes....Music has been a means in our country for upward self transcending."[27] A piece of music is sensed or captured by a listener not mainly by his auditory perception but by his total personality. There is a tendency to submit our senses as they are attracted and enraptured by the magnetising powers of the emotion packed rendering of Hindustani Classical Music. A thorough comprehension and enjoyment of Hindustani Classical Music calls for sensitivity, feeling and an atmosphere free from tensions along with knowledge of the laws and principles of this particular form of music. No doubt it is considered an art with powers to lead one into a trance onto the shores of tranquility. A *rāga* may come within the purview of various *rasas.* The specific *rāga*-impact elicited by any musical form should induce sensitivity in the listener and create that specific *rasa* or feeling which inspired the orginal creation of that particular musical form.[28] The act of listening implies aesthetic appreciation, which is none other than re-creatlon of the artist's creative act. A piece of music produces in a listener sensuous-physical experiences, which, when raised from impressions to ideas by the activity of the listener's consciousness, are transmuted into a total imaginative experience, identical with that of the renderer. Thus, when the re-creation of the listener synthesises with the artist's original creation, does the listener imbibe the true meaning of the composition. A coincidence, then, of the artist's creative spirit and the litener's feeling and interpreting capacity is the point from which religious experiences may come to the latter.

For the artist one's listeners mean people who hear one expressing oneself and understand what one seeks to express. When a person expresses something that is in one's mind, and another hears and understands what is being expressed, the hearer who understands has that same thing in one's mind too. Hence, when someone hears and understands a piece of music, one is not only understanding the artist's expression of emotions, one is exposing emotions of one's own in the same manner as the artist's. However, there is a difference between the artist and the audience in so far as expressing emotions is concerned. Both do exactly the same thing—express a particular emotion in a particular manner—the artist is one who can solve for oneself the problem of expressing emotions whereas the audience can express them only when the artist has shown them how.

It follows that a listener too on fulfilling certain preconditions, like total involvement with the rendering, can benefit by it in acquiring religious experiences. This happens when what the imaginative experience of the listener makes out of the sensations received from a piece of music, is identical with the emotions that the artist attaches to the rendering. The question is – how can we be sure of such an identity ? There seems to be no possibility of an absolute assurance; the only assurance we can have is an empirical and relative assurance which is fortified as conversation proeeeds, and based on the fact that neither party seems to the other to be talking nonsense. In spite of this difficulty, it ought to be mentioned that a determined and intelligent audience will penetrate, far enough, into the complexities of musical form, but it need not, on that account, think it has extracted the meaning of the work.

The probability of synchronising the minds of artist and audience is simplified by the artist who works out one's compositions keeping in view the audience's limitations – this consideration makes the work more comprehensible. In this way, it becomes more sharing of emotions by the artist with the audience rather than working with the one track motive of expressing his personal emotions. If what one is trying to do is to express emotions that are not one's own merely, but one's audience's as well, one's success in doing this will be tested by one's audience's reception to what one has to say. On the other hand, an artist trying to arouse certain emotions in the audience resulting in refusal by the audience to respond favourbly to these emotions proves one's failure. Therefore, an artist who attaches importance to one's audience does so because one thinks that the emotions one has tried to express are not peculiar to oneself, but shared by the audience as well, and the mode of expression is as intelligible for one's audience as is for oneself. Such an attitude, in which a renderer invities the community to participate, offers it the scope for not just to passively accept one's work, but to repeat it over again for itself, thereby stepping up chances of its acquiring religious experiences.

How music acts upon the minds of people – Lee worked on this issue by acquiring data through circulation of questionnaires. His subjects included people with diverse opinions about music. He wanted to know whether music, if at all interest arousing, conveys any meaning beyond itself or remains just music. He categorised the answers into the following : (*i*) those in whose life music means a great deal, (*ii*) those for whom it means less, and (*iii*) those in whose life it means nothing worth reckoning. According to his finding, "half the persons interrogated did answer precisely that undoubtedly music *had* a meaning beyond itself, many adding that if it had not it would constitute only sensual enjoyment and be unworthy of their consideration .... that for these persons music did not remain *just music*, but became the bearer of messages, was further made certain by a good deal often unexpectedly explicit or eloquent writing which attempted to describe the things it dealt with and the more or less transcendental spheres whence that message of music seem to come."[29] The other half of the answerers either explicitly denied or disregarded the existence of any message and insisted that music had not necessarily any meaning beyond itself. They asserted that when really interested in music, they could think of nothing else but music.

Lee enquired whether they saw anything, landscapes, moving pictures or dramatic scenes; did the music strike them as expressing the emotions or life history of the composer or performer or their own ? Or else was such emotional expression merely recognised as existing in the music without referring to any particular questions. The affirmative answers showed that according to individual cases the message was principally of one of those kinds, visual or emotional, abstract or personal, but with many alterations and overlappings. Under all circumstances the message was always a message. A great majority of the respondents said that hearing music awakened in them an emotion *sui generis*, occasionally shot with human joy or sadness analogous to the exaltation and sense of suhlimity awakened by the beautiful in other arts of nature.

Lee based his enquiry on the working hypothesis that the emotional message drawn out from music is owing to predominance of emotional interest in an individual's inner life. Contrary to this belief, people with obvious emotional traits persisted to answer that music has no message for them, while rejected the *just music* alternative without revealing any particular emotional bias. For Lee, then, "many events suggest how the desire for music as something to be listened to has gradually evolved out of a primitive need for music, something stirs the inert, or releases pent-up emotions and to induce such day-dreams as restore and quicken the soul."[30]

Lee's question and answer experiment sharply differentiates between listening to music and hearing it, between a response to music such that implies intellectual and aesthetic activity of an intense and elevating kind, and a response consisting largely of emotional and imaginative day-dreams devoid of personal and practical preoccupations, full of refreshing visions and sentimental satisfaction. These two ways of impersonal contemplative happiness can benefit humankind.

The *rāgas* of Indian music are even deemed to be the living embodiments of the Divinity, and they act as mediums enabling direct apprehension of the Absolute. The Divine forms of the *rāgas* are contemplated and the artist's concentration and meditation upon them empowers them to commune their individual soul with the universal sound of the Divine from the *rāgas*. Humankind is seen reaching its heights of achievement and hence being godlike, when involved in the act of artistic creation. Music claims superiority over the other arts as it creates a consoling and transcending attitude of mind, which in turn purifies and cuts asunder the knots of the mind, resulting in the realisation of the absolute *shabda-brahman*. "Therefore music should be taken as a means to an end, as a spiritual *sādhanā* for the attainment of the God consciousness."[31]

The aim of the intuitive artists as well as the audience should be to construct the forms of the *rāgas*, which can be spiritualised and seen in their ecstatic vision. The divine vision is the be all and end all of life for all artists and music lovers. "By the artifiicial construction of harmony we can go beyond the phenomena of sound vibrations, and perceive not sounds but immaterial relations through which can be expressed realities of a spiritual nature. We can thus lift the veil by which matter hides from us all true realities."[32]

What is more important is to find a basis for the belief that music can sufficiently stir the human organism to result in its direct confrontation with religious experiences. For drawing out a basis we must turn to Yoga. Yoga has been the accepted method for the attainment of religious experiences. What precisely happens to the mind under the influence of Yogic practice? By controlled and restrained bodily activities and fixing of attention in one direction, the mind is emptied of all content. Feelings of satisfaction, oneness, elation, ensue. These states are attained by blotting out and suppressing all physical sensation – indeed, of the entire empirical content of concentration. It is *cittavṛttinirodha*—the holding or stilling of the mind stuff. This emptiness of mind is the ideal state in *sādhanā* and is the creative void (*śūnya avasthā*) ideal for creation. Yoga really stands for the arrest and negation of all mental modifications.

From this it seems legitimate to remark that Hindustani Classical Music affords objects, in the form *rāgas* for meditation (*sādhanā*). Yoga of Patanjali lays down some requirements for reaching the yogic end—*yama* (restraint), *niyama* (observances), *āsanā* (posture), *pranāyama* (breath-control), *pratyahāra* (withdrawal of the senses), *dhārṇā* (attention), *dhyāna* (meditation) and *samādhi* (concentration). These are the aids for purging the mind of all impurities, rendering it perfectly calm and serene, so that spiritual insight into reality is possible. Some of the steps taken by the mystic to attain to the stillness of contemplation are also adhered to by a *sādhaka* of Hindustani Classical Music, which yields comparable psychic states and uprushes of divine awareness.

It is observed that a true aspirant of Hindustani Classical Music follows more or less the eight aids for spiritual attainment as prescribed by Yoga. Discipline and training in the practice of Hindustani Classical Music requires a steady and calm mind, desirable posture, withdrawal of senses, fixing of the mind on the desired object and contemplation of the object. For a dedicated aspirant of Hindustani Classical Music, it is a form of Yoga—*nādopāsana*. Fulfilment of necessary requirements yields in achieving accuracy of *svara* which is realisation of *nāda brahman*. In Ranade's *Hindustani Music Its Physics And Aesthetics*, he makes a reference to breath-control in Indian music. He says, "proper breath-control secures poise, whereas resonance depends chiefly upon proficiency in immaculate articulation. The Indian musician does not of course prescribe any particular exercises in breathing, but takes care to see that the Alāpa exercises are so graded as to develop the power of sustaining the voice with the greatest possible care. He therefore makes it a point to avoid any jerks or shocks in voice-production and develops his capacity for sustaining the breath long enough by practisng the vocalisation to slow time."[33]

A dedicated perusal of Hindustani Classical Music results in integration of body and mind and depersonalization—total nullification of differences between the renderer and rendered. Yoga also is annihilation of all thought processes. "Even if we leave aside the role of music as a means of spiritual realization, the effect of musical chords and modes (*rāgas*) is much more far reaching than our ears are able, at first, to allow us to perceive. Our ear can apparently be satisfied by a very approximate accuracy. But a perfectly accurate interval does not react only on our ears, it produces a transformation in all the cells of our body, a slowing down or an acceleration in the movements of every molecule in ourselves and in the surrounding matter."[34] Pandit Vishnu Digambar Paluskar, towards the latter part of his life, found in music the medium for his search for God.[35] The contemporary Indian musician Ali Akbar Khan says, "Real music is not for the mind or for the body, but for the spirit which exists independently of each."[36]

We have highlighted the view that Hindustani Classical Music has emotional content and is instrumental in provoking religious experiences. But this is one side of the picture which necessitates a mention of opposed views. In the West, there are the heteronomists' and autonomists' views on the meaning of music. The latter is for music as a self - sufficient realm of organised sounds which mean nothing. The heteronomists opine that music functions to denote or connote specific ideas, things and emotions, and is consequently a language. "To say then, that music *is* a language, on this theory is to say that music represents or symbolizes some concept or thing to some listener."[37]

Hanslick, considered the staunchest autonomist, allows that music can represent the dynamic properties of specific feelings. Music connot represent love, but it can represent its dynamic element of movement—its waxing or waning character. When granting to music capacities to produce the dynamic properties of feelings, or the motion accompanying psychical action, according to its momentum, speed, slowness, strength, weakness, increasing and decreasing intensity, one vital concomitant of feeling is reproducecd. So, if music is suggestive of feelings, the rest, i.e., realisation or actual feeling, is left to the interpreting or grasping capabilities of the listener. Moreover, when different movements represent distinct feelings, why dispute the capacity of music to produce feelings and emotions ? It is beyond doubt that different movements rouse different feelings, but for this the listener must be *sahṛidaya.* Experiments conducted on plant life show clearly that plants respond to music.[38] If plant life can be affected by music, is it not superfluous to say that music cannot produce feelings enough to affect and transform human beings ? Seeing the attitude of Hanslick, Morris Weitz comments : "Hanslick, consequently, is a heteronomist in this limited sense : music is a language of the dynamic properties of emotions and can be said to mean—i.e., to represent or to denote—these properties."[39]

While agreeing with Hanslick that there is nothing extra-musical in music, Dr. K.C. Gangrade, (Retired) Professor and Head of the department, Instrumental Music, B.H.U., concedes to music the power of attracting attention on the strengh of its aesthetic appeal. It is his further contention that music has been misunderstood and loosely handled making it appear as if music is vested with the power to stimulate religious experiences. In the course of a discussion, with the author, on the question 'Is music a religious stimulant?' he opined that, "Music has the great quality of immediately attracting attention, immediately start giving pleasure. It does not require any other material except the 'Notes' for its manifestation—and as a corollary it follows that everything except notes is extraneous to music. For its creation music does not look to any worldly situation or phenomenon as model for representation or as source of musical inspiration.

There is nothing moral in Music nor anything immoral. There is nothing religious in music nor irreligious.

Music, because it is pure pleasure in itself, has throughout been coupled or tagged with almost everything—but then it gets degraded to subserve something else, lofty or mean, the result being a definite loss of varying amount of its innate beauty depending upon the type and magnitude of restriction it has to put up with."[40]

"Mysticism has no necessary connexion with the arts any more than it has with such praeternatural phenomena as clairvoyance and the like. It is true that music or painting or poetry may induce a natural mystical experience. In most cases, however, this will be *per accidens* and will depend on a variety of psychological causes that elude us .... "[41] Though Zaehner agrees that music is endowed with powers to cultivate religious experiences, he attributes this power to accidents, extra-musical factors or labels the experience as an inferior form of mysticism. In his *Mysticism Sacred and Profane*, he categorises mystic experiences into three—natural, pantheistic and monistic—placing them in heirarchical order of perfection. His view that music induces natural mystical experiences is denying music the capacity of inducing the highest or purest form of religious experiences. But the question is how Zaehner arrives at the heirarchical order of mystical experiences. There being no apparent justificatlon for such a heirarchy, the seers of Hindustani Classical Music are justified in granting greatest significance to their experiences attained through music.

It transpires, thus, that Hindustani Classical Music is an art which elevates human beings to a deep moral and religious plane, free from worldly frivolity and carnal dissipation. This dispossition is triggered by some sort of experience of beauty or pleasure which actually predisposes the person for the mystical event, making one temporarily passive, so that the divine communication may occur. But, does it eliminate the possibility of contesting the stand that Hindustani Classical Music has religious potentials ? No, it seems possible to say that music is merely an aesthetic form. The ultimate concern of a musician is to achieve the aesthetic heights of a rendering. However, in Hindustani Classical Music, it is possible both for the artist and the listener (who is *sahṛidaya*) to feel a composition reaching out beyond the aesthetic. For them, the aesthetic experience, or experience of beauty, stirs the feelings that suggest and ultimately merge with the spiritual.

It is not incorrect to say that whatever music may be, effectually it certainly does not restrict itself to the bounds of simple aesthetic expression. It may be meant to limit itself till there, but experience shows it to surpass its jurisdiction and rather evoke certain states of mind, sentiments and feelings. A musical work is said to result in feeling states in the person who contemplates it. Music or any *sādhanā* mark a shift in our ordinary reality orientations. A blurring of the boundaries between self and the rest of reality is commonly experienced by both the renderer and listener of music. The distinction of 'self' and 'I' ness are obliterated. The state of self obliteration is usually triggered by experiencing goodness, truth, beauty or pleasure, which actually predisposes the person for the mystical event by taking ones mind off ordinary events and making it temporarily passive but receptive only of the reality that rushes in. When overtaken by peace and joy, followed by uprushes of reality, the person feels as if one has been seized by something, and one gains insight, love and confidence.

A piece of music elicits and accentuates this quality of being a whole and of belonging to the large, all-inclusive whole which is the universe we live in. This fact, Dewey thinks, "is the explanation of that feeling of exquisite intelligibility and clarity we have in the presence of an object that is experienced with esthetic intensity. It explains also the religious feeling that accompanies intense esthetic perception. We are, as it were, introduced into a world beyond this world which is nevertheless the deeper reality of the world in which we live in our ordinary experiences". He goes on, "I can see no psychological ground for such properties of an experience save that, somehow, the work of art operates to deepen and to raise to great clarity that sense of an enveloping undefined whole that accompanies every normal experience. This whole is then felt as an expansion of ourselves."[42]

At this point speculations about the listener's ability to acquire religious experience comes into focus. Thus far the importance of listeners in the realm of Hindustani Classical Music has been emphasised and it has been observed how they by empathetic involvement with a rendering, benefit from it, by way of having religious experiences. But it is mentionworthy that it is not necessary for every listener to benefit in this way. The spiritual experiences generated in a listener by music, instrumental or vocal, are bound to be short-lived, emphemeral or temporary, excepting in some rare cases when such experiences are lasting phenomena. The reason for this is that spiritual experience in order to be lasting requires a change in the psychic structure of an individual. It requires a good deal of emotional training, discipline and curbing of passions. This is brought about by *sādhanā*, moral and spiritual training, under the guidance or an able teacher. In this way, the works of musicians may stimulate religious experiences in others, though it is equally true that the religious potentials of a rendering received in the form of aesthetic appeal, are much less intense than that in the case of the renderer.

In other words, the chances of acquiring religious experiences are better in the case of the artist than that of the listener. This difference is solely because the former undergoes rigorous training and becomes well versed with the language of music, whereas, the listener does not usually go through any formal training, but is drawn to music by dint of its melodious scheme and aesthetic appeal. For the latter, individual interest makes music comprehensive and that is how it becomes possible for a listener to get involved with a rendering and understand it. Only those listeners with sound knowledge of the rules and principles of Hindustani Classical Music can expect to attain spiritual upliftment from it Generally, music can serve as an aid in generating spiritual feelings and emotions in prayer, worship and festivities. It may be concluded that knowledge of the principles or methods of theory and practice are essential in the field of music, because so long the significance and value of music are not realised, it remains confined to the domain of phenomenal enjoyment. Without adequate knowledge one cannot go deep into the core of music to reach its ultimate goal—to draw out its spiritual content. It is therefore very important for the listener to be *sahṛidaya.*

Aesthetic experiences are often preludes to the religious experiences—the former may culminate in the latter. But, when analysed on their own standing, as separate experiences, they are found to be qualitativelydifferent also. Their first difference ensues from the distinctive nature of the referents. The ultimate referent of religious experience as normally reported, is some spaceless and timeless reality or states of existence. Secondly, the response of the subject also differs in some respects in the two cases, e.g., in religious experience the subject experiences union or communion with the Deity, etc., having an attitude of devotion and self-surrender towards it. Further, the impact of religious experience on personality and psyche is more intense than of any aesthetic experience. However, if the aesthetic experience is generated by a religious object or reality, the two experiences coalesce and their differences are no more. An aesthetic experience normally fades or pales out to become the higher experience of spirituality. We may refer here to Gnoli who contends that, "one must not forget that, while the mystical experience is perfect fullness, in which the knots of 'I' and 'mine' are already completely undone, in the aesthetic experience the process of undoing has only just begun."[43]

Aesthetic experience and religious experience though not similar experiences, are different by merit of variance in degree —it is possible for the former to lead to the latter kind of experience. In both kinds of experiences, a communication link has been set up between the outside world and the deeper processes of the personality, of which the conscious intellect is not normally aware. When this link between reality and the depths of the personality becomes explicit, the generalised reality orientation (the conscious intellect, the automatic structure of perception) is swept aside. This resultant phenomenon is unconcerned with the origin or content of the experience, and is, rather, the common feature of both religious and aesthetic experiences. "They (L.B. Bourque and K.W. Back) hypothesize that there are at least two varieties of ecstatic experience, the religious and aesthetic. In one report they document that 47% of their sample answered the aesthetic question affirmatively, 32% answered the religious question affirmatively, and 22% answered them both affirmatively. (L.B. Bourque and K.W. Back, "Social Correlates of transcendental experiences", *Sociological Analysis* XXX, Fall, 1969, pp. 151-163). They further hypothesize that the difference between these respondents is the language they have available to them for describing the experience. Most people refer to the aesthetic element ; however, those who had both the aesthetic and religious categories available to them chose the religious. This led researchers to conclude that the experiences were the same, the only difference being in the respondents and their abilities to describe what had happened."[44]

Many have left no distinction between the aesthetic and the religious. One respondent wrote to Pratt, " "I have experienced God's presence, and by that I mean that in a state of contemplation or under the influence of music or of superb natural scenery I have been lifted out of myself in a state of pure aesthetic joy".... "Thus for many a mystic the joy of nature and the joy of the Lord are hardly distinguishable, and neither one would be complete without the other."[45] Aesthetic experience is, thus, intimately connected with the mystical - it may be a profound relation in the sense that the aesthetic experience is the first step to the mystical experience. There is "some kind of bridge, however fragile, between the finite things we so dimly grasp through aesthesis and the object of the mystical experience. .."[46]

Even if we trace a link between aesthetic experience, pleasure and spiritual experience, it cannot be doubted that all the three are clearly subjective, as their content does not submit to generalisations and universalisations. There is no consistency in their objective content, hence, for all practical purposes, the experiences are primarily subjective. But calling them subjective does not mean that they are creations or projections of the mind. Subjective implies what is experienced ; the content, as it were, and also the conditions that lead to the experiences and their response that ensue. Hanslick rightly remarks—"To represent, to mean, to refer to anything specific by means of musical sounds .... is possible only if one could find a "causal nexus between these ideas and certain combinations of sound" ; but this connection is simply not forthcoming."[47] Trying to establish any causal nexus means generalisation, to which music and its effects do not give in—there is a lack of inevitableness, exclusiveness and uniformity which does not allow for any generalisations. Agreed, that this implies receding to the realm of subjectivity, but it cannot be denied the attention it demands. Individual experiences if considered seriously may reveal significant facts about religious experiences. Keeping both these aspects—the non-availability of generalised concepts and subjective experiences—in mind, we may suggest (only) that religious experiences are possible to acquire through the proper perusal of Hindustani Classical Music, as also by its aesthetic appreciation—i.e., both renderer and listener may acquire religious experiences through Hindustani Classical Music.

Though religious experiences may be an extension of aesthetic experiences it is clear that the former may be acquired through music. However, in order that music registers its best effects on the religious side, must be accompanied by favourable extra-musical factors. In other words, the 'set' and 'setting' are very important in this respect. Devotional music is most effective in the appropriate environment, time and circumstance. That is why such music is used in religious centres and gatherings where each individual comes with reverence and submission. In the case of pure music, however, the beauty of the music and its appeal are mainly instrumental in inviting the attention, to be followed by empathetic involvement, of the listener. Added to this, the listener must have some knowledge about the basic principles of music which will facilitate proper realisation of the beautiful in music, which happens to be the spring board to spiritual realisation. Thus, music cannot on its own bring to surface the religious in us – human participation and co-operation with a rendering are of equal importance. As mentioned already the listener must be *sahṛidaya* and an artist must be fully involved in the act of rendering so that the mood and temper of what is rendered may be well manifested. This will also ensure the artist's own attainment of religious experience.

Using music for religious purposes is to the advantage of humankind because it is no harmful habit for the mental set up of individuals. As it is an agent provoking religious experiences, it offers very good opportunities for studying them, and researchers can use it unrestrictively as a medium of experiment. So far drugs have been used to study religious experiences but, their side effects pose serious problems. These difficulties may be overcome by substituting music for drugs in the study of religious experiences. It will no longer involve the individual's exposure to personal or subjective risk of addiction resulting in psychophysical damage. However, for deriving the maximum out of Hindustani Classical Music, the experient must be trained in it so that what is fed does not appear to be Greek or Latin.

REFERENCES

1. Swami Prajñānanda, *Music of the Nations* (A Comparative Study), New Delhi, 1973. p. 38.
2. *Ibid.* p. 51.
3. *Ibid.* p. 54.
4. Sumati Mutatkar, 'The Sound of Hindustani Music', *Eve's Weekly*, Special Issue Indian Culture, Bombay, Vol. xxxi No. 3. August 13-19, 1977. p. 58.
5. G.H. Ranade, *Hindustani Music its Physics and Aesthetics*, Bombay, 1971. p. 53.
6. Swami Prajñananda, *Music of the Nations*, (A Comparative Study) *op. cit.* pp. 53-54.
7. A.W. Levi, *Varieties of Experience*, New York, 1957. p. 368.
8. Usha Gupta, *Hindi Ke Krishna Bhakti Kāleen Sahitya Mein Sangeet*, Published by Lucknow University. p. 218.
9. Sumati Mutatkar, 'The Sound of Hindustani Music', *Eve's Weekly*, *op. cit.* p. 31.
10. B.C. Deva, *An Introduction to Indian Music*, *op. cit.* p. 67.
11. *Ibid.* p. 71.

12. Lalmani Misra, *Bharatiya Sangeet Vadya*, New Delhi, 1976. pp. 191-192.

13. Usha Gupta, *Hindi Ke Krishna Bhakti Kāleen Sahitya Mein Sangeet*, *op. cit.* p. 217.

14. Basant, *Sangeet-Visharad*, Hathras, 1977. pp. 136-137.

15. G.H. Ranade, *Hindustani Classical Music, Its Physics and Aesthetics*, *op. cit.* p. 105.

16. B.C. Deva, *An Introduction to Indian Music*, *op. cit.* p. 71.

17. A.W. Levi, *Varieties of Experience*, *op. cit.* p. 336.

18. Geddes MacGregor, *Aesthetic Experience in Religion*, London, 1947. pp. 187-188.

19. *Encyclopaedia Britannica*, Macropaedia, Volume I, 15th. Edition, 1974. p. 166.

20. Eduard Hanslick, *The Beautiful in Music*, *op. cit.* p. 21.

21. *The Modern Review*, Volume XXXI, Calcutta, January-June 1922. p. 596.

22. Andrew M Greelay, *Ecstasy a Way of Knowing*, New Jersey, 1974. p. 54.

23. E.R. Goodenough, *The Psychology of Religious Experiences*, New York, 1965. p. 151.

24. B.C. Deva, *An Introduction to Indian Music*, *op. cit.* p. 87.

25. R. Gnoli, *The Aesthetic Experience According to Abhinavagupta*, Varanasi, 1968. pp. xxiii-xxiv.

26. B.C. Deva, *An Introduction to Indian Music*, *op. cit.* p. 72.

27 R.G.K., 'Splendours of Indian Music—Are they Vanishing? A Rasika's Alapana', *Illustrated Weekly of India*, Volume CI 40, November 9-15, 1980. p. 7.

28. Usha Gupta, *Hindi Ke Krishna Bhakti Kāleen Sahitya Mein Sangeet*, *op. cit.* p. 221.

29. Vernon Lee, 'Varieties of Musical Experience' (From *Music and its Lovers*, by V. Lee, E.P. Dutton & Co., Inc., New York, 1938. pp. 23-34) E. Vivas & M. Krieger (ed) *The Problems of Aesthetics a Book of Readings*, New York, 1966. p. 299.

30. *Ibid.* p. 304.

31. Swami Prajñānda, *Music of the Nations*, *op. cit.* p. 53.

32. A. Danielou, *Introduction to the Study of Musical Scales*, New Delhi, 1979. p. 9.

33. G.H. Ranade, *Hindustani Music its Physics and Aesthetics*, *op. cit.* p. 121.
34. A. Danielou, *Introduction to the Study of Musical Scales*, *op. cit.* p. 15.
35. A.I.R. Varanasi, programme commemorating the 109th. death anniversary of Pandit Vishnu Digambar Paluskar.
36. Robert E. Ornstein, *The Psychology of Consciousness*, London, 1975. p. 167.
37. Eduard Hanslick, *The Beautiful in Music, op. cit.* p. x.
38. Usha Gupta, *Hindi Ke Krishna Bhakti Kāleen Sahitya Mein Sangeet*, *op. cit.* p. 68.
39. Morris Weitz (ed.) in his introduction to Eduard Hanslick, *The Beautiful in Music*, *op. cit.* p. xii.
40. Extract from author's discussion with Dr. K.C. Gangrade.
41. R.C. Zaehner, *Mysticism Sacred and Profane*, New York, 1971. pp. 35-36.
42. John Dewey, 'Art as Wholeness', (From John Dewey, *Art as Experience*, New York, 1934. pp. 187-195) in A.W. Levi, *Varieties of Experience*, *op. cit.* pp. 401-407.
43. R. Gnoli, *The Aesthetic Experience According to Abhinavagupta*, *op. cit.* p. xxv.
44. Andrew M. Greelay, *Ecstasy a Way of Knowing*, *op. cit.* p. 85.
45. J.B. Pratt, *The Religious Consciousness : A Psychological Study*, New York, 1921. p. 356.
46. Geddes MacGregor, *Aesthetic Experience in Religion*, *op. cit.* pp. 132-133.
47. Eduard Hanslick, *The Beautiful in Music*, *op. cit.* p. x.

7

Religious Experience and Expression

The Problem Stated : Expressibility of Religious Experiences

The opening chapter of this work is an exposition of the characteristics of religious experiences, which are said to constitute their very essence. The previous chapters have been centred around an inquiry into the practical implications of some of these characteristics in the light of the genesis of religious experiences. Keeping within the same frame-work it is proopposed to examine 'ineffability' as a characteristic *vis-a-vis* the expressibility of religious experiences.

Religious experiences are held to be evasive of expression in intelligible terms. This view is well supported in spite of the sizeable literature of their inner life and experiences, produced by those who had religious experiences and also their desire to express themselves. "One of the best-known facts about mystics is that they feel that language is inadequate, or even wholly useless, as a means of communicating their experiences or their insights to others. They say that what they experience is unutterable or ineffable. They use language but then declare that the words they have used do not say what they want to say, and that all words as such are inherently incapable of doing so."[1] In spiritual experience the perfected seers attain a state of pure silence, and Buddha provides the best available example. This mystical silence is at once a mystery and a problem to the intellectual world. "Indeed, beyond all apparent sense perception, even beyond all thought that moves in mental images, they find, they say, a higher, more illuminating experience. This they declare to be ineffable."[2]

Before going into the details of this multi-faceted issue, the meaning of ineffability in the context of religious experiences must be discussed. For this it is necessary to explain the meaning of experience and language, as also to examine some specific views. Experience can be said to be "a human activity related to the purposes and interests of the one who experiences, and it was understood as an interpreted product of multiple transactions between man and the environment. Moreover, stress was placed on the social and funded character of experience in place of the older conception of experience as a private content confined to the mind of an individual. On this view, experience is not confined to its content but includes modes or dimensions that represent frames or meaning—social, moral, aesthetic, political, religious—through which whatever is encountered can be interpreted."[3] Therefore, experiences had through the senses are always socially shared, whereas experiences of the religious kind are allegedly not convertible into articulate from. If ever they are socially expressed, they are expressed to a certain extent and not completely.

The invariable concomitant of any experience is expression and religious experiences are no exception. "To accumulate, organize, and communicate experience is fundamental in the functions of the human mind ..."[4] In association with language religious experience finds its one outlet to humankind. "Once you seek to communicate your feeling to others (or even to make their meaning articulate to yourself), you have to employ language and general ideas, and the function of thought is to see that those general ideas in themselves true and not merely a reflection of your own subjective feeling."[5] For effective expression different symbolic and subtle terms are used. Putting it otherwise—language, being the only sensible mode of communication among individuals, plays a significant role in keeping alive this relation between society and those gifted individuals with special capabilities and insight.

Language is the system by which patterns of meaning are communicated through patterns of sounds or symbols—symbols here stand for written language—of experiences. Words and symbols constitute the basic units of language. (Later the representational value of symbols will be considered). Owing to its functional characteristic, language which is the medium of communication, is by its nature intersubjective rather than subjective. "Thus language is originally and essentially nothing but a system of signs or symbols, which denote real occurrences, or their echo in the human soul."[6]

After analysing the situation Paul R. Clifford advances an explanation for the aforesaid ineffability of religious experiences. He may be quoted thus—"However far the range of our knowledge, there is a realm beyond our understanding, and this will always remain so, simply because we are subject to earthly conditions which of themselves set the bounds to our comprehension. This is obvious, it may be said, once we realize that we are inextricably involved in the subject-object relationship, which makes it impossible to comprehend anything as it is in itself; and the knowing subject remains unknowable in himself for exactly the same reason."[7] A oneness of opinion regarding the ineffability of religious experiences is to be found in the traditions of East and West alike. Mystics and scholars from all over the globe have corroborated this either from experience or deep study of the problem. R.C. Zaehner is one according to whom language has no words appropriate for satisfactorily describing religious experiences.

The Upanishadic traditions propound the idea of inherent oneness of individual souls (*jīva*) and the universal soul (*Ātman*). Here again religious experience is self-discovery or self-realisation. In the Vedic traditions Brahman is taken to be the changeless, causeless *sat cit ānanda* (existence, truth, pure delight) basis of the universe. It is the absolute truth and everything ultimately converges at that point. The state of realisation of this vital oneness (*mokṣa, nirvāna*) is the highest any individual can attain. It is possible for the soul in an embodied state to reach this state, called *jīvanmukti.* Ignorance or *avidyā* impedes the attainment of this highest state. "Hinduism admits that the unquestionable content of the experience is a *that* about which nothing more can be said. The deeper and more intimate a spiritual experience, the more readily does it dispense with signs and symbols."[8]

Buddha taught the possibility of human attainment in *nirvāna* an experience or consciousness which was not generated by the activity of the sense. The fact that Buddha very often used to say (vide *Brahmajāla-sutta*) that he had a profound experience of things 'far beyond', which is 'comprehended only by the wise' and 'not grasped by mere logic', may be taken to mean that his extra-empirical experience can neither be logically proved with arguments nor be expressed in empirical terms and language. These grounds have laid the foundation for followers like the Mādhyamika to raise a philosophy of mysticism and transcendentalism out of the very silence of Buddha. The beginnings of the dialectic are traceable in the direct teachings of the Buddha. He pronounced some problems to be insoluble or inexpressible (*avyākṛta*). T.R.V. Murti contends that the Mādhyamika dialectic was anticipated in essentials by Buddha. The Mādhyamikas have but systematically formulated and drawn out their implications.

Regarding reality the Mādhyamikas maintain a negative stand, advancing a contention that all is void (*śūnya*). Their doctrine of *śūnyavāda* has been misunderstood to mean a total negation of reality as far as the universe is concerned. But their view is not really nihilistic in temper, nor does it deny all reality. For them, the apparent phenomenal world perceived by us is unreal. Behind this phenomenal world there is a reality which is not describable by any character, mental or non-mental, that we perceive. Being devoid of phenomenal characteristics it is called *śūnya*. Both Upanishadic traditions and Buddhism "speak of the ultimate as devoid of empirical determinations, as incomparable to anything we know ; silence is their most proper language."[9] The former's way of defining Brahman as 'neti neti' is what cannot be grasped by speech, thought or senses. Brahman is *nirdharmaka* and knowledge of it is *paramārthasatyā*. "Paramārtha Satya or Absolute Truth is the knowledge of the real as it is without any distortion (akṛtrimam vastu-rūpam). Categories of thought and points of view distort the real ... The paramārtha is the utter absence of the function of Reason (buddhi) which is therefore equated with saṁvṛti. The Absolute truth is beyond the scope of discursive thought, language and empirical activity ; and conversely, the object of these is saṁvṛti satya. It is said : "The paramārtha is in fact the unutterable (anabhitapya), the unthinkable, unteachable ,etc."[10]

According to Buddhism independence and non-dependence on anything else for its existence and origination are the criteria that mark the real. But everything that can be known is dependent on some condition. So, what seems real is not real, yet it cannot be rejected as unreal. *Śūnyatā* or voidness is the name for this indeterminable, indescribable real nature of things. The indescribable nature of things is deduced from the fact of their being dependent on other things or conditions—theory of dependent origination (*Pratītyasamutpāda*). "The Mādhymika theory of the phenomenal nature of the world follows from the doctrine of pratityasamutpāda, or dependent origination. A thing is a mass of dharmas following one another in unbroken succession .... Dharma alone exist, but they are doomed to destruction .... Nothing is by itself. Everything depends on something else. The Mādhyamikas do not dismiss all dharmas as well as their collections as unreal, though they look upon them as phenomenal and momentary."[11] *Pratītyasamutpāda* has received different interpretations at different times. According to the Mādhyamikas it "is not the principle of temporal sequence, but of the *essential dependence* of things on each other, i.e., the unreality of separate elements (naissvābhāvya, dharma-nairātmya). The entire Mādhyamika system is a re-interpretation of Pratityasamutpāda. It is now equated with Śūnyata—the empirical validity of entities and their ultimate unreality."[12]

The term *śūnya* is variously understood. It is in a sense nothingness, and in another sense, a permanent principle, transcendental and indefinable, immanent in all things. The former is true of the world of experience ; the latter of the metayphysical reality. *Śūnyavāda* may also be interpreted as a theory of relativity which declares that no thing, no phenomenon experienced, has a fixed, absolute, independent character of its *own* (*svabhāva*) and, therefore, no description of any phenomenon can be said to be unconditionally true. Moreover, Buddha's teachings regarding dependent origination, impermanence, etc., apply to the phenomenal world, things observed in ordinary experience. But the Mādhyamika contention is that these teachings of the Buddha are inapplicable when *nirvāṇa* is attained. The nature of *nirvāṇa*-experience which takes one beyond ordinary experience cannot be describ ed, it can only be suggested negatively with the help of words which describe our common experience. It transpires that the Mādhyamikas accept the existence of a transcendental reality (like the noumena of Kant) behind the phenomenal world that is free from change, conditionality and all other phenomenal characters. Nagarjuna, therefore, describes *nirvāṇa* with a series of negatives.

It may be noted that in its conception of twofold truth, denial of the phenomenal world, negative description of the transcendental and the concept of *nirvāṇa* as the attainment of unity with the transcendental self, the Mādhyamika approaches very close to Advaita Vedānta.

Silence as the only expression of the highest mystical state raises controversies. It is alleged that silence was a cloak for negative rationalism and also a device to escape those metaphysical questions to which adequate answers were not available. The so-called silence of Budha and his aversion to speculative theories cannot be adduccd as evidence of his not having a philosophy. In this context it becomes necessary to grasy the significance of mystical silence. "Words do not denote the absolute in any recognisable sense. The Absolute is incommensurable and inexpressible ; it is utterly transcendent to —Śunya."[13] When the real *puruṣa* in human beings transcends its finite form and name, to merge in the supreme *puruṣa*, one cannot but be silent. In such spiritual experience one's individuality, egoism, mind and senses are cast off. This is a state where the experiencer, the experience and the experienced merge to unite. A state without duality leaves no scope for words. Hence, the height of religious experience is pure silence. Buddha's "silence can only be interpreted as meaning the consciousness of the indescribable nature of the unconditioned reality."[14]

A common feature of the Eastern systems is the unanimous acceptance of the incapacity to define the nature of the absolute with the help of intellect, in rational terms. And religious experience according to these traditions is encounter with the absolute. So it is seen how the ultimate reality cannot be comprehended or described in words. Corroborating this Rudolf Otto says: "What is true of the strange nothingness of our mystics holds good equally of the śūnyam and the śūnyata, the void and the emptiness of the Buddhist mystics. The void of the Eastern mystic like the 'nothing' of the Western mystic is a numinous ideogram of the 'wholly other'. Nothing can be said of it since it is 'absolutely and intrinsically other than and opposite of everything that is and can be thought.' "[15]

The discussions and exposition so far show how the terms nirvāṇa, mokṣa, liberation, jivanmukti, self-realisation, god-realisation, Absolute, insight, unity, and so on, are very singificantly related to religious experiences. These terms all may be used in a slightly different but legitimate sense to characterise or represent the same things from different perspectives. Mokṣa, liberation, nirvāṇa, are actually the resultant of religious experience - the climax. Nirvāṇa is the negation of the empirical being bound by the law of karma or saṁsāra. It is an inexplicable state which can be attained even here and now by the complete destruction of thirst (*taṇhā*) and the defilement of mind. Likewise, self-realisation and god-realisation imply the cognitive aspect (*prajñā*) of the religious experience, when all doubt and misgivings are no more and the truth is revealed. What is known or experienced is the absolute and unity, and insight facilitates or is the special ability by dint of which such experiences are possible. These terms are used by different schools to bear the same meaning—it is only a variance of perspective and not content.

The ineffability of the experience, however, has no impact on the mystic's certainty of what one has experienced. The degree of certainty is directly proportionate to the intensity and duration of the experience. The noetic quality of the religious experience is responsible for the accompanying certitude of what has been experienced, though linguistic expression may be not be adequately patterned to carry and convey their content. Thus, the meaning of ineffability in the context of religious experiences is the problem of expression surfacing in the form of numerous inter-connected questions It is imperative to acquaint ourselves with some of these questions as raised by Stace in his *Mysticism and Philosophy*. He questions —"What is this difficulty about the use of language which the mystic feels ? Why can he not express himself in words ? And how is it that, if he cannot describe what he experiences, he nevertheless does write and speak adout it often with great eloquence and force ? What are his words actually describing if they are not describing his experiences and insights ? How do his words function ?"[16]

With these questions in focus Stace seeks to evaluate whether mystics and sometimes their critics are really justified in upholding the ineffable character of religious experiences. Is it true that religious experiences defy expression, articulation, translation or representation in terms of imagery or thoughts ? Is ineffability in the context of religious experiences absolute or partial ? In his opinion an examination of the major documents of the world's mystical literature will amply reveal that the alleged ineffability of mystical experience cannot be explained by any of the psychological principles which apply to our common everyday consciousness. If they are right in contending their special kind of consciousness to be such that it denies articulation in the terms of ordinary consciousness, thereby remaining 'un-understood', we must examine the rational possibilities that corroborate their stand.

Stace commences his analysis with a consideration of the Emotion Theory, according to which the difficulties in confining the content of the experience to words is attributable to the emotional aspect of religious experiences. The mystic experiences profound blessedness and joy ; sometimes in extreme cases, ecstasy and rapture are concomitants of the experience. So also are the feelings of awe and reverence – for what is sacred and holy in the experience. Emotions are known to be shadowy and elusive and less sharply outlined in to the conceptual structures of thought. Therefore, the depth of the mystic's emotions defy expression in words.

Though this theory advances a salient point, it is not the complete explanation for mystical ineffability, because observation testifies that religious experience is neither only emotion, nor chiefly emotional. It is also some logical difficulty and not merely emotional difficulty that hinders the mystic's free expression of the experience in intelligible words.

It has been held impossible to convey to a person without religious experience their nature or message. This impossibility of communicating a religious experience is likened to the impossibility of communicating the nature of colour to a blind man. The Spiritual Blindness theory holds the non-mystic to be spiritually blind, while the mystic who tries to convey one's experience has spiritual vision. This difference causes ineffability. In a way this theory is a predicament applicable to any kind of sensory or non-sensory experience. The fact that it applies equally to every kind of experience, which by and large are made articulate, makes this theory useless as an explanation for the ineffability of religious experience. Secondly, by terming non-mystics spiritually blind, the theory does not explain the eneffability of religious experience. It rather exposes some radical defect or incapacity of the human understanding mechanism. This explains ineffability as the non-mystic's failure to frame the idea which the mystic attempts to share.

According to these theories which attribute ineffability to the basic human incapability of conceptualisation, mystic experiences are inherently incapable of being conceptualised. The experience can be had directly but cannot be abstracted into concepts. Difficulty in comprehension is owing to the fact that the experience has in it no distinguishable items—the experience being unique cannot be expressed as concepts. Immensity and sublimity as part of the experience are also instrumental in making it ineffable. This granted would mean encouraging the view that ineflability is an exaggeration intended to express the emotions of the experiencer. On the one hand, then, the mystic does attempt to express oneself because one is observed to make use of language which appears to be descriptive of the experience. But, the question—How do the words of the mystic function if they are unable to describe their experience ?—remains to be answered. In this context the Dionysian Theory and the Theory of Metaphor needs to be looked into.

Dionysius "taught in an extreme form the view that no words apply to the mystical experience, or to God."[17] He sought to express God's transcendence of all words by the continual use of the words 'super' or 'supra'—e.g. God is neither existent nor non-existent, but he is super-existent. However, inconsistencies within itself renders this an unsatisfactory theory. It is not out of place to regard these theories to be versions of the view that the mystic's language is symbolic. Only, in Dionysius's theory the relation between symbol and the concept symbolised is causal, whereas the Metaphor Theory implies a relation of resemblances. The latter finds support in the fact that the language used by mystics often tends to be metaphorical. Rudolf Otto in his *The Idea of The Holy* has developed the metaphor theory impressively. Religious experience of what he calls the 'numinous' is incapable of conceptualisation. Even so, the religious person sees some resemblance, though faint, between a characteristic of the religious experience and some non-religious quality of something in the natural world, the name of which is used to metaphorically represent the corresponding religious quality.

This theory is also open to objections. It is possible for a metaphor to express some unconceptualisable feature of religious experience owing to some mutual resemblance. Wherever there is a resemblance a concept is possible. But use of metaphors according to this theory. is for something that cannot be conceptualised. Use of metaphors imply a preconceived awareness of what they symbolise. And this holds good for one who is to understand some metaphorical expression. Thus, the association between metaphor and the corresponding concept it resembles must be known *a priori* by both who expresses and understands. This alone can ensure any sensible and successful dialogue regarding religious experiences. "The metaphor can only operate to bring before his mind what he already knows or has experienced. It cannot produce a knowledge or experience which he did not have before."[18] When such prior knowledge is not there, we have what is usually called 'meaningless metaphor'. This theory like the Dionysian theory implies absolute ineffability, which further suggests all descriptive words to be metaphorical. Taking religious experiences to be inherently unconceptualisable, the metaphor theory has proved its failure in explaining their ineffability.

According to Stace the theory that the language of the mystic is symbolic has behind it an enormous weight of authority and tradition. To a certain extent the emotion theory is not without an element of truth. "It may well be that whoever experiences, at any rate for the first time, the blessedness or joy—the peace which passeth all understanding—which the mystical consciousness brings, may be rendered for the moment almost speechless by the depth of his emotion."[19] What mystics variously call the intellcct, understanding or reason, they agree, is incapable of handling religious experience. Language has been moulded by the intellect as a tool of expression for its special purposes. Thus, ineffability is partially the result of emotional block, while the mystic's difficulty with words is based on logical problems.

Stace's theory is founded on the question – "What is it about the understanding – other than the mere fact that it is the faculty of concepts—which produces in the mystic a sense of extreme difficulty with language, a feeling that the words which he actually uses never succeed in expressing what he wants to say ?[20] There are in reality two problems associated with the alleged ineffability, and the failure to distinguish between them has made them both insoluble. "First, there is the problem of whether words can be used *during* the mystical experience. Secondly, there is the problem whether they can be used *after* the experience when it is being *remembered*." Of this he opines that, "we cannot speak of it when we have it, but we can afterwards."[21] After the experience is over, the experiencer is back to the plane of ordinary sensory-intellectual consciousness, which enables one to contrast both the states of consciousness. A probable confusion between, and, inability to differentiate, the two separate situations has led to the theory that a remembered mystical experience cannot be spoken of except in symbolic language. Remembered experiences are expressed to a high degree of success and effectivity. In spite of this, a difficulty in using words to express religious experiences is felt, making the mystics call their experiences ineffable.

The question is then of explaining the mystic's difficulty with language. The mystic's language is both metaphorical and ambiguous, which is mainly because one feels some hindrance in using language to communicate one's experiences. The one possible reason for the human understanding's incompetancy in tackling religious experiences Stace attributes to the laws of logic which are characteristic rules of the operation of understanding. Mystics are observed to disobey the laws of logic. The laws of logic do not apply to religious experience. Owing to this, religious experiences are very often paradoxically presented. Use of paradoxes subject the experiencer to embarrassment because one is a logical being, except, maybe, in one's moments of 'vision'. This makes one blame language. "The explanation is ... that he confuses the paradoxicality of mystical experience with ineffability. But the basis of the psychological explanation lies of course in the logical difficulty of the paradoxes."[22] However, this theory formulated by Stace has been objected to as he admits that where there is no multiplicity there can be no concept and therefore no word. But his theory implies that certain words are literally descriptive of the experience and therefore must express concepts. To this he replies that concepts arise only when the experience is remembered and thc remembered experiences of different persons resemble each other, making it possible to classify them.

These theories scrutinised by Stace seem to stand for the various ways in which the issue may be viewed. As they have made way for further discussion we will undertake a systematic discussion in the sections to follow. The specific modes of expression, the kinds of expression, as also the factors that determine expression, shall all be subject to scrutiny in this chapter.

Desired And Spontaneous Expressions

"So far as the mystic's needs go toward the perpetuation of his experience, no exegesis, no apologetic is required. And all mystics I have known, in literature and in person, have tried to talk about their experience."[23] However, founded on their problems with expression, both mystics and their critics, or let us say, non-mystics, seem to be convinced that religious experiences are ineffable. The conviction that religious experiences are ineffable is not absolute and it is hoped the ensuing discussions will enlighten us in this regard.

Whatever may be remarked regarding the status of religious experiences is possible on the basis of what is evident about them from their diverse expressed forms. In other words, any attitude, whether appreciation or criticism, regarding the value, validity or cognitivity of religious experiences, rests on the observation and evaluation of sensible expression. Their reality is questionable because, unlike other experiences they are not always intelligibly expressed.

There are two points which are aimed at being highlighted and discussed within this frame of reference—religious experience and expression.

1. It is possible to classify the expressions of religious experiences into well-defined categories-(a) desired and intentional, and (b) spontaneous and unintentional.

2. The impacts of religious experiences as observed suggests that they are on occasions reasonably well expressed.

Expressions included in the first category are those used with the intention of conveying the content of an experience, whereas the second category implies the irresistible and impulsive consequence of the experiences—their natural concomitants as it were. The former kind of expressions are observed to result from the remembered part of the original experience. The actual experiencing "is not a thinking state ; it is merely a form of immediate experience. It cannot yield knowledge until it is correctly interpreted. Its true meaning must be brought to light by intellectual operations which are not mystical. In the mystic state one does not think, he does not cognize, he is simply immediately aware—of what ? Of the fullness of some concrete experience."[24] This feature of expression has been ackowledged by Radhakrishnan in his *An Idealist View of Life*. "So long as the experience lasts, the individual remains rapt in contemplation, but no man can rest in that state for all time.... Scarcely is the seer assured of the unique character of the experience than he is caught in the whirl of desire and temptation, discord and struggle. During the vision, its influence was so potent and overwhelming that he had neither the power nor the desire to analyse it. Now that the vision is no more, he strives to recapture it and retain in memory what cannot be realised in fact. The process of reflection starts. He cannot forget the blessed moments which have a weight for the rest of his life and give to his beliefs a power and a vividness."[25] During the experience thinking and rationalisation approach extinction and may disappear altogether.

As mentioned already, Stace, too has differentiated between the experiencing (during) and remembering (after) states of religious experiences. It is his contention that the latter state may be expressed in words.

The remembered experiences are urged by one's subjective desire to convert the experiences in articulate form. In this way, mystics are concerned with giving philosophical form or exposition to their experiences, however remote the expressions may seem to be from its original presentation. Expressions, when they are the medium for conveying and publicising religious experiences, evince an act of purposeful and rational utilisation. Expressions of this kind, then, are the outcome of rationalisation. The sequence is like this — there is an experience, but after the experience is over, the subject realises the value and and deeper meaning of what was experienced. One begins to get the feeling that humankind in general could be benefited by one's experience. This arouses in one a desire to pass on incoherent and comprehensive form the essence of the experience. This entire process from its earliest stage when the desire to express develops upto formal expression, is apparently a rational one. However, in order to be successful in fulfilling the desire for expression, the mystic must keep in mind comprehensibility and coherence in using the linguistic apparatus. This must obviously involve rationalisation.

Paul Schmidt's[26] division of religious language on the basis of their distinctive use seems to be equally applicable to the category of rationally expressed forms of religious experiences. He calls the two aspects evocative and invocative. Similarly, well thought out expressions of religious experiences are found to have twofold impact evocative and invocative. The evocative ones are such that they call forth attitudes or reactions from the listener. And a good example of this is the sermon or devotional songs which are expressions capable of evoking specific attitudes among listeners. As against this, the in-vocative ones secure attitudes in the person who experiencs. Prayer, meditation, confession, etc., are all those kinds of expression that invoke awareness of new attitudes, hopes and meaning.

Expressions that fall within the second class are concomitants of the intense experience, which can neither be resisted nor controlled and must be manifested. "The religious mystic experiences some unusual organic responses which accompany an alteration in the rhythm of his body. Its fluctuations are less marked and the tension of the organs also ceases, producing a greater harmony of the physical functions."[27] The details of some of the spontaneous expressions of religious experience have been looked at in Chapter I. Therein they were dealt with as responses to the experience. So, the responses are the spontaneous expressions—they come naturally, flow out as it were. Usually the spontaneous expressions appear on the subject's bodily or physical condition. In the realisation of the highest kind "The tension of normal life disappears, giving rise to inward peace, power and joy. The Greeks called it ataraxy ... the Hindu term '*Śānti*' or peace...is a positive feeling of calm and confidence, joy and strength in the midst of outward pain and defeat, loss and frustration. The experience is felt as profoundly satisfying where darkness is turned into light, sadness into joy, despair into assurance."[28] Such inward realisation is evident from the subject's calm, serene and composed disposition. No longer is the individual affected by adversities. "In the state of being merged with God he feels himself to be beyond good and evil. Whatever emotions he has felt as he moved towards his revelation, in the moments in which he actually experiences it he is endowed with an indescribable sense of peace and an unshakeable conviction of the reality of his experience."[29]

So, one form of the spontaneous expression springs from the deeply felt impact of the divine experience. They are externally visible in the form of total detachment, contentment, introversion, tolerance, etc.. Alongside these there is, in general, loss of control over speech, bodily movements and voluntary activities. The body is often recorded to sway in rhythmic motion. The impact is perceptible "at various levels of human development and manifolds itself in various attitudes and dispositions. It may, for instance, express itself in the feeling of dependence."[30]

We have seen how this particular expressive form ensues without pre-warning and as a cocomitant of religious experiences. In great art and emotional mysticism the impulse systems are modified and selected by one predominant thought or feeling. "In the familiar types of religious mysticism, imagination selects and orders the impulses and combines them into a stable poise .... Thus outbursts of song during states of rapture are common among religious mystics, with whom, as with poets, "the sense of musical delight" is evident. It is here that we find a similarity of mental experience in the poet and the religious mystic. But the religious mystic has a superior power of organizing experience. Like the true poet, the religious mystic is impersonal and detached, but his integration of the impulses is more profound. This engenders a stronger feeling of acceptance and certainty in the case of religion."[31]

Expressions which are manifestations of bodily and personality changes are not expected to have any cognitive import. They have no knowledge bearing capacity about any referent and therefore have no cognitive value except for the fact that they suggest the occurrence of a spiritual experience. They are the indicators from which it can be concluded that a subject is having some divine experience. As the external reaction of drugs and other intoxicants are similar, often genuine religious experiences are passed off as mental aberrations. In our discussion of drugs and music we have already tried to explain why this kind of controversy persists.

So far we have taken into account only one form of the spontaneous expressions. Apart from their psycho-physical manifestations, spontaneous expressions appear in the form of poetic, artistic or musical outbursts. It is a recorded fact that religious experiences activate the creative urge in human beings in which various sentiments like devotion, awe, reverence, submission, wonder, appeal, etc., are expressed. These expressions are founded on richness of feelings and mood, which sets the ball rolling and the devotional song, poem or other artistic creations ensue. In devotional songs we find a depiction of the rich variety of feelings and in their subtle and varying shades we find the emotional aspect of humankind in the heights of its supremacy. Religious experiences, then, manifest themselves as praise, adoration, acknowledgement of the supremacy and excellence of the divine, feeling of joy and peace. All of these are explicit in some artistic form, whether musical or poetic or even as paintings and sculptures.

The creative arts that result from religious experiences certainly leave an impact on other minds because all of these are publicly comprehensible expressions. In this way spontaneous expressions of religious experiences do partially carry some message for society.

After having dealt with the two kinds of expressions possible in the case of religious experiences we are led to the conclusion that non-mystics and lay persons all have some idea about the nature, content and message of religious experiences. Whatever we have said in the context of categorising the modes of expression rests on the contention that the lay person too is aware of the 'hows' and 'whys' of religious experience. This is because there are certain modes of expression that appear in specific codified patterns making them generally comprehensible. Dr. Radhakrishnan may be quoted here—"If experience is the soul of religion, expression is the body through which it fulfils its destiny."[32] Further, "If mystical experiences are removed from the realm of religion, this would of course affect the notion and interpretation of religion itself. For it is not open to doubt that such experiences, when interpreted as divine inspirations, become the sources of many religious ideas and phenomena, if not of entire religions."[33]

Religions resting on revealed truths, like *śrutis*, are the outcome of the highest kind of religious evperience bestowed upon individuals known as seers and prophets. Revelations give birth to the dogmas, norms, rituals, practices, etc., that are so much a part of religion. "Religious experience receives its initial, practical expression in the forming of the cult that provides an orderly framework for the worship of the religious object."[34] Also, "Most enduring, historical to religious traditions find their roots in the religious experience and insight of charismatic individuals who have served as founders; the sharing of their experience among disciples and followers leads to the establishment of a religious community."[35]

The social or public dimension of religious experience is a fact and it need not be visualised as opposed to comprehensible expression nor considered to be wholly an individual affair. The climax of the social dimension of expression is to be understood thus : "In all of the world religions, religious experience receives its most enduring expression in the form of social scriptures and the body of commentary through which they ore interpreted. Mythological and symbolical forms of expression are older than conceptual forms and systems of doctrines. Myth takes the form of a story and represents the imaginative use of materials drawn from sensible experience in order to express a religious meaning surpassing the sensible world....primary forms of religious experience — legends, parables, confession, lamentation, prophetic vision."[36]

Besides the mentioned forms of expression, those who have encountered religious experience also try to formulate specific paths which when traversed judiciously would bring God-realisation or self-realisation. Thus, based on their personal experience mystics are able to show us the path that leads to experiences of divinity. This is evinced by the age-old yogic practices, which start off with bringing under control the body, which eventually leads to control and elevation of the mind. So we see how dogmas, and the very formation of creeds and the prescribed path to God are available to us from religious experiences. All this then is the legitimate contribution of religious experiences. Therefore, it is justified to maintain that ordinary human beings have comprehended and benefited from religious experiences.

Symbols, Metaphors, Analogies and Paradoxes in Religious Expression

Religious experience is the direct apprehension of reality, and knowledge of it comes from the subjective reports of mystics. The descriptions of mystics are full of figures of speech, paradoxes, symbols, analogies and contradictions. Religious experience "tends to formulate itself...into contradictory statements simultaneously asserted as true. The language in which religious experience tends to express itself is not the language of mathematics or even of the empirical sciences but of parable and paradox which still claims to convey truth."[37] Religious experiences are so profound and indescribable as to be hostile to all attempts at ordinary expression. As a means of articulation mystics have fallen back upon symbols, paradoxes, analogies, etc.. The mystic defines the real paradoxically, as the indefinable. It is that which is all that the finite is not, that which refuses to be caught in the net of any predicate.

An experience outside the realm of space and time is indeed difficult to convert in comprehensible terms belonging to the realm of time and space. Even so, in the previous section it was seen how religious experiences have been partially understood. "We may well suppose that the mystic finds it impossible to state clearly in ordinary language what it is that he experiences about the fact which underlie the appearance of time and change and duration."[38]

Here, in this section, attention is focused upon expressions which are products of rational thinking. "Though the tools of sense and understanding cannot describe adequately, creative imagination with its symbols and suggestions may be of assistance. The profoundest wisdom of the past is transmitted to us in the form of myths and metaphors which do not have any fixed meaning and therefore can be interpreted as life requires. The seers...by letting their imagination work on experience, devised symbolic conceptions such as crossing the ocean of saṁsāra, ascending into heaven, meeting God face to face. Plato expressed his deepest convictions, which were incapable of proof in the language of poetry, saying, 'Not this perhaps, but something like this must be true.' If we insist on interpreting these symbols literally, difficulties arise. But if we go behind the words to the moods they symbolise, agreement is possible."[39]

So "man for an incalulable length of time has possessed a 'language, which enables him to express his sense of the 'sacred' in a way that no other language can – the medium of symbols and primordial imagery."[40] Those who have tried to speak of the Godhead have got themselves entangled in the use of paradoxical language. A good example is given in Meister Eckhart's attempt at conveying the meaning of God and Godhead. "I am the cause that God is God. God is gotten of the soul, he's Godhead of himself; before creatures were, God was not God, albeit he was Godhead which he got not from the soul.

When I subsisted in the Ground, in the bottom, in the river and found of Godhead, no one asked me where I was going; there was no one to ask me.

God in the Godhead is spiritual essence, so elemental that we can say nothing about it except that it is naught.... God in the Trinity is the living light in its radiant splendour."[41]

From what has been said above some interesting consequences ensue.

1. The mystic resorts to symbolic language; one uses terms of sense-perception to express what one regards completely supersensible.

2. Bold paradoxes are used, e.g., God is luminous darkness; the mystic's experience is a sweet pain, or a most active passivity.

3. It is sometimes argued with the non-mystical investigator of mysticism that none can know who lacks the experience out of which the mystic draws one's certainty.

What exactly is understood by symbols and paradoxes? Putting it very briefly, "A symbol is the expression of some theme that cannot be expressed in any other or better way."[42] Expanding this it may be put thus – "when a sound or gesture becomes so related to an event as to mean that event, it becomes a symbol and its meaning or significance is precisely that relation to that event."[43] An individual is gifted with the innate ability to arbitrarily attach specific meanings to things, sounds, words or acts, that are not intrinsic to the items themselves. "Much of the extraordinary imagery of religious language seems to be an attempt to express what taken literally is fantastic, contradictory and ridiculous, but which is an attempt to convey the sense of what transcends all statements."[44] "...the symbolic language of musticism is an large measure derived from the activity of the unconscious which, being strongly instinctual by nature, furnishes symbolical forms whic are emotionally suited to experiences of a sublimated libidinal kind."[45] Also "Archetypes are 'dominants, which, operating within the collective unconscious, 'create' those symbolic patterns by which man expresses his reactions to the numinous and the mysterious."[46] Paradoxical expression raises contradictions leaving the description unresolved and in doubt. To express the profoundness of the supreme reality some quality is asserted and the same denied.

The oft-used analogy is that of human love as this takes us closest to religious experiences. Love can become an experience deep and profound, a portal through which we enter the realm of the sublime. To have one's heart and mind absorbed in love seems to unveil the mystery of the universe—"love is the notion that comes closest to what is experienced in the mystical encounter with God."[47] "The unity the mystic grasps in his interlude of insight is best compared with the powerful, compassionate, absorbing unity of human love. Indeed, whatever it is out there that the mystic *sees* convinces him that it is the model of human love, which is but a pale reflection of it."[48]

The tendency to use human love, at times sexual love, as the analogy to express religious experiences is found in most religious traditions. "The Divine communion is sought to be translated in terms of human love. The Vaishnava cult of

Bengal and the Sufi cult among the Muhammadans, for instance, have developed a rich poetic literature embodying religious raptures which easily pass for human love lyrics."[49] In fact, "It has long been taken for granted in India that sexual union and mystical love in what appears to be a sexual form are the highest (because the most natural) manifestations of the ultimate reconciliation of all opposites in the One which is beyond all dualities—sexual union in the sphere of matter, mystical rapture in the sphere of spirit."[50]

Many mystics, particularly Christian ones, have compared the experience of love and the mystic episode to marriage. For an example we take into consideration a passage from Ruysbroeck's *Adornment of the Spiritual Marriage* : "When we have thus become seeing we can behold in joy the coming of the eternal Bridegroom .... And the coming of the Bridegroom is so swift that he is perpetually coming and dwelling within with unfathomable riches ; and ever coming anew in His Person, without interception, with such new brightness that it seems as though He had never come before. For His coming consists beyond time, in an eternal Now, which is ever received with new longings and new joy. Behold, the delight and the joy which this Bridegroom brings with Him in His coming are boundless and without measure, for they are Himself."[51] Therefore, the mystic experience which claims to be unique "is possible to convey in some measure its general character by the analogy of the relationship of human love and friendship. In this way I can get some notion of why the mystical experience is ineffable, even if I have no mystical experience myself, because I know what it is to have a friend and to be loved by my friend. Any one who has been in love with a person of the opposite sex and whose love has been reciprocated knows how different is this experience from the more immature experience of being 'in love with love'. Compared with such a sexual experience, all other sexual experience seems auto-erotic. The mystic is saying, in effect, that the relationship between his experience of God and what often passes for 'religious belief' is analogous to the relationship between 'real' human love that more or less auto-erotic experience that often passes for it."[52]

The frankness of the mystical writers in using language borrowed from sexual love can be very misleading. A reader is inclined to wonder whether the outpourings of the mystics are not attempts to express repressed or thwarted sexual love. In this way "It is sometimes claimed that these religious experiences are simply disguised sexual predicaments—warped sexual desire gives these experiences the structure they have. But sexual desires can hardly be a sufficient condition for the occurrence of the experience, for many people with very strong and even with very warped sexual urges do not have religious experiences. Even if they did, this would not establish that they were only about sex and not about God. Perhaps, since sex is a relatively permanent drive in human beings, God took this sure route to show His presence to man : to reinforce the idea of God, to stamp it in, so that everyone would have it."[53]

Freud pioneered the view that the sexual allusions in the writings of saints and mystics are so blatantly obvious that religious activity of this nature must be a fairly direct substitute for sexuality. It is obvious then, his "contention that religion is nothing but a sublimation of the sexual libido seems to receive support from the kind of language most frequently used in certain forms of mystical prayer and experience."[54] But manifestations of repression expressed themselves in a much more veiled form. The difficulty with Freud is that, "His attitude to religion was full of sweeping generalizations determined by an inability to grasp the difference between, on the one hand, religiosity and religious observance under the coercion of fear, and, on the other, revealed religion."[55]

Further, "The use of such language seems to be in the nature of a sublimated sexual activity. It is true that the control of the sexual impulses forms an essential part of the preparation for mystical prayer, and that it is possible that the use of erotic language may be an indirect means of satisfying these deflected sexual impuleses, but even so there are other explanations. For instance, the use of erotic language in religion may possibly have its origin in the ancient fertility rites associated with religion in agricultural and pastoral societies. But, perhaps, it is safer to suggest that the desire for and the sense of, mystical union find their most natural expression in erotic language just because there is no other kind of language sufficiently vivid and sufficiently instinctual to serve as the sublimated expression of man's sense of union with the Beloved.

The word 'love' in a mystical context implies a belief in the existence of a metaphorical reality with which it is 'natural' for the soul to seek union. In the same way as the sexual instinct implies the existence of human partner with whom physical satisfaction is possible, so mystical impulses imply the existence of a divine lover, and if this is so, the language of erotic union is natural in such contexts."[56] The fact is that the nomenclature of earthly love is the nearest available mechanism for the expression of its divine equivalent.

Before closing this section it must be pointed out that words may be used either to designate an object or evoke a sentiment. In the evocative, when it becomes sentimental, the word is used for the sake of the sentiment attached to the word rather than for the purposes of designating some object. In ordinary language the word ought properly to fade out of sight as soon as it has served its proper function of referring to some object. This distinction is important in the context of understanding the symbolic and paradoxical expressions of religious experiences.

The experient of a religious experience feels an inseparable compulsion to communicate and also to explain what happened to oneself. However, such communications are invariably accompanied by certain difficulties, partly because of the nature of the experience itself, and partly because of the limitations of human language—hence the existence of symbolism which enables the experient to express the logically inexpressible. We may refer here to Happold who has beautifully summed up and assessed the problem. "Our ordinary language has evolved to describe a common sense world of sense-experience. When it became necessary to express a view of the world as a space time continuum, a new language, a new symbol-system, had to be invented. But the Divine ground of all existence is not contained in a space-time continuum ; it is also out of space and time and different both in kind and degree from the worlds which the languages of commonsense experience and of mathematics and science have been framed to describe. As yet no 'spiritual calculus' is available, a language of symbol and paradox, which may be alien and incomprehensible to one not accustomed to it. The Divine Ground can be spoken of only in a language of polarity, a language of opposites, as non-personal and personal, supranatural and trans-natural, other and not other, without and within, transcendent and immanent, as Eternal Rest yet evolving activity."[57]

This being the state of affairs, the mystic's account of his experience is not always well received by others. Rather, they are misunderstood. However, on closer examination their significance is realised. Andrew M. Greelay is one who initially paid no heed to what mystics said but later came to understand them. "I will admit that my own tendency was to dismiss the language of mysticism as highflown rhetoric, a rhetoric that became dull with constant repetition. "Love is fine", I said to myself, "but that seems to be all those people can talk abo it." It was only when I met some real, live mystics and became convinced that we must take them seriously indeed and listen quite carefully to what they say that I came to understand that their rhetoric was not an exaggeration but rather an understatement of what they had experienced."[58]

The various points discussed above lead to the conclusion that "what can be handed on to others is not the vision itself, but the inadequate symbols in which the seer tries to represent what he has seen and to preserve it in his memory. Language was not meant for such purposes, and contemplatives sometimes feel that there is a kind of profanation in speaking of things which 'it is not lawful for man to utter'. It is difficult to communicate such experiences to those who have never known anything of the kind themselves. But we may listen to them with the same humility and confidence that we show to great poets and musicians. We never think of questioning their good faith."[59]

Some Reflections

We have seen how religious experience makes the experient feel an inescapable compulsion to communicate and also to explain what one went through. Such endeavours at communication are confronted by certain difficulties—on the one hand, because of the very nature of the experience, and on the other, because of the limitations of human language. These difficulties are in turn responsible for the existence of symbolism, which enables one to express one's spiritual experience. Also, desired expressions of religious experiences are the product of ratiocination, based on the objective of conveying the content of what was experienced. The fact that sometimes expressions are deliberate and desired, for which symbols and figurative language is used, leads us to conclude that certain factors are actively involved in any expression of religious experiences.

"Something is directly experienced but it is unconsciously interpreted in the terms of the tradition in which the individual is trained. The frame of reference which each individual adopts is determined by heredity and culture. Again, there is no such thing as pure experience, raw and undigested. It is always mixed up with layers of interpretation. The alleged immediate datum is psychologically mediated."[60] Religious experiences are described in terms of the experient's personal setting—one's concerns, interests, attitudes, feelings, capabilities, traditional, cultural and social background as also one's faith and belief. The mystical expressions are coloured by the teachings received by the mystic—every religion confirms itself through its mystics.

In this way "if we, compare and contrast the statements made by religious mystics of various times, races, and religions, we find a common nucleus combined with very great differences of detail. Of course the interpretations which they have put on their experiences are much more varied than the experiences themselves. It is obvious that the interpretations will depend in a large measure on the traditional religious beliefs in which various mystics have been brought up."[61] The apparent differences in the experience of different mystics is only a difference on the thought level and not in the essence of the experience. Although the experience in content is the same among all, there is variety in their account of the experience. This difference should be ascribed to the difference in the medium adopted by them in conveying the experience. Descending from the spiritual heights, the mystics convey their experiences in terms and forms typical of their cultural and religious heritage. It is striking how "Commitment is an important feature of religious language ..."[62]

The account of a Christian mystic would be coloured and clothed by the concepts and terminology of Western culture and Christian religion. The presentation of a Hindu mystic would be tainted by the peculiarities of Hindu mythology and culture. For example, the Vaishṇava speaks of the cowherd, the Brindāvan and the river Yamunā. "Where we are told that the souls have felt in their lives the redeeming power of Kṛṣṇa or Buddha, Jesus or Mohammad, we must distinguish the immediate experience or intuition which is mixed up with it. St. Theresa tells us that after her experience she learned to understand the Trinity. Surely she would not have recognized the revelation as that of the Trinity if she had not already known something of the Trinity."[63]

Interpretation and influence of psychical, cultural and religious factors holds good in the case of revelations also. The diversity of revelations Dr. R.S. Misra attributes to the inherent "existential situation of man."[64] In every revelation of Reality it is an individual who receives it or who perceives it. And an individual not only *receives* it but also *shapes* it. One also contributes something to it. One makes one's own response to it. And in this process the original experience of Reality undergoes some sort of modification. One is endowed with a particular psychic structure and one is conditioned by one's finitude. So when one has some experience or when one knows something, it is conditioned by one's psychic structure and one's finitude. It means that it is shaped and modified in accordance with the psychic structure of the individuals and the other finite conditions." Thus, every act of knowledge or experience involves an element of construction .... This is also true of the transcendental experience or revelations .... God is supposed to speak to them (*ṛṣis*, prophets, seers, etc.)* not in some transcendental language but in their own language, the language which they understand and speak. It really means that the message which is supposed to be communicated by God to his chosen men is received by them under the conditions of their own historical and finite existence and is interpreted accordingly."[65]

As pointed out by Dr. Misra, this is the first level of interpretation in the case of revelation—when the message is being received. Further conditioning and modification takes

* Bracket author's.

place when the experience is sought to be expressed in language. When put in language "the living experience of a transcendent Reality has to be formulated in concepts and words and through symbols, myths, etc., and is thus conditioned by them. The main difficulty involved in a religious language is that here the transcendental experiences have to be described and articulated through the words which are primarily meant for secular use."[66]

An interesting fact emerged when we cited the example of St. Theresa who said she would not have recognised her revelation to be that of the Trinity if she did not have prior knowlaedge of it. There seems to be certain preconceived ideas on the basis of which the experient recognises one's experience. Without them, no objective meaning could be attached to the qualitative aspect of the experience. Like in Plato the 'Idea' is something there and worldly experience complying with it are recognised accordingly. This preconceived notion of objects experienced helps in expression and interpretation.

The experiences are all perhaps the same—though there may be some differences owing to the intellectual interpretation they undergo. This clearly explains how "The Christian interprets the experiences in terms of a pre-existent Christian orthodoxy in which he has been reared, the Hindu in terms of more characteristically Indian ideas, and the Buddhist in terms of conceptions which may have come from pre-Aryan sources or were possible atleast in part freshly minted by the Buddha himself."[67] So, it must be understood that the difference between experience and interpretation is vital. Interpretation means anything which the conceptual intellect adds to the experience for the purpose of comprehensibility. What is added may be only classificatory concepts, or a logical inference or an explanatory hypothesis.

Buddha is probably the only exception as he is marked out as the one who admitted the reality of the spiritual experience, yet refused to interpret it as a revelation of anything beyond itself. He reports the experience rather than interpreting it, though, strictly speaking, there are no experiences which escape interpretation. It is only a question of degree. Buddha keeps closest to the given and is content with affirming that a deeper world of spirit penetrates the visible and tangible world.

It is no exaggeration to hold that religious experience is interpreted, by those who have it, in terms of the dogmas which constitute their prior set of beliefs and training. Moreover, different individual mystics with their individual outlooks and temperaments tend to emphasise different aspects of the experience. In this way the role of the different factors prove that :

1. these factors are eventually responsible for the form in which we lay persons can best comprehend religious experiences.
2. psychic and environmental factors are active in bringing about religious experiences as also in expressing them.

(We have seen in an earlier chapter how the psychic structure, psychological and environmental factors subject an individual to having religious encounters.)

In this chapter both the spontaneous and desired kinds of expressions have been discussed. Spontaneous expression available in the form of devotional works like those of Mirabai and Tyagaraja are undoubtedly of great value to human life. But this type of expression of religious experience does not tell much about the nature of the experience, or shall we say, the nature of 'what was experienced'. This is because devotional works of this kind are spontaneous outbursts of emotion and intense feeling in the form of praise and adoration accompanied by awe and wonder. The other spontaneous expressions as apparent on the experient's body and personality tell us merely that the person is undergoing some divine experience. Unlike either of these, the intentional expressions do carry something regarding the actual experience. This is possible because the intellectual expression follows the actual experience and is not any accompaniment. Religious doctrines, like philosophical doctrines, are the expressions of experiences already had. In this way, from the direct experiences of mystics and prophets we have before us the various religious doctrines, dogmas, rituals as also the methodologies that facilitate religious experiences. "No one can deny that the lives of some persons have been radically and permanently altered as a result of religious experience, and it is supposed that the consequences in human deeds of that altered life attest to the genuineness of the religious experience."[68]

In spite of this, a cloud of doubt hovers in the minds of many with regard to expressibility of religious experiences. These experiences are allegedly subjective and strictly private. But, based on what has been said above, it is our humble submission that the so-called privacy of religious experiences do not prohibit or even impede communications and understanding. Even "The so-called "public" world is only a construction out of the many private worlds. I can, subject to certain limitations, compare my private colour experiences with your report of yours, but so can I compare my experiences of fear or anguish, my thought habits or associations, my reasoning processes, with the reports which other people give of theirs."[69] Much of the rationalistic criticism of religious experiences and revelation is due to a confusion between symbolic statements and literal truths—what has been figuratively presented when taken literally is bound to be misleading.

Modern philosophy has reached the point when its assumed function is analysis and clarification. This of necessity implies its interest in language, expression and cognitivity. Pioneered by the Vienna Circle, the logical positivists established their foundational tenet thus—the sole criterion of the meaningfulness of any statement is the possibility of verifying it by sense-experience. As religious experiences—broadly speaking, metaphysics on the whole—do not succumb to empirical verification they are rejected as nonsensical by Ayer. Apart from the usual charges against Ayer for his attitude towards religious experiences, there are a few observations which we wish to present.

Ayer, in granting that "the mystic does not give us any information about the external world ; he merely gives us indirect information about the condition of his own mind",[70] has actually accepted the vital significance of religious experiences. Though subjective, the condition of the mystic's mind itself is sufficient to prove the intense impact of the experience. On the contrary, sense experiences in day to day life does not apparently have any such striking or permanent impact on an individual except occasionally.

Moreover, the cognitive value that the positivists are in search of and which according to them is the only test of meaningfulness and validity, seems rather limited and narrow—there being no justifieation for this. Like aesthetic, moral and musical experiences, religious experiences are based mainly on human emotions and feelings. Yet, they do not end there. They are impressive enough to induce permanent changes in the person. Ficticious or nonsensical experiences cannot possibly be instrumental in affecting such drastic changes as evinced in the lives of saints and mystics. It makes them immune to all provocations of sensory delight. The validity or truth of such experiences is known to all from the impact they have on the human mind. In such instances when change is affected as a result of direct experience or indirect report, the genuineness of the subject's discovery, in all probability, can be held to be empirically determined. We must note here

Ayer's charge that if the mystic had acquired any information from one's experience, one would be able to express it and also indicate in some way or other how the genuineness of one's discovery might be empirically determined. This charge has been overruled, we suppose, following the discussions above.

Taking for granted the language of science, particularly physics, to be the norm for all language, was probably another misleading assertion on the part of the logical positivists. Language cannot be limited to express the science alone—it is a means to communicate all types of experiences and the religious ones are no exception.

Ayer in *The Central Questions of Philosophy*, a book that came in the early seventies, has conceded—"You can say, if you please, that the information which they (religious experiences)* yield is incommunicable to those who are not equipped to receive it, but this also puts an end to the argument. So long there is no intelligible proposition before us, there is nothing to discuss."[71] Lack of linguistic apparatus or ability to comprehend cannot certainly be the mark of meaninglessness. A person with no prior knowledge of mathematics cannot indulge in any successful discussion on the subject, because the mathematician's statements are presupposed to be 'not-intelligible propositions'. This example does show us the actual sistuation that prevails in the case of religious experience—language—comprehensibility triangle. Another striking point that evolves from this example is that logical positivists have probably exerted too much criticism in the case of religious experiences, because mathematics is a subject dealing with abstract concepts that cannot be empirically verified—yet it passes unquestioned.

The test of truth stands fulfilled when the person concerned envisages reality and changes accordingly. It is no unheard

* Bracket auther's

of situation when an individual goes astray and finds no meaning in life or living. But one's whole approach to life is radically changed when 'love' enters one's life. This experience of 'love', failing to be empirically verified, should be deemed nonsensical and meaningless because, by dint of its non-verifiability it loses cognitive import. But, in our opinion, statements made with reference to any love experience cannot be meaningless or nonsensical. This should be granted at least on the subjective plane if not objectively, because the significance of that particular love experience may have no public significance. But 'God' and ' religion' are popular concepts, so statements in this context coming directty from those who have experienced receive greater approval and weightage than the experience of 'love'. So, we see how the value of these experiences is evident from their effects.

Religious language then "in spite of all its limitations and inadequacies, serves a necessary function inasmuch as it provides a ladder by which one can reach the Divine It is with this end in view that the mystics, saints and prophets all over the world have described their experiences of God and religious philosophers have tried to formulate definite concepts and views about him, though they fully realised the wisdom of maintaining complete silence ... Even Wittgenstein had to speak a lot in order to communicate the truth of silence."[72] Wittgenstein evinces a broader outlook in his analysis of language and its uses. His recognition of silence as the ultimate resort when sensible expression fails is commendable. In the *Tractatus* Wittgenstein argued that there is something which cannot be put into words but which nevertheless shows itself. "There are, indeed, things that cannot be put into words. They *make themselves manifest*. They are what is the mystical."[73] However, his ultimate conviction is "What we cannot speak about we must pass over in silence."[74] This goes so close to the professed silence in the Buddhist and Vedāntic traditions.

It is important to recognise that one could have either of two reasons for keeping silent. One reason is simply that one does not wish to talk nonsense and one will be doing so, if one talks about the mystical. The other is that one does not wish to trivialise the mystical by talking about it in not so comprehensible terms. Wittgenstein's reason seems to be the latter and not the former. And this is evinced by his statement (6·522—As quoted above) which is incompatible with the conclusion that he thought of the mystical as nonsensical. Unlike the positivists Wittgenstein displays a regard for the mystical and has no intention of dismissing it as meaningless or nonsense. Therefore, silence makes sense in the realm of religious experiences, but rejecting them on the basis of linguistic failure does not seem fair.

REFERENCES

1. W.T. Stace, *Mysticism and Philosophy*, London, 1961. p. 277.
2. G.A. Coe, *The Psychology of Religion*, Chicago, 1916. p. 269.
3. *Encyclopaedia Britannica*, Macropaedia, Volume XV, 15th. Edition, 1974. p. 648.
4. G.A. Coe, *The Psychology of Religion*, *op. cit.* p. 269.
5. D.M. Edwards, *The Philosophy of Religion*, Calcutta, 1968. p. 89.
6. Paul F. Schmidt, *Religious Knowledge*, The Free Press of Glencoe Inc., 1961. pp. 7-8.
7. Paul R. Clifford, *Interpreting Human Experience*, London, 1971. p. 18.
   Pratt is of the opinion that "the mystic is justified in his constantly reiterated assertion that his deepest religious experiences are indescribably – ineffable." J.B. Pratt, *The Religious Con-*

sciousness ; *A Psychological Study*, New York, 1921. pp. 345-346.

8. S. Radhakrishnan, *An Idealist View of Life*, Bombay, 1971. p. 79.

9. T.R.V. Murti, ***The Central Philosophy of Buddhism***, London, p. 19.

10. Ibid. p. 244.

"In the *Lankāvatāra-sūtrā* (*sagāthaka*, 167) it is stated that the real nature of objects cannot be ascertained by the intellect and cannot, therefore, be described." Datta and Chatterjee, *An Introduction to Indian Philosophy*, University of Calcutta, 1968. p. 144.

11. S. Radhakrishnan, *Indian Philosophy*, Vol. I, Bombay, 1977. pp. 646-647.

12. T.R.V. Murti, *The Central Philosophy of Buddhism*, *op. cit*. pp. 7-8.

13. *Ibid*. p. 231.

14. *Ibid*. p. 48.

15. Rudolf Otto, *The Idia of The Holy*, E.T., p. 30. Quoted from S. Radhakrishnan, *Indian Philosophy*, Vol. I, op. cit. p. 701.

16. W.T. Stace, *Mysticism and Philosophy*, *op. cit*. p. 278.

17. *Ibid*. p. 288.

18. *Ibid*. p. 293.

19. *Ibid*. p. 295.

20. *Ibid* p. 296.

21. *Ibid*. p. 297.

22. *Ibid*. p. 305.

23. Agehananda Bharati, *The Light at The Center*, New Delhi, 1977. p. 46.

24. H N. Wieman, *Religious Experience and Scientific Method*, London, 1971. p. 15.

25. S. Radhkrishnan, *An Idealist View of Life*, *op. cit*. p. 74.

26. Paul F. Schmidt, *Religious Knowledge*, *op. cit*. p. 86.

27. Radhakamal Mukherjee, *The Theory and Art of Mysticism*, Delhi, 1960. p. 26.

28. S. Radhakrishnan, *An Idealist Vew of Life*, *op. cit*. p. 73.

29. Arthur Guirdnam, *Christ and Freud A Study Of Religious Experience and Observance*, London, 1959. p. 34.
30. J.R. Puri, 'Experimental Approach to the Study Of Religion', Harbans Singh (ed.), *Approaches To the Study of Religion*, Seminar Papers, Punjabi University, Patiala. p. 108.
31. Radhakmal Mukherjee, *The Theory and Art of Mysticism*, *op. cit.* p. 39.
32. S. Radhakrishnan, *An Idealist View of Life*, *op. cit.* pp. 70-71.
33. Frits Staal, *Exploring Mysticism*, Penguin Books, London, 1975. p. 184.
34. *Encyclopaedia Britannica*, Macropaedia, Vol. XV, op. cit. p. 650.
35. *Encyclopaedia Britannica*, Micropaedia Vol. VIII, *op. cit*, p. 649.
36 *Ibid.* pp. 650-651.
37. Daya Krishna, 'Religious Experience, Language and Truth', Sidney Hook (ed.), *Religious Experience and Truth –A Symposium*, London, 1962. p. 234.
38. C.D. Broad, *Religion, Philosophy and Psychical Researeh, Selected Esays*, London, 1953. p. 196.
39. S. Radhakrishan, *An Idealist View of Life*, *op. cit.* p. 76.
40. G.S. Spinks, *Psychology and Religion*; *An Introduction to Contemporary Views*, London, 1963. p. 63.
41. F.C. Happold, *Religious Faith and Twentieth Century Man*, Penguin Books, 1966. p. 127.
42. G.S. Spinks, *Psychology and Religion*; *An Introduction to Contemporary Views*, *op. cit*, p. 66.
43. H.N. Wieman, *Religious Experience and Scientific Method*, *op. cit* p. 331.
44. Harold H. Tittus, Maylon H. Hepp, *The Range of Philosophy, Introductory Readings*, New Delhi, 1974. p. 311.
45. G.S. Spinks, *Psychology and Religion*; *An Introduction to Contemporary Views*, op. cit. p. 51.
46. *Ibid.* p. 63.
47. Geddes Macgregor, *Introduction To Religious Philosophy*, London, 1960. p. 181.

48. Andrew M. Greelay, *Ecstasy A Way of Knowing*, New Jersey, 1974. p. 74.

49. Radhakamal Mukherjee, *The Theory and Art of Mysticism*, *op. cit.* p. 121.

50. R.C. Zaehner, *Drugs, Mysticism and Make-Believe*, London, 1972. p. 66.

51. F.C. Happold, *Mysticism A Study and an Anthology*, Baltimore, 1963. p. 89.

52. Geddes Macgregor, *Introduction to Religious Philosophy*, *op.cit.* pp. 178-179.

53. Kai Nelson, *Reason and Practice — A Modern Introduction to Philosophy*, New York, 1971. p. 198.

54. G.S. Spinks, *Psychology and Religion; An Introduction to Contemporary Views*, *op. cit.* p. 125.

55. Arthur Guirdham, *Christ and Freud, A Study of Religious Experience and Observance*, *op. cit.* p. 31.

56. G.S. Spinks, *Psychology and Religion, An Introduction to Contemporary Views*, *op. cit.* p. 125.

57. F.C. Happold, *Religious Faith and Twentieth-Century Man*, *op. cit.* p. 124.

58. Andrew M. Greelay, *Ecstasy A Way of Knowing*, *op. cit.* p. 78.

59. W.R. Inge, *Mysticism in Religion*, London, 1969. p. 34.

60. S. Radhakrishnan, *An Idealist View of Life*, *op. cit.* p. 78.
V. Varadhachari is of the opinion that "The profound religious experiences are of course, psychologically mediated and the Divine reveals itself within the framework of the devotees innate prejudices." V. Varadachari, *Psychic Research Occultism and Yoga*, Madras, 1970. p. 93.

61. C.D. Broad, *Religion, Philosophy and Psychical Research Selected Essays*, *op. cit.* p. 193.

62. Paul F. Schmidt, *Religious Knowledge*, *op. cit.* p. 55.

63. S. Radhakrishnan, *An Idealist View of Life*, *op. cit.* p. 77.
Quoted from Evelyn Underhill, *Mysticism*, p. 132.

64. R.S. Misra, 'Religion, Reality and Truth' in the reprint: *Religious Language and Other Papers*, R.S. Misra, Dept. of Philosophy, B.H.U. p. 60.

65. *Ibid.*
66. *Ibid.* p. 63.
67. W.T. Stace, *Mysticism and Philosophy, op. cit.* p. 35.
68. Paul F. Schmidt, *Religious Knowledge, op. cit.* p. 55.
69. W.T. Stace, *Mysticism and Philosophy, op. cit.* p. 59.
70. A.J. Ayer, *Language, Truth and Logic*, Penguin Books, 1974. p. 157.
71. A.J. Ayer, *The Central Questions of Philosophy*, Penguin Books, 1977. p. 5.
72. R.S. Misra, 'Religion, Reality and Truth', from the reprint *Religious Language and Other Papers*, op. cit. p. 64.
73. Ludwig Wittgenstein, *Tractatus Logico-Philosophicus*, translated by D.F. Pears and B.F. McGuiness, London, 1961. p. 73 – 6.5 22.
74. *Ibid* p. 74 – 7.

Bibliography

Books

Akhilananda, Swami : *Mental Health and Hindu Psychology*, George Allen & Unwin Ltd., London, 1952.

Alexander, Franz : *Fundamentals of Psychoanalysis*, George Allen & Unwin Ltd., London, 1949.

Arapura, J.G. : *Radhakrishnan and Integral Experience*, Asia Publishing House, Calcutta, 1966.

Argyle, Michael and Beit-Hallahmi, Benjamin : *The Social Psychology of Religion*, Routledge & Kegan Paul, London, 1975.

——— : *Religious Behaviour*, Routledge & Kegan Paul, London, 1958.

Ayer, A.J. : *Language, Truth and Logic*, Penguin Books, Middlesex, England, 1974.

——— : *The Central Questions of Philosophy*, Penguin Books, Middlesex, England, 1977.

Baker, Canon A.E, (Collected and Edited with an Introduction) : *Religious Experience and other Essays and Address* William Temple, James Clarke and Co. Ltd., London, 1958.

Ballantyne, J.R. and Deva, Govind Sastri : *Yoga Sutras of Patanjali*, Susil Gupta (India) Private Ltd., Calcutta, Secood Edition : Fourth Reprint, 1963.

Bandopadhyaya, Shripada : *The Music of India*, D.B. Taraporevala Sons & Co. Private Ltd., Bombay, 1958.

Beardsworth, Timothy : *A Sense of Presence*, The Religious Experience Research Unit, Manchester College, Oxford, 1977.

Baillie, John : *The Sense of the Presence of God*, Gifford Lectures, 1961-62, Oxford University Press, London, 1962.

Behari, Bankey : *Sufis, Mystics and Yogis of India*, Bhavan's Book University, Bharatiya Vidya Bhavan, Bombay, 1971.

Bendit, Laurence J. : *Paranormal Cognition*, Its Place in *Human Psychology*, Faber and Faber, London. 1944.

Bennet, Charles A. : *A Philosophical Study of Mysticism*, An Essay (Reprinted with a preface by Rufus M. Jones), Yale University Press, New Haven, 1931.

Besant, Annie : *Mysticism*, Theosophical Publishing Society, London, 1914.

Bharati, Agehananda : *The Light at the Center, Context and Pretext of Modern Mysticism*, Bell Books, Vikas Publishing House Pvt. Ltd., New Delhi, 1977.

Bhatt, V.M. : *Yogic Powers and God Realisation*, Bhavan's Book University, Bharatiya Vidya Bhavan, Bombay, 1964.

Bhattacharya, H.M. : *Principles of Philosophy*, Published by the University of Calcutta, 1959.

Brain, Russell : *Nature of Experience* (The University of Durham, Riddell Memorial Lectures), Oxford University Press, London, 1959.

Broad, C.D. : *Religion, Philosophy and Psychical Research, Selected Essays*, Routledge & Kegan Paul Ltd., London, 1953.

Brown, L.B. (ed.) : *Psychology and Religion, Selected Readings*, Penguin Education, Middlesex, 1973.

Brown, Stuart C. : *Do Religious Claims Make Sense*? SCM Press Ltd., London, 1969.

Butler, Dom Cuthbert : *Western Mysticism* (2nd. Edition with Afterthoughts), Harper Torch Books, Harper & Row, Publishers, New York, 1966.

Caird, John : *An Introduction to the Philosophy of Religion*, Glasgow, Jackson, Son & Ltd., 1936.

Choudhary, Kamakhya Prasad Singh : *Modern Indian Mysticism*. Motilal Banarsidass, Delhi, 1981.

Clark, W.H. : *The Psychology of Religion*, The Macmillan Co., New York, 1958,

Clifford. Paul R. : *Interpreting Human Experience. A Philosophical Prologue to Theology*, Collins, St. Jamesis Place, London, 1971.

Coe, George Albert : *The Psychology of Religion*, The University of Chicago Press, Chicago. Illinois, 1916.

Cutler, Donald R. (ed.) : *The World Year Book of Religion, The Religious Situation*, Volume 2, Evans Brothers Limited, London. 1969.

Cooke, Deryck : *The Language of Music*, Oxford University Press, London, 1959.

Danielou, Alain , *Introduction to the Study of Musical Scales*, Oriental Books Reprint Corporation, New Delhi, 1979.

Dasgupta, Surendranath : *Yoga as Philosophy and Religion*, Motilal Banarasidass, Delhi, 1973.

——— : *Hindu Mysticism*, Motilal Banarasidass, Delhi, 1976.

Davies, John Booth : *The Psychology of Music*, Hutchinson of London, 1978.

Datta, D. and Chatterji, S. : *An Introduction to Indian Philosophy*, University of Calcutta, 1968.

Datta, Dhirendramohan : *The Chief Currents of Contemporary, Philosophy*. The University of Calutta, 1961.

Dewcy, John : *Experience and Nature*, The Paul Carus Lectures First Series. 1925, Oxford Book Company, New Delhi, 1965.

Diamond, Malcolm Luria : *Coutemporary Philosophy and Religious Thought An Introduction to the Philosophy of Religion*, McGraw—Hill Book Company, New York, 1974.

Deussen, Paul : *The System of the Vedānta*, Authorised translation by Charles Johnston, Motilal Banarasidass. Delhi, 1972.

Deva, B. Chaitanya : *An Iutroduction to Indian Music*, Publications Division, Ministry of Information and Broadcasting, Government of India, New Delhi, 1973.

Ducasse, C.J. : *A Philosophical Scrutiny of Religion*, The Ronald Press Company, New York, 1953.

Dunlap, Knignt : *Mysticism, Freudianism and Scientific Psychology*, St. Louis, C.V. Mosby Company, 1920.

Durant, Will : *The Story of Philosophy*, Ernest Benn, London, 1929.

Edwards, D. Miall : *The Philosophy of Religion*, Progressive Publishers, Calcutta, 1968.

Ewing, A.C. : *The Fundamental Questions of Philosophy*, Allied Publishers Privatc Limited, Bombay, 1967.

Eysenck, H.J. (ed.) : *Experiments with Drugs, Studies in the Relation between Personality, Learning Theory and Drug Action*, Pergamon Press, London, 1963.

Faber, Heije : *Psychology of Religion*, Translated by Margaret Kohl from the Dutch Cirkelen om een geheim, SCM Press Ltd., London, 1976.

Ferre, Frederick : *Basic Modern Philosophy of Religion*, George Allen & Unwin Ltd., London, 1968.

Flew, Aatony : *New Approach to Psychical Researcl*, Watts & Co., Johnson's Court, London, 1953

Flew, Antony and Macintyre, Alistair (ed.) : *New Essays in Philosophical Theology*, SCM Press, London, 1955.

Flower, J. Cyril : *Psychological Studies of Religious Questions*, William Norgate, London, 1924.

Forem, Jack : *Transendental Meditation*, E.P. Dutton & Co., Inc., New York, 1974.

Frazier, Allie M. : *Issues in Religion, A Book of Readings*, American Book Company, New York 1969.

Freud, Sigmund : *The Future of an Illusion*, Translated by W.D. Robson-Scott, The International Psycho-Analytical Library Edited by Ernest Jones, No. 15, Published by the Hogarth Press, and the Institute of Psycho-Analysis, London, 1943.

——— : *Totem and Taboo*, Kegan Paul, London, 1938.

Fromn, Erich : *Psychoanalysis and Religion*, Yale University Press, New Haven, 1977.

Fuller, J.F.C. : *Yoga : Study of the Mystical Philosophy of the Brahmins and Buddhist*, Sri Sadguru, Delhi. 1988.

Galloway, George ; *The Philosophy of Religion*. T & T Clark, Edinburgh, 1960.

Ghose, Sisirkumar : *Mysticism and Society A Point of View*, Asia Publishing House, Delhi, 1968.

——— : *Mysticism : Views and Reviews*, Clarion Books, New Delhi, 1987.

Glock, Charles Y., and Stark, Rodney : *Religion and Society in Tension*, Rand McNally & Company, Chicago, 1965.

Gnoli, Raniero : *The Aesthetic Experience According to Abhinavagupta*, The Chowkhamba Sanskrit Studies Vol. LXII, The Chowkhamba Sanskrit Series Office, Varanasi, 1968.

Goedenough, Erwin Ramsdell : *The Psychology of Religious Experiences*, Basic Books, Inc., Publishers, New York, 1965.

Gosvami, O. : *The Story of Indian Music Its Growth and Synthesis*, Asia Publishing House, New Delhi, 1957.

Greelay, Andrew M. : *Ecstasy A Way of Knowing*, Prentice-Hall, Inc., Englewood Cliffs, New Jersey, 1974.

Grensted, S.W. : *The Psychology of Religion*, The Home University Library of Modern Knowledge, Oxford Univerity Press, London, 1952.

Guenther, Herbert V. : *Buddhist Philosophy in Theory and Practice*, A Pelican Original, Penguin Books, Published by special arrangement with Shambala Publications, Inc., Berkeley, California, 1972.

Guirdham, Arthur : *Christ and Freud, A Study of Religious Experience and Observance*, George Allen & Unwin Ltd., London, 1959.

Gupta, Usha : *Hindi ke Krishna Bhakti Kaleen Sahitya Mein Sangeet*, Lucknow University, Lucknow.

Haber, Ralph Norman, and Fried, Aharon H. : *An Introduction to Psychology*, Holt, Rinehart and Winston, Inc., New York, 1975

Hacker, P.M.S. : *Insight and Illusion, Wittgenstein on Philosophy and the Metaphysics of Experience*, Clarendon Press, Oxford, 1972.

Hall, Calvin S. : *A Primer of Freudian Psychology*, A Mentor Book, The New American Library, New York, 1955.

Hanslick, Eduard : *Beautiful in Music* (Translated by Gustav Cohen), Edited, with an Introduction by Morris Weitz, The Bobbs-Merrill Co. Inc., A Subsidiary of Howard W. Sams & Co., Inc., Publishers, Indianadolis, New York, 1957.

Happold, F.C. : *Religious Faith and Twentieth-Century Man*, Penguin Books, England, 1966 (Middlcsex).

——— : *Myticism A Study and an Anthology*, Penguin Books, Middlesex, 1977.

Havens, Joseph (ed.) , *Psychology and Religion : A Contemporaay Dialogue*, D. Van Nostrand Company, Inc., New York, 1968.

Heidbreder, Edna : *Seven Psychologies* Kalyani Publishers, Ludhiana, 1971.

Heywood, Rosalind : *The Sixth Sense: An Inquiry into Extra-Sensory Perception*, Chatto and Windus, London, 1959.

Hicks, John H. : *Philosophy of Religion*, Second Edition—Foundation of Philosophy Series, Published by Prentice-Hall, Inc., New Jersey, 1973.

Hiigard, Earnest R., Atkinson, Richard C., Atkinson, Rita L. : *Introduction to Psychology*, Oxford and IBH Publishing Co., New Delhi, 1953.

Hocking, William Ernest : *The Meaning of God in Human Experience, A Philosophic Study of Religion*, New Haven : Yale University Press, 13th Printing, 1955.

Hook, Sidney (Ed.) : *Dimensions of Mind a Symposium*, Collier Books, New York, 1961.

——— : *Religious Experience and Truth, A Symposium*, Oliver and Boyd Ltd., London, 1962.

Hospers, John : *An Introduction to Philosophical Analysis*, Allied Publishers Private Limited, New Delhi, 1971.

Hudson, Donald W. : *A Philosophical Approach to Religion*, Published by Macmillan, London, 1974.

——— : *Wittgenstein and Religious Belief*, Macmillan, London, 1975.

Huxley, Aldous : The *The Perennial Philosophy*, Chatto and Windus, London, 1946.

Huxley, Julian : *Religion Without Revelation*, C.A. Watts & Co. Ltd.. London, 1967.

Idries, Shah : *World of the Sufi ; An Anthology of Writing about Sufis and their work*, London, Octagan Press, 1979.

Inge, W.R. : Mysticism in Religion, Rider and Company, London, 1969.

Jacobi, Jolande : *The Psychology of C.G. Jung, An Introduction with Illustrations*, Kegan Paul, Trench, Trubner & Co. Ltd., London, 1942.

Jacobi, Jolande (Selections Edited) : *C.G. Jung Psychological Reflections*, Harper Torchbooks, The Bollingen Libray, Harper Row, Publishers, New York, 1961.

James, William : *The Varieties of Religious Experience, A Study in Human Nature*, with a new Introduction by Reinhold Neibuhr, Collier Books, New York, 1961.

——— : *The Will to Believe, Human Immortality and other Essays on Popular Philosophy*, Dover Publications, Inc., New York, 1956.

Johnson, Paul E. : *Psychology of Religion*, Abingdon Press, Nashville, New York, 1945.

Johnstone, Ronald L. : *Religion and Society in Interaction, The Sociology of Religion*, Prentice-Hall, New Jersey, 1975.

Jung, C.G. : *Psychology and Religion*, Yale University Press, New Haven, 1965.

——— : *Psychology of Religion : West and East*, The Collected Works of C.G. Jung, Volume II, Translated by R.F.C. Hull, Routledge and Kegan Paul, London, 1953.

——— : *Psychology of the Unconscious*, Authorised translation, with Introduction, by Beatrice M. Hinkle, Routledge and Kegan Paul Ltd., London, 1951.

——— : *Modern Man in Search of a Soul*, Routledge and Kegan Paul Ltd., London, 1962.

——— : *Freud and Psychoanalysis*, The Collected Works of C.G. Jung, Translated by R.F.C. Hull, Routledge and Kegan Paul, London, 1961 (Volume IV).

——— : *The Archetypes and the Collective Unconscious*, The Collected Works of C.G. Jung, Volume IX, Part I, Translated by R.S.E. Hull, Routledge and Kegan Paul, London, 1959.

Keeling, S.V. (Ed.) : *Philosophical Studies by the Late J. MCT. Ellis Mctaggart*, Edward Arnold & Co., London, 1934.

Ladriere, Jean : *Language and Belief*, Translated by Garrett Barden, Gill and Macmillan Ltd., Dublin, 1972.

Lata, Prem : *Chaitanya Mahaprabhu*, ESS ESS Publication, New Delhi, 1988.

Leuba, James H., : *The Psychology of Religious Mysticism*, London, Kegan Paul, Trench, Trubner and Co. Ltd., New York : Harcourt, Brace and Co., Inc., 1925.

Levi, Albert William : *Varieties of Experience*, The Ronald Press Company, New York, 1957.

Lewis, H D. : *Our Experience of God*, Collins, London, 1974.

MacMurray, John : *The Structure of Religious Experience* (1936, Reprinted 1971), Faber and Faber Limited, London, 1936.

MacGregor, Geddes : *Introudction to Religious Philosophy*, Macmillan & Co. Ltd., London, 1960.

——— : *Aesthetic Experience in Religion*, Macmillan & Co. Ltd., London, 1947.

Mandell, Arnold J. and Mandell, Mary P. (Ed.) : *Psycho-chemical Research in Man, Methods, Strategy and Theory*, Academic Press Inc., New York. 1969.

Masih, Y. : *Freudianism and Religion*, Thacker Spink & Co. Pvt. Ltd., Calcutta, 1964.

Maslow, Abraham H. : *Religions, Values, and Peak-Experiences*, The Viking Press, New York, 1970.

Masters, R.E.L. and Houston, Jean : *The Varieties of Psychedelic Experience*, Anthony Blond, London, and Holt, Rinehart and Winston, New York, 1966.

Matilal, Bimal Krishna : *Logical Illumination of Indian Mysticism* : An Innaugural Lecture Delivered before the University of Oxford on 5th. May, 1977, Oxford University Press, Delhi, 1977.

McDermott, Robert A. (Ed.) : *Basic Writings, of S. Radhakrishnan*, Jaico Publishing House, Bombay, 1972.

McPherson, Thomas : *The Philosophy of Religion*, Von Nostrand Reinhold Company Ltd., London, 1971.

Meland, Bernard E. : *The Secularization of Modern Cultures*, Oxford University Press, New York, 1966.

Menen, Aubrey : *New Mystics and the True Indian Tradition*, Thames and Hudson, London, 1974.

Miles, T.R. : *Religious Experience*, Macmillan, London, 1972, New Studies in the Philosophy of Religion.

Miller, L. (Ed.) : *Philosophical and Religious Issues : Classical and Contemporay Statements*, Dickenson Publishing Co. Inc., California, 1971.

Miller Jonathan (Ed.) : *Freud the Man, His World, His Influence*, Weidenfeld and Nicolson, London, 1972.

Misra, Lalmani : *Bharatiya Sangeet Vadya*, Bharatiya Jñanpith Prakashan, New Delhi, 1976.

Misra, R.S. : *The Integral Advaitism of Sri Aurobindo*, Banaras Hindu University, Banaras, 1957.

——— : *Studies in Philosophy and Religion*, Bhāratiya Vidya Prakasana, Varanasi, 1971.

Montague, William Pepperell : *The Ways of Knowing or The Methods of Ph'losophy* (The Method of Mysticism), Muirhead Library of Philosophy, George Allen and Unwin Ltd., London, 1962.

Mukherjee, Radhakamal : *The Theory and Art of Mystictsm*, Asia Publishing House, New Delhi, 1960.

Muller, F. Max : *Theosophy or Psychological Religion*, Asian Educational Services, New Delhi, 1978.

Munshi, K.M. & Diwakar, R.R. (General Editors) Rao Nagaraja, P.; Gopalaswami, K.; Ramakrishnan S. (Editors) *Radhakrishan Reader, An Anthology*, Bharatiya Vidya Bhavan, Bombay, 1969.

Murti, T.R.V. : *Central Philosophy of Buddhism*, George Allen & Unwin Ltd., London, 1955.

Naravne, V.S. : *Modern Indian Thought*, Asia Publishing House, Bombay, 1967.

Nielsen, Kai : *Reason and Practice — A Modern Introduction to Philosophy*, Harper and Row, Publishers, New York, 1971.

——— : *Contemporary Critiques of Religion*, Macmillan, London, 1971.

Nuys, Kelvin Van : *Science and Cosmic Purpose*, Rider and Co., London, 1951.

O'Brien, S.J. : *Varieties of Mystic Experience An Anthology and Interpretation*, Holt, Rinehart and Winston, Canada, 1964.

Olson, Robert G. : *An Introduction to Existentialism*, Dover Publications, Inc., New York, 1962.

O'Maley, L.S.S. : *Modern India and the West*,Oxford University Press, Oxford, 1968.

Ornstein, Robert E. : *The Psychology of Consciousness*, Jonathan Cape, London, 1975.

Osborn, R. : *Freud and Marx A Dialectical Study*, with an Introduction by John Strachey, Victor Gollancz, London, 1937.

Otto, Rudolf : *Mysticism East and West*, Living Age Books, Meridian Books, New York, 1960.

——— : *The Idea of the Holy*, An Inquiry into the non-rational factor in the Idea of the Divine and its Relation to the Rational, Translated by John W. Harvey, Oxford University Press, London, 1952.

Pandit, M.P. : *Tradition in Sadhana* : *Studies in Tantra, Veda, Yoga Philosophy and Mysticism*, Sterling, New Delhi, 1988.

Parker, DeWitt R. : *The Principles of Aesthetics*, Appleton-Century-Crofts, Inc., New York, 1946.

Passmore, John : *A Hundred Years of Philosophy*, Penguin Books, First Published 1957, reprinted 1978, Middlesex.

Patanjali, V. : *Thoughts on Indian Mysticism*, Sagar Publication, New Delhi, 1978.

Patrick, G.T.W. : *Introduction to Philosophy*, George Allen and Unwin Ltd., London, 1968.

Perumpilly, Fr. Marcel George O.F.M. Cap. : *Psychological Needs in Religious Life*, Kerela, 1974.

Prajñānanda, Swami : Music of the Nations (A Comparative Stduy), Munshiram Manoharlal Publishers Pvt. Ltd., New Delhi, 1973.

Prasad, Ramchandra : *Acharya Rajneesh, The Mystic of Feeling*, Motilal Banarasidass, Delhi, 1970.

Pratt, James Bisset : *The Religious Consciousness* : *A Psychological Study*, The Macmillan Company, New York, 1921.

Price, H.H. : *Essays in the Philosophy of Religion*, Based on the Sarum Lectures 1971, The Clarendon Press, Oxford, 1972.

Rader, Me'vin (Ed. with Introduction and Notes) : *A Modern Book of Esthetics An Anthology*, Holt, Rinehart and Winston, Inc., New York, 1973.

Radhakrishnan, S. : *The Hindu View of Life*, Upton Lectures Delivered at Manchester College, Oxford, 1926, George Allen and Unwin Ltd., London, 1948.

——— : *An Idealist View of Life*, George Allen and Unwin (India), Bombay, 1971.

——— : *The Philosophy of Rabindranath Tagore*, Good Companions Publishers, Baroda, 1961.

——— : *East and West in Religion*, George Allen and Unwin Ltd., 1958.

——— : *Religion in a Changing World*, George Allen and Unwin Ltd., 1967.

——— : *The Religion we Need*, Varanasi, 1963.

——— : *Eastesn Religions and Western Thought*, Second Edition, Oxford University Press, London, 1940.

——— : *The Bhagavadgīta*, George Allen and Unwin (India) Private Limited, Bombay, 1971.

——— : *Indian Philosophy*, Volume I any Volume II, George Allen and Unwin Ltd., London, 1977.

Rajneesh, Bhagawan Shree : *Psychology of the Esoteric, The New Evolution of Man*, Orient Paperbacks, New Delhi, 1978.

——— : *The Eternal Quest*, Orient Paperbacks, New Delhi, 1980.

Ramanujachari, C. : *The Spiritual Heritage of Tyagaraja* with an Introductory Thesis by V, Raghavan, The Ramakrishna Mission Student's Home, Madras, 1957.

Ramsey, Ian (Ed.) : *Prospect for Metaphysics*, Essays of Metaphysical Exploration, Philosophical Library Inc., New York, 1961.

Ranade, G.H. : *Hindustani Music Its Physics and Aesthetics*, Popular Prakashan, Bombay, 1971.

Randall (Jr.), John Herman and Buchler, Justus : *Philosophy : An Introduction*, New York, 1944.

Ricoeur, Paul : *Freud and Philosophy, An Essay on Interpretation*, Translated by Denis Savage, Yale University Press, New Haven, 1970.

Rhine, J.B. and Pratt, J.G. : *Parapsychology Frontier Science of the Mind*, Blackwell Scientific Publications, Oxford.

Robinson, Edward (Ed.) : *This Time Bound Ladder*, The Religious Experience Research Unit, Manchester College, Oxford, 1977.

——— : *Living the Questions*, The Religious Experience Research Unit, Manchester College, Oxford, 1978.

Rolland E. Romain : *Life of Ramakrishna*, Advaita Ashram, Calcutta, 1979.

Roth, John K : *Problems of the Philosophy of Religion*, Chandler Publishing Company, Toronto, 1971.

Russell, Bertrand : *Mysticism and Logic*, (and other Essays), Penguin Books, London, 1953.

——— : *An Inquiry into Meaning and Truth*, Penguin Books, Middlesex, 1973.

——— : *History of Western Philosophy*, George Allen and Unwin Ltd., London, 1975.

Santayana, George : *Reason in Religion*, Volume III of The Life of Reason or the Phases of Human Progress, Collier Books New York, 1962.

——— : *Reason in Art*, Volume IV of The Life of Reason or the Phases of Human Progress, Collier Books, New York, 1962.

Seashore, Carla : *Psychology of Music*, Dover Publications Inc., New York, 1967.

Schmidt, Paul F. : *Religious Knowledge*, The Free Press of Glencoe, Inc., 1961.

Schneider, Louis : *Sociological Approach to Religion*, John Wiley & Sons, Inc., New York, 1970.

Schneider, Herbert Wallace : *Religion in 20th. Century America*, Harvard University Press, Cambridge, 1952.

Schultz, Duane P. : *A History of Modern, Psychology*, Academic Press Inc., New York, 1969.

Selbie, W.B. : *The Psychology of Religion*, Oxford Handbooks of Theology, At the Clarendon Press, Oxford, 1926.

Shankar, Uday : *Personality Development*, Atma Ram & Sons, Delhi, 1981.

Singh, Harbans (Ed.) : *Approaches to the Study of Religion*, Seminar Papers, Guru Govind Singh Department of Religious Studies, Punjabi University, Patiala.

Singh, Ravindra : *I Was a Drug Addict*, Orient Paperbacks, New Delhi, 1979.

Scharf, Betty R. : *The Sociological Study of Religion*, Hutchinson University Library, London, 1973.

Schuon, Frithjof : *Gnosis : Divine Wisdom*, Translated from the French by G.E.H. Palmer, John Murray, London, 1959.

Sircar, Mahendranath : *Hindu Mysticism according to the Upaniṣads*, Oriental Books Reprint Corporation, New Delhi, 1974.

Sivananda : *Sadhana A Text Book of the Psychology and the Practice of the Techniques to Spiritual Perfection*, 2nd. Edition, Motilal Banarsidass, Delhi, 1967. (Reprint 1978).

Smart, Ninian : *The Religious Experience of Mankind*, Collins, The Fontana Library of Theology and Philosophy, London, 1970.

Smith, Henry Clay : *Personality Development*, McGraw-Hill Book Company, New York, 1974.

Spinks, G.S. : *Psychology and Religion; An Introduction to Contemporary Views*, Methuen & Co. Ltd., London, 1963.

Staal, Frits : *Exploring Mysticism,* Penguin Books, Middlesex, 1975.

Stace, W.T. : *Mysticism and Philosophy,* Macmillan and Co. Ltd., London, 1961.

Stratton, George Malcolm : *Psychology of the Religious Life,* George Allen & Co. Ltd., London, 1911.

Tagore, Rabindranath : *The Religion of Man,* Unwin Books, London, 1961.

Tennant, F.R. : *Philosophical Theology* Vol. I, Cambridge : At the University Press, 1928.

Thakur, Shivesh C. (Ed.) : *Philosophy and Psychical Research,* Muirhead Library of Philosophy, London, George Allen & Unwin Ltd., 1976.

Thouless, Robert H. : *An Introduction of the Psychology of Religion,* Second Edition, Cambridge : At the University Press, 1956.

——— : *An Introduction to the Psychology of Religion,* Third Edition, At the University Press, Cambridge 1971.

Tilleard-Cole, R.R. and Marks, J. : *The Fundamentals of Psychological Medicine,* Medical and Technical Publishing Co. Ltd., Lancaster, 1975.

Titus, Harold H. and Hepp, Maylon H. : *The Range of Philosophy,* Introductory Readings, Affiliated East-West Press Pvt. Ltd., New Delhi, 1974 (Second Edition).

Tripathi, S.M. : *Psycho-Analytic Concept of Religion,* Ajanta Publications, Delhi, 1979.

Underhill Evelyn : *The Mystic Way, A Psychological Study in Christian Origins,* J.M. Dent & Sons, Ltd., London & Toronto, 1914.

——— : *Mysticism a Study In the Nature and Development of Man's Spiritual Consciousness,* Methun & Co. Ltd., London, 1911.

Urmson, J.O. : *Philosophical Analysis,* Oxford University Press, London, 1969.

Varadachari, V. : *Psychic Research Occultism and Yoga*, Madras, 1970.

Vivas, Eliseo and Krieger, Murrary (Ed.) : *The Problems of Aesthetics*, A Book of Readings, Holt, Rinehart and Winston, New York, 1966.

Vivekananda, Swami : *Raja-Yoga*, Advaita Ashrama, Calcutta, 1978 (Seventeenth Impression).

Webb, C.C.J. : *Religious Experience*, A Public lecture delivered in the hall of Oriel College on Friday 19 May 1944, Oxford University Press, London.

Wieman, Henry Nelson, *Religious Experience and Scientific Methods*, Southern Illinois University Press, Carbondale and Edwardsville, Feffer and Simons, Inc., London, 1971.

Weitz, Morris : *Problems in Aesthetics*, An Introductory Book of Readings, The Macmillan Company, London, 1970.

Wittgenstein, Ludwig : *Tractatus Logico-Philosophicus*, Translated by D.F. Pears & B.F. McGuinness with the Introduction by Bertrand Russell, Routledge and Kegan Paul, London, 1978.

Wolman, Benjamin B. : *Contemporary Theories and Systems in Psychology*, Jointly published by Harper & Row, New York, and John Weatherhill, Inc., Tokyo, 1960.

Wood, Ernest : *The Intuition of the Will*, The Theosophical Publishing House, Madras, 1949.

Wright, William Kelly : *A Student's Philosophy of Religion*, The Macmillan Company, New York, 1958.

Wuthnow, Robert : *Experimentation in American Religion*, *The New Mysticisms and their Implications for the Churches*, University of California Press, Berkeley and Los Angeles, 1978.

Yinger, Milton J. : *The Scientific Study of Religion*, The Macmillan Company, Collier-Macmillan Ltd., London, 1970.

Zaehner, R.C. : *Drugs, Mysticism and Make-Believe*, Colliers, London, 1972.

Zaehner, R.C. : *Mysitcism Sacred and Profane, An Inquiry into Some Varieties of Praeternatural Experience*, Oxford University Press, New, York, 1971.

——— : *Hindu and Muslim Mysticism*, Schochen Books, New York, 1969.

Journals

Berthold, Fred (Jr.) : The Meaning of Religious Experience, *Journal of Religion*, Vol. 32, 1952.

Bertocci, Peter A : Existential Phenomenology and Psychoanalysis, *The Review of Metaphysics*, A Philosophical Quarterly, Vol. XVIII, No. 4, Issue No. 72, June 1965.

Crossan, John Dominic : Parable as Religious and Poetic Experience, *The Journal of Religion*, Vol. 53, No 3, July 1973.

Hardy, Sir Alister : *Science, Religion and World Unity*, Religious Experience Research Unit, Manchester College, Oxford.

Hay, David and Morisy, Ann : Reports of Esctatic, Paranormal, or Religious Experience in Great Britian and the United State – A Comparison of Trends, *Journal for the Scientific Study of Religion*, Volume 17, No. 3, September 1978.

Hay, David : Religious Experience Amongst a Group of Post-Graduate Students – A Qualitative Study, Religious Experience Research Project, Religious Experience Research Unit, Manchester College, Oxford.

Hood, Ralph W. (Jr.) : Anticipatory Set and Setting : Stress Incongruities as Elicitors of Mystical Experience in Solitary Nature, Situations, *Journal for the Scientific Study of Religion*, Vol. 17, No. 3, 1978.

——— W. (Jr.) : Eliciting Mystical States of Cousciousness with Semistructured Nature Experiences, *Journal for the Scientific Study of Religion*, Vol. 16, No. 2, 1977.

Kagal, Ayesha : The Story of the Drug Addict, *Sunday Review, The Times of India*, June 27, 1982.

Miles. T.R. : On Excluding the Supernatural, Reprint, Ref. Stud. I, pp. 141-150.

Krishna, Daya : Mysticism and the Problem of Intelligibility, *Journal of Religion*, April, 1954.

Needleham, Jacob : Religion and the Recovery of Experience, *Review of Metaphysics*, Vol. 23, 1969-70.

Mutatkar, Sumati : 'The Sound of Hindustani Music', *Eve's Weekly*, Special Issue Indian Culture, August 13-19, 1977, Vol. XXXI.

Perry, Charner M. : Language and Thought, *The Monist*, Vol. XXXVIII_ Jan. 1928.

R.G.K. : Splendour of Indian Music – Are they Vanishing ? A Rasika's Alapana, *Illustrated Weekly of India*, Vol. CI 40 Nov. 9-15, 1980.

Ray, B.N. : The Cognitive Value of Religious Experience, *Philosophical Quartely*, Vol. IV, No. I April 1928.

Robinson, Edward : Tolerating the Paradoxical, A Scientific Approach to Religious Experience, The Religious Experience Researh Unit, Manchester College, Oxford, 1978.

Schneiderman, Leo : Psychological Notes on the Nature of Mystical Experience, *Journal for the Scientific Study of Religion*, Vol. VI, No. 1, April, 1967.

Schamb, Edward L. : Interpretation of Religion, *The Monist*, Vol. XXXIII, Jan. 1928.

Smith, Huston : Do Drugs have Religious Import, *The Journal of Philosophy*, Vol. LXI, No. 18, October 1, 1964.

Weiss, Paul : 'Religious Experience, *Review of Metaphysics*, Vol. XVII, No. 1, Issue No. 65, Sept. 1963.

Wainwright, William J. : Mysticism and Sense Perception, *Religious Studies*, 9, 1973.

Encyclopaedias.

Encyclopaedia Britannica.

Encyclopaedia of Religion and Ethics.

Encyclopaedia of Philosophy.

Eysenck, H.J. Arnold, W., Meili, R. : Encyclopaedia of Psychology.

Ferguson, John : Illustrated Encyclopaedia of Mysticism and the Mystery of Religions.

Ferm, Vergilius (ed.) : An Encyclopaedia of Religion.

Fodor, Nandor : Encyclopaedia of Psychic Science.

Gaynor, Frank (ed.) : Dictionary of Mysticism.

Index